Wicca 333
Advanced Topics in Wiccan Belief

Wicca 333
Advanced Topics in Wiccan Belief
Part One of a Master Class in Wicca

(Revised and Expanded)

Kaatryn MacMorgan-Douglas

COVENSTEAD PRESS　　　**BUFFALO, NEW YORK**

Wicca 333: Advanced Topics in Wiccan Belief
Revised and Expanded

ISBN: 978-0-6151-7535-5
All Rights Reserved, ©2007 Kaatryn MacMorgan
Earlier version (ISBN 0-595-27170-7) ©2003 Kaatryn MacMorgan

Books by Kaatryn MacMorgan-Douglas:

All One Wicca (Fall 2001, Fall 2007)

A Master Class in Wicca:
      Wicca 333 (Spring 2003, October 2007)
      Wicca 334: (December 2007)

The Ethical Eclectic (July 2007)

I dedicate this work to the Schumakers and Catherine D'Imperio — some people have beliefs, other people live them. As always, it would be impossible without my loving families: at home, at Temple University, at University of Buffalo and on the Net. No book will ever have dedication space for all who've touched, inspired, helped, rescued, taught and befriended me, and for that I thank the ones whose names *are* my prayers.

Contents

Introduction.. i

Topic One: The Wiccan Rede: An Adult View.............. 1

Topic Two: All Paths Lead to the Same Place and All gods
are One God, right? 18

Topic Three: Wicca's Real History............................ 49

Wicca in Practice I: Asking Questions 68

Topic Four: Wicca is not Celtic & Other Simple Truths ... 74

Topic Five: The Religion of The Great Mother Goddess and
Wicca 98

Topic Six: Pagan, pagan, Wiccan, wiccan and other
silliness 122

Wicca in Practice II: Gleaning Good Source Material......140

Topic Seven: Rational Wicca and Irrational Magic.........147

Topic Eight: Wicca and Creationism...........................164

Topic Nine: The Science of Belief 186

Wicca in Practice III: Mental Experiments and Validity
Testing 213

Topic Ten: Wicca and Science 219

Topic Eleven: Proselytizing 239

Topic Twelve: Wicca 666: Facts about Satanism for the non-
Satanist 255

Wicca in Practice IV: Forming an Ethical Code............ 273

Appendices 276

Introduction: What is this book?

I was once asked by a student what I would put in an upper-level college seminar on Wicca, what discussions I'd wish to have with the class and what I think people with a firm grounding in Wicca would appreciate learning from me. Since I'm an opinionated person, this was actually easy for me to address, and I ended up with a veritable sheaf of discussion topics. Around the same time that I was doing this, a friend of mine was graduating from college and helping her professor write a proposal for a two-part upper level course in English literature. The course was designed to be twelve weeks long with five classes a week. Each week would be divided into different topics with each class addressing a different part of that topic. A few extra weeks would be dedicated to testing and paper writing.

On her advice, I decided to go through my sheaf of Wiccan topics as if I were crafting a similar course, narrowing it down to twelve interesting topics I felt were well suited to someone with a firm foundation in Wicca. When I was finished, I had come up with two sets of topics, which I divided into two groups: "keepers" and "laters." The keepers were things I felt I could explain and teach about clearly with a minimum of further research. All I felt I needed to discuss these topics in depth were my personal library, websites of high quality I've recommended in the past and personal experience. The "laters" included things like "The Biblical nature of exclusionary Christianity," which would require quotations from obscure texts in foreign languages--or would require, at the least, common texts in translation. I had a deep interest in discussing these things, but simply did not feel I could teach about them, either through my lack of experience or because the materials would require so much prefacing and disclaiming that they'd be rendered nonsensical. I tried to create a coherent but eclectic collection of topics, ranging from the history of Wicca and its beliefs to Wicca's relationship with other religions, to more complicated topics from Psychology and Biology with relevance to Wicca.

In addition to these twelve topics, I've also included four "Wicca in Practice" topics, which are some basic concepts in advanced learning. The "Wicca in Practice" topics are one part psychology, one part study technique and a dash of experiential advice. They should be helpful for Wiccans and non-Wiccans alike, but aren't vital to the material herein.

This work is **not** an introductory text, so the material will often make an assumption about what you know. If you were in a classroom, this would be where you could raise your hand to ask for additional explanation. In *Wicca 333*, I can't answer your raised hand, but I do answer emails to Kaatryn@MacMorgan.org. Some of you will find these topics not sufficiently advanced for your perceived level, and at least one topic herein is so very rudimentary to members of my own tradition that I willingly risk offending them to make sure other Wiccans are up to speed. Please understand the book is for a wide range of people, not any one person.

If I can make my way slowly through the Iliad with one C+ semester of Ancient Greek, three grammar texts, two translations and an online dictionary, a beginning student can make his or her way through this book with considerably less. To make things a tad easier, this book contains several appendices including a glossary of terms, a self-test of basic facts and a list of persons mentioned with a brief discussion of who they are. Again, as fans of *All One Wicca* know, I'm always willing, if not always able, to answer complicated questions by email, and I can be reached at the address above.

Who is This Book For?

As mentioned above, this work is for the advanced student or the beginning student with access to assistance. As so-called advanced books in the past have shown, the concept of intermediate or advanced students vary from author to author. I would say that the minimum preparation to read this book without assistance would be a year and a day of study with a group, or being a well-read solitary practitioner with a group of friends, online or off, to bounce ideas off of. At the least, this solitary practitioner would have read or been exposed to the main concepts of Margot Adler's *Drawing Down The Moon*, Ronald Hutton's *The Triumph of The Moon*, Gerald Gardner's *Witchcraft Today* and at least one introductory Wiccan text, such as Scott Cunningham's *Wicca: A Guide for the Solitary Practitioner*, Raymond Buckland's *Complete Book of Witchcraft*, or, of course, *All One Wicca*.

In Appendix III you will find a self-test. This is not a test of Witchy-ness, nor is it a test of proficiency in Wicca. It represents topics that intermediate to advanced students should've been exposed to, even to a slight degree. If you glance through it and find you have no idea what any of these things are, it might indicate that the material herein will be beyond your depth. If you read through it and are familiar with all the concepts, you may find parts of this book below your level of expertise. If you find yourself in the middle, you're probably smack dab in the center of the target audience. I leave it to *you* to find the answers, because if I don't publish them, I know you haven't been cheating.

Who is Kaatryn MacMorgan-Douglas?

From the mid-1990s, until a couple of years ago, I was the acting head of The Church of Universal Eclectic Wicca (CUEW.) As of 2007, and this edition of this book, I am a few years past the ten-year mark that indicates part of the transition between Priestess and High Priestess in the tradition to which I belong, Universal Eclectic Wicca (UEW). Despite this passage, I don't really think of myself as a High Priestess. I'm more of a lowly researcher. In addition to my status with CUEW, I am the author of the tradition's textbook, *All One Wicca*, which has been published numerous times, in multiple editions, and is also available in a free partial edition at http://www.allonewicca.com.

Although I grew up feet from the campus of Syracuse University in Syracuse, New York, I graduated with a B.A. from Temple University in Philadelphia, Pennsylvania, where I double majored in Biology and Psychology, as well as minoring in Ancient Mediterranean Studies. In 2005, I got off of my butt and completed a second BA in Anthropology from the State University of New York at Buffalo, and I anticipate and am engaged in further studies, probably finishing another degree this year. However, as an older student, I know that absolutely nothing is written in stone.

I speak English proficiently, (even though my editor may swear otherwise) can muddle my way through French, and horribly mangle Ancient Greek, Classical Latin and Modern Cornish. In addition, in the short time between the first and second editions of this book, I started to pick up some Czech after a fantastic trip to the magical city of Prague. I can crochet, write

HTML and simple JavaScript, make bread by hand and machine, make mead, can peaches, do simple calculus, read tarot and much more... but I can't juggle.

I have been a practitioner of Ceremonial Magic, an Atheist, a Rationalist, a Skeptic, a Hellenic Reconstructionist, a mom, a partner, homeless, poor, undereducated, overeducated, aggressive, passive, passive-aggressive and several thousand other adjectives throughout my life and I still am a few of them.

None of these adjectives, statistics or factoids is enough for you to accept what I say as gospel. I'd rather not begin with the phony caveat of "your mileage may vary" and I don't believe the ranting of the anti-scholastic camp that claims "there are no facts in religion," but I am *not* a pope, a goddess, a powerful channel bringing you the voice of space aliens, or whatever your personal kink regarding perceived leadership is. If you disagree with me, do the research yourself; I've cited my sources for those very reasons. If you want to agree with me, don't repeat what I said, but read it for yourself in other sources. Do not accept what *I* say, or for that matter what *any* author says simply because you see it on a printed page. Accept it *if and only if* it matches *your* research and *your* experiences.

Why Wicca 333?

This book is called Wicca 333 for several reasons. On the one hand, certain elements within the anti-Wiccan community will go out of their way to find a reference to Satan in any number that appears in a Wiccan book. On the other hand, as any Ceremonial Mage or scholar of the book of Revelations knows, "333" *really* means nothing. The best these elements could do is say that 333 is one-half of 666, so Wicca 333 is therefore half as diabolical as any other book on Wicca. I like that idea. In a way, Wiccan books are often diabolical: they may contain erroneous data, bad history, and even outright lies on occasion. This diabolical behavior isn't the doing of Satan, but the doing of a bad publishing system that sometimes favors Wiccan books that are put out fast and appeal to the lowest common denominator. We guarantee, therefore, that Wicca 333 will contain, at a minimum, less than 50% of the diabolic data found in other works.

If you seriously believe that I named this work Wicca 333 to give fundies an excuse to rant or give myself an excuse to poke fun at my favorite target, you don't need a book on Wicca, you need to purchase a book about curing your gullibility. While it is true that I thought the title would get you thinking, and maybe even get some fundies to advertise my book for free, my use of the number 333 in the title has nothing to do with numerology, 666 or neo-Christianity. In fact, it comes from an anecdote several of my students have been subjected to:

When I attended college, my university was one in which freshman level classes began with 0, sophomore classes with 1, and so forth. My best and worst upper-level courses shared the course number 333. These two classes, in two different fields, represented the amazing diversity between what two people considered upper level work and a high grade. In one, your grade was determined by showing up to a class, discussing your feelings and writing several short opinion papers. In the other, your grade was determined by two tests of the material and an intensive final project in which you had to combine several hours of lab work with a basic knowledge of multi-media presentation and the hard-science behind your work. In both, I received an A. In the first, my A was one of a dozen out of a class of 20, and in the second it was one of only two or three. While my GPA treated both classes equally, they were *not* equal.

You can use this work like that first class, you can read it, form opinions, and maybe talk about it with a friend and you will receive the emotional equivalent of an "A." After all, you did the work of reading, so you deserve it! You can also use this work like the second class, read it, do research, understand the philosophy behind it and maybe explain it to your friends or students in depth. In doing so, you get the same "A," but *you* know that you did more than just read the book; you used it as a springboard into something more.

Like the university, which described a senior-level class in broad enough terms to make my 333s equal, an author can only put the material out there and hope that you use it as best you can. To me, 333 will always represent the possibility of learning a huge amount of information, as well as the possibility of doing nothing more than regurgitating the words of a teacher. Unlike college classes where you are at the whim of a professor's interpretation of upper level, the decision in this case is yours. I think you can guess where I'd like you to take it…

Kaatryn MacMorgan-Douglas

Topic One: The Wiccan Rede: An Adult View

What is the Rede, anyway? Does the Wiccan Rede really teach us "harm none?" Does the idea of harming none make any sense? How long has it been a part of Wicca? What forms does it have? How do we discuss it with people who are not Wiccan?

What is the Rede:

[It seems almost silly to begin a book on Wicca for the advanced student with "What is The Wiccan Rede?" In theory, any Wiccan with more than a few weeks of study would know what it was, but based on observations of websites, books and students, as well as discussions with other teachers, some people are clearly confused or mistaught regarding the Rede, so I will begin our discussion of the Rede with what may be review for most, but should clear up any confusion for the rest. I will also attempt to explain where the confusion stems from, using traditional Wiccan interpretations of the Rede. These interpretations have been fairly widely published by a slew of authors, past and contemporary, and they match the teachings involving the Rede in those of the major established traditions of Wicca that use it. -KMD]

In 1975, the faith poem *Rede of the Wiccae* appeared in *Green Egg Magazine*.[1,2]It consists of twenty-six numbered lines, two of which name and clarify preexisting beliefs in the Wiccan community, namely The Rule of Three and The Wiccan Rede. *Rede of the Wiccae* was written by Gwen Thompson (1928-1986), the founder of the New England Covens of Traditionalist Witches[3] (NECTW). The work was allegedly passed down to her in said form by her grandmother, and according to NECTW was published with the intention of setting the record straight on the true nature of Wiccan belief.

---

[1] *Green Egg Magazine* Vol. III. No. 69 (Ostara 1975).
[2] Chapter endnotes have been changed to footnotes in this edition for the ease of the reader. Mostly, this decision was based on Al Franken's description of how Ann Coulter lies with endnotes in his book *Lies and the Lying Liars who tell Them.* I'll never use endnotes again, promise.
[3] http://www.nectw.org

The poem is deceptively simple, and some have claimed that its simplistic nature is reflective of the simple people who wrote it. Wiccan Priest and English literature scholar Tamryn Wyrmstar[4] shuns the idea that it is simple because it was written by simple country folk, and refers to that concept as "typical urban American prejudice." He breaks each line of the poem into one of four categories, noting that they appear in complete sets of twelve, ten, two and two, corresponding exactly to the makeup of a large coven: twelve outer court members, twelve inner court members including a Priest[5] and Priestess and a single pair above them all, which can be seen as either the High Priestess and High Priest, Witch Queen and Witch King, or the God and Goddess themselves, depending on the tradition.

Wyrmstar labels these categories Advice, Ritual Practice, Ritual Language and The Naming of the Laws. The first and largest group, Advice (*With the fool no season spend or be counted as his friend.[6]*) corresponds to the rough metaphysical information shared with the outer circle of a traditional group, information that is bound only lightly by oath, if at all. He comments on his website[7] that most of this material is not only *not* oathbound, but is common folklore of the British Isles. In other words, *Wiccae* is based on folk beliefs found outside of Wicca, such as avoiding fools and casting stones in water to divine the future. Wyrmstar also points out that only one of these pieces of writ is a prohibition, reminding us of the advanced outer court position of Caller.[8] (Wyrmstar freely admits this may be stretching the corresponding of the lines of *Wiccae* to coven positions a bit far.)

---

[4] [Eke Name] http://www.angelfire.com/rant/ingwitch/
[5] By "priest and priestess" we are understood to mean those positions with similar titles, such as "high priest and priestess" in those groups where leadership is not broken into normal and "high" priests.
[6] Rede of the Wiccae, line 21.
[7] http://www.angelfire.com/rant/ingwitch/
[8] Also called Lady's Hand, Scribe, Guardian and Squire, this position was often held by a priest-in-training, who would, in ritual situations, be in charge of making announcements such as "Let none who do not come into this circle in perfect love and perfect trust remain."

The next two groups of lines—the ten pieces of Ritual Practice (*When the Wheel begins to turn – let the Beltane fires burn*[9]) and the two lines of what he calls Ritual Language—correspond to the factoids and information an inner court member would know, someone above the level of initiate, familiar with the basic practices within the group. These lines are specific to Wicca and indicate that a level of training has occurred. This is made more obvious in the two lines of Ritual Language which correspond roughly to two pieces of traditional circle casting spoken by the Priestess (*Merry meet an merry part; bright the cheeks an warm the heart*[10]) and the Priest (*Bide the Wiccan laws ye must in perfect love an perfect trust*[11]) or divided between the Priest and Priestess within ritual.

We turn our attention to the second leader pair, the one Wyrmstar considers most important to Wicca as a whole, in wondering what, exactly, The Wiccan Rede is. The first of these two lines, line 23 (*Mind the Threefold Law ye should – three times bad and three times good*), exemplifies the concept of naming a law. We see the common Wiccan notion of threefold return given the name "The Threefold Law." When confronted with those people who claim *Wiccae* is The Wiccan Rede itself, not the tradition-specific faith-poem published under the slightly different title of *Rede of the Wiccae*, Wyrmstar indicates that only line 23 and the last line of *Wiccae* follow the same pattern, and clearly the pattern of line 23, that of a law's name, followed by its content, is something that few people will claim is erroneous. If, therefore, line 23 gives the name "The Threefold Law" to "three times bad and three times good," then line 26, if it shares the same pattern, must give the name "The Wiccan Rede" to "An it harm none, do as you will."

This, in my mind, at least, settles the debate over whether Wiccan authors and teachers mean the entire 26-line poem or instead the eight words in the last line of the poem when they refer to the "Wiccan Rede." Although

[9] Rede of the Wiccae, line 16
[10] Ibid, line 22.
[11] 9. Ibid, line 1.

dismissed by some who argue such things as an easy way out, I also find striking evidence for the fact that the poem is *not* The Wiccan Rede itself in the simple fact that *Rede of the Wiccae* was published under *that* title, not as *The Wiccan Rede*. A good study of such a debate, however, requires a building up of a full body of evidence in favor of one's position, and these two factors aren't enough to fully lay the specter of the idea of *Wiccae* as the Rede itself to rest. For that last evidence, we need to consider historical validity.

A term or phrase is considered historically valid when it can be shown that it has been used a particular way for a majority of its existence. For example, the slang term "bad," in the sense of meaning something that was cool, hip or interesting, certainly has not taken up a significant percentage of the amount of time that the word "bad" has been in use. The use of the word "bad" to mean *good*, then, while an existing colloquialism, does not have the weight of time and practice behind it required to make the common definition of the term bad be "something cool, hip, or interesting." We could break down the term into a statistic, saying that bad had been used for, oh, fourteen hundred years, and only has had the new definition for twenty-five, and that percentage of time (<0.02%) would represent the historical (or temporal) validity of the new definition. (We'd also examine the percentage of the population using it a certain way, versus another, but that's another type of validity.)

With something like the term "The Wiccan Rede" this is a little easier. Wicca, at less than a century old, does not have a long-standing lexicon, and the term "The Wiccan Rede" has an even shorter age than the religion itself. Taking the appearance of the law in the poem in 1975 as the literal date of the law's creation (which is actually overly parsimonious, as it is assuredly extant in 1964!), we see the first significant, widespread and *common* use of The Wiccan Rede to mean only the phrase "An it harm none, do as you will" (or a mild variation on it with thous and the like) within ten years in the widely available *Buckland's Complete Book of Witchcraft* and at that time, we see *Wiccae* still called by its title by NECTW. Therefore, the weight of historical validity is on the side of those who say The Wiccan Rede is the eight words Buckland mentions—and not the poem with an already existing title—because we see this division between the two things existing long before they are seen as the same. In addition, since there was no huge hue and cry regarding the phrase as it appears in several author's work in the 1970s, despite the existence of contemporary criticism of the same work for other reasons, those claiming the use of the term "The Wiccan Rede" to mean the poem itself has historical validity are stuck in a position of having done too little too late to prove their case. Indeed, all the early publications refer to the eight words as "The Wiccan Rede" and the poem by its proper title[12].

Admittedly, this is not proof positive that the use of the term "The Wiccan Rede" to refer only to the eight-word phrase is correct, only proof that it is the *most common understanding* of the term, the one supported by the weight of publication, history and maybe even by its use in Thompson's poem. Certainly, from a scholastic point of view, calling *Rede of the Wiccae* "The Wiccan Rede" is inaccurate simply because that is not the title the author (or authors) referred to it by. Wyrmstar shoots off one final shot here, however, noting that Thompson was kind enough to provide us with an alternate title (*The Counsel of the Wise Ones*) and that if it were her intention that it be called "The Wiccan Rede," she would've called it that in at least one of her titles for it.

For the purposes of this book, and in the majority of writings within the Wiccan community, "The Wiccan Rede" refers to the phrase "An it harm none, do as you will," and *Rede of the Wiccae* refers to the twenty-six lines that appeared in "Green Egg" more than a quarter of a century ago.

How long has it been in Wicca?

As mentioned before, The Wiccan Rede first appears in Wicca in wide publication by the 1980s, either as the named law in *Rede of the Wiccae* or later in *Buckland's Complete Book*

---

[12] The only real resolution to this would be for NECTW to *publicly* state the Rede and Rede of the Wicca are different in *their tradition*, which would stop this blather altogether.

of Witchcraft as well as a handful of other books and private publications as an independent entity, depending on your view of history. It doesn't appear in any of Gerald Gardner's works. It is not mentioned in *most* books on Wicca before 1975. And it doesn't appear in any books of shadow, made public or shared to reputable sources, written before 1975. It is certainly *not* in Gardner.

The closest thing to "the Rede" in Gardner's books is an oft-quoted line from *The Meaning of Witchcraft* (1959) in which Gardner states that his witches lean toward "the morality of the legendary Good King Pausol, 'Do what you like so long as you harm no one.'" However, if this were a "Law" of Gardner's Witchcraft, it is at least surprising that he never used it as a defense of Wicca in his many press appearances and writings. The truth is that he discussed it as a morality that witches were merely inclined to, *not* as their prime directive, or their law of laws. In fact, Gardner goes on to state that his witches followed an important law regarding a prohibition of baneful magic—unless used to prevent a greater harm—and *contrasted this* with the morality of Good King Pausol.

John J. Coughlin, author of *Out of the Shadows: An Exploration of Dark Paganism and Magick* (1stbooks, inc, 2001) and editor of *The New York City Pagan Resource Guide*[13], has explored the origins of the phrase in-depth in his ongoing work *The Evolution of Wiccan Ethics*[14]. In this revolutionary material, he analyzes the existing published works of Early Modern Wicca[15] for any indication of an original Rede. His work indicates that the phrase "Eight words The Wiccan Rede fulfill, an it harm none, do as you will," was around, if not in common Wiccan parlance, in the early 1960s, the earliest published use of it discovered so far being a mention of the quote in volume one (1964) of *Pentagram*, generally at-

---

[13] http://www.waningmoon.com/guide/
[14] http://www.waningmoon.com/ethics/index.shtml
[15] The use of the phrase Modern Wicca here is not reflective of a belief in an ancient Wicca, but establishes a lack of belief that the Wicca being practiced today is anything *but* modern. In other words, Modern Wicca refers to Wicca that exists at this point in time, not any Wiccas of the past, real or (most likely) imagined.

tributed to a speech by Doreen Valiente at a dinner sponsored by *Pentagram*. This speech is further quoted in Hans Holzer's 1969 *The Truth about Witchcraft* (Doubleday).

This leaves us with the rather unsatisfactory conclusion that The Wiccan Rede was probably created in the early 1960s, possibly as solitary practitioners began to pop up, and the pre-existing moral restraint by virtue of consensus-building began to disintegrate. While there is no proof that it was the holy writ it is now, it certainly existed, even if we cannot accurately determine how it got into common usage. However, what we *can* do to get an idea of how it may have been added to Wicca in general is to examine how it came to be added to the laws of publicly accessible groups that began without it. UEW is once such case study that I, at least, needn't go far to examine.

Although differing in many significant ways from its original group, Universal Eclectic Wicca can be said to have been born in 1969 as a group called the Silver Chalice community[16]. When it was founded, one High Priest, Gérard Greyarrow, insisted that the rule "Do freely that which causes no harm" be enumerated into the beliefs of the group. Since Greyarrow had read Holzer's book, it is likely that the idea that this was an appropriate Wiccan belief for a fledgling group came from that book. Later, in the 1970s, the phrase "that which may harm is done with restraint" was added to the phrase in *The Fifteen Creeds of a Silver Chalice Witch* (which was later renamed *The Fifteen Creeds of Silver Chalice Wicca*.[17]) In the mid 1980s, when *Buckland's*

---

[16] This is not a claim of 1969 being the definitive age of UEW. For all intents and purposes, I believe UEW is a tradition that begins *tomorrow*, and the day after that. There are significant differences between past and current incarnations of UEW, and I think claiming UEW is an unbroken tradition from the 1960s is a big mistake. It's not unbroken…it's reincarnated. I don't think I can translate for Wiccans of the 2000s how radical UEW was in the 1980s in saying it went, at best, to 1969, when other groups were falling over themselves to say they, in 1956, 1954, 1953, were *the* American Wiccan tradition. UEW has never claimed to be old, unfortunately, our claims of definite youth are now seen as old!

[17] The progression of the Silver Chalice Fifteen Creeds is detailed on CUEW's website, http://www.cuew.org, where it is listed under "foundational documents" in the clergy handbook.

Complete Book of Witchcraft was added to the reading list, The Wiccan Rede as "An it harm none, do as thou wilt" became standard teaching in UEW, and then was later enumerated as one of the Five Points of Wiccan Belief, UEW's core theology[18].

This idea, that it began as a sort of bleed-through from the early 1960s, possibly even from Valiente's speech, and then developed separately from the point of initial contact, later being brought back into line when widely published works on Wicca began to appear, seems highly logical, and matches the progression of many traditions of Wicca itself. It seems likely that if the grassroots "witches" of the mid 20th century could spark the creation of many varied traditions that would later adapt to conform to a form of Wicca that came to be in the 1980s, the Rede could do the same.

This renders the idea of when it came to be in Wicca largely moot, because the separate evolution of redes, leading to an eventual conformity to the published Rede makes the entire concept a sticky one. Does Gardner, mentioning the beliefs of "Good King Pausol," establish a first Rede? Does Silver Chalice's "Do freely that which causes no harm" qualify as The Wiccan Rede? Does it pop into existence the moment Valiente mentions it? We can't really answer these questions with anything more than personal opinion. All we can say is that it doesn't begin to be seen as a common thread in Wicca until the mid-1980s, and that it is still, currently seen as a common Wiccan belief.

[In my personal opinion, Raymond Buckland is primarily responsible for the elevation of the Rede to the status it has today. Others, such as Scott Cunningham, would build upon the idea of the Rede as Wicca's Prime Directive, but I feel that Buckland single-handedly moved it from obscure sub-reference to commandment-like sacred writing, and I feel that is a contribution we as a community should honor him for.-KMD]

---

[18] The Five Points, enumerated as such, date to about 1992, although the concept is older.

Reading the Rede:

Having established the Rede as the eight words "An it harm none, do as you will," and having admitted defeat when discussing the date of its addition into Wicca, we can go on the brief tangent of evaluating it for what it is today. As mentioned previously, one could claim it nonsensical to have a discussion of The Wiccan Rede at the beginning of an advanced work, but a quick perusal of any Wiccan message board will uncover people claiming years of experience in Wicca who seem to have a basic lack of understanding as to what those words mean.

People without experience in Middle English (fake or otherwise) sometimes see "An it harm none, do as you will," and incorrectly believe it states "harm none." While such a mistake is in syntax, we'll ignore that for a while and treat the phrase as if it does say "harm none." The goal of the Rede, in this version, is to do no harm to others, to the world around oneself and to the individual, which seems quite admirable. People who believe this feel they can move through the universe being creatures of growth and light, doing harm to nothing via sensible eating, sensitive life decisions and a complete embracing of a better-than-the-rest ideology. They sneer at leather and videogames, cars and eating meat, even at people's decisions to have children in their attempt to harm none.

In reality, harming none fails as a mature theological construct[19]. If you breathe, you harm microbes that die upon contact with your respiratory tract. If you eat, you harm animals, plants, yeasts and microscopic molds living on most foods. If you reproduce, you create a drain on resources. If you don't reproduce, you don't pass on your genes and can be seen as harming your ancestors. In the most extreme case, if you go out to the forest and die (hav-

---

[19] In this line and some that follow, I've replaced the term theology (in the first edition) with Wyrmstar's better term, theological construct, which he defines as a belief, practice, ethic or other religious concept that serves the purpose of strengthening or enforcing the basic concepts of the religion or philosophy about the divine that spawns it. I'm not quite enough of a structuralist to see religion in this way, but it is a better term for this instance than that I would've used and needs less explanation.

ing, of course, ceased to breathe and eat), you kill the plants you land upon by over-fertilization, and create a smell that, at the least, will lower property values.

To this reality, our misunderstood harm-noners defend their actions by claiming that "harm none" is a goal, not a commandment. This, say those who see the Rede as the prime belief of Wicca, reduces The Wiccan Rede to a suggestion, to mere advice, not the rule of thumb it has been in Wicca in the past. Beginning Wiccans surf the net or pick up books to hear one group say that absolutely nothing must be harmed in order to live at one with the Rede while still others say that breaking the Rede, even once, makes a person not a Wiccan. These two points of view, both incorrect from a strictly grammatical reading of the Rede, are completely incompatible.

It is not surprising, then, that our newbies are confused. In reality, the Rede states "An it harm none, do as you will." This is really a very literal statement. "An it harm none," which means "If it does no harm" or "Those things/actions that do no harm," followed by "do as you will." It is not "do only those things that harm none" — a theological construct that makes no sense — but instead "do those things that cause no harm as you will." That statement does not speak to those actions that do cause harm; those things are covered in the rest of the religion. In *All One Wicca*, I reduced this to a rhyme of my own, attempting to make the point painfully clear: "Do as you will, if it harm naught. If it harm some, do as you ought"... with the "ought" defined by the rest of the religion.

In her (no longer online) *Read the Rede, Reed*, Wiccan Priestess and critic "Alpha" gives the "real" meaning of The Wiccan Rede as:

> You are aware of your thoughts and actions, so you know your will, a thing deeper than want — animals want — things that think, that are completely sentient on the human or higher level have will: intention and desire, based on knowledge of the self. Everyone who can know their will can do their will-act within their intention, desire and knowledge of self to achieve an end.
>
> Wiccans, however, are obliged to attempt to live in a manner that works with their faith. Their will is limited by

choice. They may do freely, as their will dictates, only those things that harm none. They are limited in doing those things that can cause harm by the dictates of their faith. Those dictates are not stated in the Rede, those dictates are given elsewhere in their faith, The Wiccan Rede speaks only to those things which they can do willy-nilly, to their heart's content, without even having a spare thought for their faith-those things in the category of "that which harms none."[20]

In discussing a more mature and historically relevant Wiccan Rede then, we see it not as a suggestion or commandment, but a simple how-to statement: Live your life so that you do freely those actions which cause no harm; those actions with the potential to harm are done only in a manner that corresponds to the rest of your religion. It is not a statement of what not to do, but what to do. It's not a prohibition or a thou-shalt-not, but a way to live and act.

Does the Rede Work?

The Rede, defined as above, works as a theological construct because it is not restrictive. When theology is spoken in terms of *don't*s, it becomes mere convention, a set of rules. The study of the gods, and the pursuit of a relationship with them is not about *not* doing things (although some things may be prohibited) but about *doing* things. You don't have a set of rules, but a set of mores, beliefs and ethical concepts. It's not a collection of prohibitions ("Don't drink a certain thing, don't sleep around or don't lie") but instead a collection of guidelines ("Remain in control of yourself, honor your obligations and tell the truth"). In some ways, these ideas are more restrictive.

I'm fond of giving my students clips from movies or telling them to sit through a movie only to make one lesson be the extent of my suggestion. A few years back, there was a really dreadful movie called *The Thirteenth Warrior*, in which Antonio Banderas played a prince strongly dedicated to Islam whom fate throws together with a number of Germanic warriors. It's dreadful and full of horrible stereotypes, but

[20] Formerly at http://rw.faithweb.com

has a scene, maybe three minutes long, which illustrates the distinction between a theological prohibition and a theological sanction.

In the scene, the Germanic warriors, being typical stereotypes of their folk, are getting drunk, falling all over each other and basically having a good time. Banderas, of course, is commanded not to drink of the "grain or the vine," but since these Germanic warriors are drinking mead, which is made from honey, he's off the hook.

He's following his prohibition to the letter if he drinks the mead: he's been told to not drink specific things, and mead isn't one of them. His choice then becomes whether to follow the letter of the law, assuming his god knew about mead and it wasn't prohibited for a reason, or the perceived spirit of the law, assuming his god meant that he wasn't supposed to drink at all. Both situations require some degree of hubris: he's making an assumption about what a god[21] thinks. If his god had, instead, said "remain in control of your senses at all times" the situation would not be reduced to trying to know what he thinks, but instead would dictate deciding to drink or not based on how it would affect you. This revised commandment would be much more expansive, not simply concerning grain, or fruit, or even honey, but applying to *all* things which had the capacity to cause loss of control, from drinks and drugs to bad decisions.

The Wiccan Rede is one such rule: It does not say "don't hurt people or things," because that can be reduced to a question of what does and does not hurt people and things, and also ignores those things that both harm and help at the same time. Instead, it says that those things that harm nothing can be done as you will, and leaves to your discretion

---

[21] Throughout this work, "God" refers to the deity allegedly named "God" in the Abrahamic Pantheon, whereas "god" refers to any deity, including that one when his proper name is not being used — god of Abraham, for example. When discussing the Ubergod, this capitalization will also be used, as it is an Abrahamic "God" concept, or the concept of the "real God." To make this really clear, I have added many articles (the, his, of) to the word god, and further standardized the capitalization in this edition. All gods are treated equally herein.

the rest of the possible actions (and inactions) in any given situation.

Contrary to the insistence of some who are unfamiliar with Wicca and consider it illogical because of the perceived prohibition against all harm, Wicca is about *doing* those things that do no harm *freely*. This is a highly effective policy. If I wish to drink small amounts of alcohol, something I personally find pleasant, and if I do so in such a way that I am doing no genuine harm (the alcohol is not purchased from gangsters, I am not breaking a just law in consuming it, nor drinking an amount large enough to cause permanent harm to my body, nor am I driving while under its influence, drinking it at an inopportune time or am I made incapable of controlling my actions by the consumption of it), then I am not prevented from doing so as I will. If I wish to take an antibiotic, doing terminal harm to several otherwise innocent streptococci bacteria, I am also not prevented from doing so, although my faith teaches I must take full responsibility for the action—I willingly kill the bacteria, I take full responsibility for the harm done them, and I accept fully any ramifications for having harmed them.

With knowledge of The Wiccan Rede as what it is—as an invitation to do that which harms none rather than a prohibition against harm at all costs—we can see that it works quite well, thank you very much!

Discussing the Wiccan Rede with Others

In his now-defunct essay *Neo-Pagan Witchcraft and Hellenismos: a Comparison*, Drew Campbell, author of the book *Old Stones, New Temples*, listed two of the common beliefs of Neo-Pagan Witchcraft (including Wicca) as a "Universal Prohibition of Harm" and the belief that this is somehow expected of all people. This misconception (indeed a lifetime search of over 200 traditions of Witchcraft and Wicca and research for four books has not found even one group with these beliefs) is founded on the often-sloppy method by which we Wiccans discuss The Wiccan Rede with others.

I am not immune from this sloppiness myself. I have often read back over early emails where I described my ethical bent as "harm none" with the unfounded belief that the person on the other end would somehow know what I meant by it. This "you know what I mean" syndrome is prevalent within a lot of early Wiccan literature, and if you frequent online communities or chat rooms that attract younger Wiccan members you'll often see it. We describe our beliefs in short hand, using "harm none" to describe The Wiccan Rede and "Karma" to describe the concept of return or the so-called Law of Three, knowing darn well that these terms are not really appropriate.

I blame this sloppiness for the bizarre belief Campbell and other persons in both the Reconstructionist and Anti-Wiccan Christian communities attribute to Wiccans: that we are strange Neo-Pagan Jains, following beliefs about harm that make no sense. Indeed, I have seen unaffiliated young Wiccans state unequivocally that they harm nothing at all; their arguments quickly dismantled by people who ask them, for example, how the destruction of soybeans for their tofu burger does not harm the soybean.

We are, therefore, both irresponsible to our communities and to our future generations of Wiccans when we speak this way, and must be ever vigilant when discussing the Rede to prevent future misconception. Several good online primers on The Wiccan Rede exist, and few established Wiccan traditions do not explain the meaning of The Wiccan Rede on day one. I strongly suggest that students read up on The Wiccan Rede, ask people who describe the beliefs in simplified terms what, exactly, they mean and try to avoid sloppiness in the future. This is the first step toward a true interfaith dialog — speaking your beliefs clearly enough to allow discussion of them by others.

Recommended Reading for Topic One:

Wiccan Ethics and The Wiccan Rede: What Sayeth the Rede?
http://www.paganlibrary.com/ethics/wiccan_ethics_rede.
php
If that link does not work, try:
http://www.sacred-texts.com/bos/bos661.htm
http://www.witchvox.com/basics/rede.html
http://www.waningmoon.com/ethics/rede.shtml

All One Wicca, Chapter one.

[If links do not point to current websites, check the supporting website for this work at http://www.macmorgan.org]

Discussion Questions for Topic One:
[These questions are not questions of "reading comprehension," I see reading comprehension questions as insulting for adults, and I assume that if you had difficulty understanding something you've read you have the capacity to go back and try to work through it on your own. These discussion questions are for use by groups like my own teaching circles, which will often read one or two sections of a book and then discuss it the next time they meet. As such, they may be reproduced as necessary, as long as their source is mentioned.

I appreciate those who have emailed me to ask for permission to use them, and I'd also like to thank the many who submitted or suggested questions.-KM]

1.1. How valid is a discussion of The Wiccan Rede in an advanced work?

1.2. Have you ever had an experience where your idea of the Rede was very different from someone else's?

1.3. If you are a member of an established tradition, do you know when the Rede was added to that tradition?

1.4. How valid do you feel a literary approach to *The Rede of the Wiccae* is?

1.5. Do you think the Rede sometimes doesn't work? Why or why not?

1.6. Do you have any personal experiences, perhaps with other religions, where you felt the letter of a rule was divorced from the spirit of it? (Like the example from "The Thirteenth Warrior.")

1.7. Do you have any personal experiences of people who dismissed the Rede, or Wicca, as illogical, based on the belief that it taught that people could not make any actions without fear of harm?

1.8. How might *you*, personally, help foster a better understanding of Wicca amongst newbies and people outside the community? Is it your job to do so—why or why not?

1.9. The term "Rede" is often translated as advice or counsel. When it appears in Middle English, the people giving that counsel are usually judges, gods and priests. Do you think *that* type of advice is different from what we might give friends or relatives, and what does that say about those who dismiss the Rede as "mere" advice?

Topic Two: All Paths Lead to the Same Place and All gods are One God, right?

Are all gods really one big Ubergod? How is this belief harmful? How did it get into Wicca? Why do some people really hate it when I say that? What's the big deal, anyway? What is Universalism? Monotheism? Henotheism?

All gods are One God: The Evolution of a Belief

Dion Fortune is generally credited with coining the phrase "All gods are One God." Fortune was a ceremonial magician and author who was often unkind in her views of nascent Modern Paganism, and whose organization, the Society of Inner Light, has worked overtime to distance itself from the Modern Pagan community. The repetition of one of her key phrases, out of context, by Modern Pagans is both humorous and troubling. On the one hand, this concept of all gods really being one God works well with the psychotherapy and the Jewish Mysticism that Fortune made her living peddling, but on the other, we must ask ourselves if non-Abrahamic religions have a reason to accept as gospel the teachings of Abrahamic religions.

Wicca evolved at a time when psychotherapy and the study of the mind were in its infancy, and just as we now look to biological science and secular ethics, current hot button topics, to answer the questions of our time, people in Fortune's time looked to psychotherapy and the diluted Judaism of the Western Ceremonial Magical traditions to answer their questions. There is nothing innately wrong with this concept: we use the tools we have to analyze the world around us. Sadly, for those evaluating the usefulness of Fortune's materials, psychology has moved far past Freud and Jung, and the pillaging of Jewish culture by non-Jews has fallen out of favor (unless you are Madonna.)

In the mid-twentieth century, just as Gardner's groundbreaking works on Early Modern Witchcraft were taking root, the study of comparative theology was still hampered by the Eurocentric concept that polytheism was inherently lesser and that monotheism was greater: the natural evolution of religion, representing progress. From this point of view, polytheistic religions are more primitive and represent cultures that are less advanced than our own (with "our own" being defined primarily as white, male, English-speaking and Christian).

Calling this belief "evolution" is particularly poignant, because Charles Darwin perhaps expresses this prejudice best in his *Descent of Man*, when he refers to the necessity of the development of increased mental reasoning capacity in man, and explains:

> The same high mental faculties which first led man to believe in unseen spiritual agencies, then in fetishism, polytheism, and ultimately in monotheism, would infallibly lead him, as long as his reasoning powers remained poorly developed, to various strange superstitions and customs.[22]

Even Frazer's *The Golden Bough*, loved by much of the Pagan community, is slanted with the idea that monotheism is the inevitable conclusion of polytheism. The concept that a monotheistic society was the natural development of a civilized culture—its innate rational order—was deeply ingrained in religious studies long before the time Gardner wrote his first book.

It is not surprising, then, that early Wicca is portrayed as polytheistic with the caveat that by polytheistic we *really* mean that it is the religion of many gods that *everyone knows* are really just attributes, faces or interpretations of the one *real* god. This stems from Wicca's desire to go with the science of its time. Sadly, modern anthropologists generally consider the popular anthropology of the time of early Wicca hogwash, and the inability of some Wiccan scholars to separate the discussion of their religion from the discussion of those anthropological materials has caused some people to dismiss Wicca as part and parcel of that very same hogwash.

Rather than using the "all gods are one" argument to defend themselves from being viewed as primitive, modern polytheistic Wiccans see polytheism as a valid approach to

---

[22] 1. Darwin, Charles, *Descent of Man*, 1871 Available online: http://www.infidels.org/library/historical/charles_darwin/descent_of_man.html

divinity in its own right. For those Wiccans who are polytheistic (and we will discuss those who are not later) the
concept of all gods being one God is not only incorrect, but
also offensive, often flying in the face of personal experiences of the divine. To the follower of Apollo, there is no
question that Apollo and Zeus are discrete entities, and the
insistence that both are, for example, mere facets of the god
of Abraham, not only makes no sense, but may be seen as
offensive, attributing acts committed by one god to another.

It's not as offensive when the things are characteristic of
the deity in question. Few Hellenic Reconstructionists or
other followers of the ancient gods of Greece will deny that
Zeus probably would've smitten the city of Sodom for abusing its guests (and, indeed, most Biblical scholars agree that
the "sin" of Sodom is abuse of the guest/host relationship)
or that Apollo would rain down plague if a king refused to
do as he asked, but it is unlikely they would agree that their
god would condemn someone to hell for not following
them or that any one god would do all the often contradict-
ing acts of the god of Abraham. For the liberal polytheist, it
is really very simple: just as you and I are discrete entities of
the big thing called humanity, Apollo, Zeus, Loki, Inanna
and Venus are discrete entities of a big thing called divinity.

Just as you are not I, Apollo is not Inanna. Claiming he
is, to someone who has experience with one or both, is ludi-
crous. We find ourselves once again put in the position of
making decisions regarding the validity of the beliefs of
other persons, and anytime we find ourselves in that position we're on shaky ground. Put simply, in order to rea-
sonably make claims about one person's religious belief,
you have to have replicable proof that yours is correct and
replicable proof that theirs is not. One lasting lesson I
learned as an atheist is that if a god comes down to you and
personally tells you what is and isn't true, and expects you
to teach it to others without more than words, that god is
either cruel or insane. In other words, unless you are provided the proof to demonstrate it at the level another person can comprehend, the information is meant for you
alone.

This is, perhaps, the core element of Wicca's theology that so aggravates people trying to persuade its adherents that they need a new faith, the simple belief that if the divine wished you to change religions, it would give you decent reasons to do so. We believe that the words and messages we get from the divine, if any, are for us alone, and don't dictate the beliefs we should teach others. This is why Wicca often teaches the replicable mechanics of religion instead of making claims about the nature of god(s).

Believing all gods are one God becomes particularly dangerous when we make assumptions about the validity of other people's religions. There are religions that have been practiced for thousands of years with little change. These faiths often teach very particular things about their gods, and if we are to shuck thousands of years of teaching, and say that hundreds of thousands of persons are wrong, and have historically been wrong, we need damned good proof of that claim. Since we don't have that proof, the rational study of religion suggests that the persons who know a religion best are its practitioners, and our own faith is only right when it does not speak to the validity of the faith of others.

This is one of the paradoxes of faith that Wicca acknowledges. Neither is it challenged by the concept that people can claim their gods are the only gods that exist (and are probably right), while at the same time others can claim that all gods exist (and are also probably right). The mechanics of this are more detailed than I wish to get at this point, but suffice it to say that most of us take the position that all religions are equally valid until they make claims about another religion… in which case they need to provide more than words if they expect to be seen as more valid. We take a scientific approach: it *may* be that one faith is actually more valid than another, but until significant proof arrives, we cannot make such a claim beyond the subjective level. A faith can only be more or less valid *for us*.

Related to the idea that all gods are one God is the belief, often mislabeled as Universalism, that all paths are different roads to the same destination, or are different ways of seeing the same path. Like the false polytheism of the apologists that teaches that all gods are one as a form of excuse for not following a monotheistic path, the false universalism of the single path is often taught of by people who simply have no strength in their own belief. It is an easily repeatable belief that works better as a catchphrase than as an actual theology. One need only imagine the religious beliefs of terrorists or other extremists to quickly realize that their paths absolutely must not lead to the same place as the paths of the righteous. While it is a nice catchphrase to say we're all going to the same place, it's not very logically solid- do you want seventy-two virgins? I don't. What on earth would I do with them?!?

One method of separating catchphrase theology from the genuine article is to question it, as simply and as directly as possible. Catchphrase theology is full of exceptions to the rule, and questions soon draw these exceptions out. We saw an example of catchphrase theology in the first topic when The Wiccan Rede was reduced to harm none. People who teach this are often quick to add exceptions such as unless there is no other way or unless it is in self-defense. Another type of exception is what I like to call "the on the spot rewrite" where, for example, we are told The Wiccan Rede can be interpreted differently for intention and action, or that The Law of Three, which does not hold up well under observation, is actually misinterpreted by everyone and means retribution in body, mind, and spirit, not that things are multiplied by three.[23] These rewrites and exceptions indicate that the catchphrases are highly imperfect, whereas a good theological point of view will fall into place neatly, even when faced with paradoxes.

All religious and spiritual paths cannot lead to the same place not because, as we might fear at first, one destination is better than the other, but because few religious or spiritual paths claim the same, or similar, ends. One path may

---

[23] Both of these examples come from Philosophy of Wicca by Amber Laine Fisher. The "Body, Mind and Spirit" comment is particularly heinous, as it is so obviously NOT what was meant when Porter said "three times bad and three times good" and Fisher actually claims that *all* the Wiccan elders teaching otherwise are confused or teaching the confusion of their elders!

teach that it leads to a paradisiacal afterlife, another to eventual reincarnation as a planet, another to self-knowledge, another to life with a particular god. On the surface, these paths can all be seen as leading towards a similar place, but to agree that they are all one would be a sort of consensual delusion. If, for example, one religion teaches that the ultimate reward in the afterlife is to be reincarnated as a planetary biosphere, it would have to follow that those expecting to encounter a heavenly paradise when they die would find planethood heavenly... despite the fact that "heaven," if it is embraced by a religion at all, will have its own, distinct religious character—a character that may not include reincarnation as anything, let alone a planet.

Even this is limiting our argument to just those paths that make attainment of a particular afterlife their goal. In order to accept that the paths that lead to an afterlife are really the same as those that make no claims about the afterlife, we have to develop tricks of thinking. For example, we must learn to believe that a person who suggests he is trying to better know himself is *really* trying to find heaven, no matter what he says. Claiming to know what another person really means—while dismissing that person's own claims—is why Wiccans are often accused of religious imperialism. It is neither easy nor pleasant to become aware of one's inner imperialist.

To take this down to a more basic level, a Familial Magical Tradition with which I am familiar teaches that every member of that family is a reincarnation of other family members who came before them. They teach that there are an unlimited number of common souls within that family but only three powerful souls, who only have only existed simultaneously at a few rare points in history. These people teach that when these souls do not incarnate, they stay in this world as protectors of the family's interests, causing sudden changes in fortune, like winning the lottery, to maintain the family. They are fickle in their assistance, however. As an example, land in the family name for centuries was foreclosed upon after bad decisions and purchased by the bank. Twenty-five years later, it was found to have archeological import and purchased by a heritage society who promptly named a member of the same family curator. This family curator was then able to purchase the land at a discount once the heritage society had gotten all the items of interest from it, and discovered it was more a drain on resources than a thing to be preserved.

To hear the current owner of the land speak, the existence of these helper spirits is directly responsible for her owning her grandfather's land today. The thought of them being anywhere but directly around her seems bizarre, almost blasphemous, because these perfect souls maintain perfection by directing all of their focus toward the assistance and betterment of that family. Comparing this belief to those that teach that perfection comes by freeing oneself of worldly attachments — like family — or those that teach that the end goal of life is removal from the world of men, you can see why those in this family grow uncomfortable when told that all paths lead to the same destination. It just doesn't make sense.

The idea that all paths lead to the same place is an interesting theory that nonetheless fails in practice. It may allow us to tell the proselyte who comes to the door to go away on the basis that regardless of what he says we *know* we can't be improved by changing to his path, but in general, we don't really believe that all paths *are* equal. We may all go to the same place, according to our own theology, but not because all paths are equal. We can only really make the claim that we all go to the same place and that all religions have the same goal if we assume other faiths are wrong.

Let's take another (extreme) example, in order to pinpoint our own prejudices regarding all paths being one. Archaeology has shown that a very small number of ancient peoples committed mass human sacrifice, and that this was probably the sacrifice of captured warriors from opposing tribes. Few if any of us will claim that a religion of massive human sacrifice[24] is a path that is just as good as our own

---

[24] I use this example because most religions that involved human sacrifice did it in small quantities and are less objectionable. Few of us, for example, feel the same way about massive execution of enemies to appease bloodthirsty gods as we do about ancient dying king cults, which treat the rare

religion. While some teach that the practitioners of those ancient religions will still go to their particular afterlife of choice, few people would want to be in communion with such a practitioner.

We end up in the same position as we were with the idea of all gods being only one God, where we essentially have to take the word of the peoples who are practicing their religions until they try to speak for the next guy over. This can be difficult for those of us who come from a Western or Abrahamic position of progress and exclusion: we *want* to be the number one faith, the most right, the most sacred, the most advanced. These are valid desires as long as you understand those superlatives to apply only to you. It is the most right faith *for you*, the most sacred faith *for you* and the most advanced faith *for you*.

Believing all paths are one path can be seen as a sort of reaction to fundamentalism: if all paths are one, religious strife is unneeded. We, as practitioners of non-Abrahamic religions, cannot understand Protestant Christians blowing up Catholic Christians (and vice versa) because they are both Christians. We cannot understand the various sects of Islam at war with each other in the Middle East, or even understand strife between them and Jews, or between sects of Jews, because they are all Abrahamic religions with the same goals. This strife happens amongst faiths that generally acknowledge the other faith as having similar theological goals, so as you can imagine, similarity between non-related religions cannot be expected to cause peace. We *want* all people to go to the same place, to have equality in this world and the next, but like the statements regarding deities, we cannot make qualitative statements about theological destinations without both internal proof (which is good enough for our inner beliefs) and external proof

sacrifice, of a willing person, as the metaphysical equivalent of throwing oneself on a hand grenade. You'll note, however, that I refuse to name this action as the act of any *one* people, because there is no proof it was the practice of an entire population. Rather than offend anyone, I prefer instead to see those mass executions in the same light as the Witchcraze and Holocaust- the hysterical actions of a populace under the control of charismatic leaders.

(which is required of people expecting to comment upon the religions of others). How we find those proofs is a matter of philosophy, and we have to acknowledge the possibility that we may not find either in this life.

Universalism Defined, the Paradox of UPG and an Introduction to our Imaginary Friends

Wicca is best described as a Universalist religion. Universalism in this sense refers to the idea that mankind does not truly need "saving." As I explained earlier, it does *not* refer to the idea that all gods or paths are equivalent, although even in that sense it usually teaches all paths have some element of truth in them. In its earliest Christian form, unaffiliated with Unitarianism, Universalism began with the acknowledgement of a paradox within Christianity: that an All-Loving deity would have a hell. Universalism came to grips with this paradox in several ways, all of which assumed their god loved everyone. The first way was the belief that persons would be given a second chance after death to be saved, presumably with more information. We can assume then, that in this version of Universalism, which has strong overtones of Christianity, the hapless Pagan would get shown the "reality" of Jesus and the rest before going to hell and would have a chance to admit his mistake and go to heaven with the rest of the world.

In the next version of Universalism, people of all religions who are essentially good people go to heaven, and people who are bad go to hell. This version settles a lot of the issues Pagans have with Christianity, especially the idea that a deathbed conversion could get a Hitler in the pearly gates... while Buddha, Gandhi and billions of non-Christians roasted far below. Many extreme Christians highly object to this belief, and righteously proclaim that the greatest of works don't mean a hill of beans to their god.

In a third version of Universalism, humanity has misinterpreted the words of the Abrahamic deity and there is no hell at all, but a place without that god. Once there, a chance to be made one with that god presents itself. Comparing this to the two beliefs above, you can see how this is a compromise: bad people still go to a sort of minimum security hell, but they can get out once they have a chance to be saved. Most forms of Universalism all agree on one thing: positive people go to heaven

Liberal Universalism, which is the category Wicca most often falls under, is the belief that mankind is "saved," as it were, by mere existence of being born. "God made me," says one Universalist slogan, "and God doesn't make junk." The mechanics of this Universalism vary. For Christian Liberal Universalists, the belief may be that Jesus died for everyone and thus everyone is saved, or that, like one of the beliefs above, second and third chances for salvation exist. For the non-Christian Liberal Universalist, hell may not exist at all, and we are not all saved so much as we are not all in any danger to begin with.

This form of Universalism, prevalent in Modern Universalist thought (though fairly alien to historical Universalism), also teaches that positive things exist in most religions, and we can learn these positive aspects with a little exploration. Since it teaches that we aren't going to hell, the price of wrong turns during exploration is negligible. With no penalty for searching, we can seek in all faiths for the elements of truth, not just our own.

This seeking from all faiths is called "eclecticism," and when it occurs without any sort of moral guideline, it can render a religion nonsensical. Indeed, the babbling of dozens of nonsense Wiccan materials, which teach that Wicca is whatever you wish it to be, is one symptom of eclecticism without guidelines, and splinter groups hiving off of the Unitarian Universalist Church are another. Ideally, we are Universalist and eclectic within a religious framework. Neither Universalism nor eclecticism teach that all paths and gods are equivalent, just that most things can be approached from multiple vectors.

As I have stated, Wicca accepts the existence of several paradoxes, and this idea of multiple vectors leads to another paradox: the paradox of Unverified Personal Gnosis (what I and others refer to simply as UPG). Rather than see paradoxes as flaws in the faith, we see them as opportunities for meditation and study. Our worldview says that it is best to use the entire mind in our spiritual pursuits, and things that are not easily solved (or are not solvable at all) are not ignored or disregarded, but used as windows to personal exploration. Like the Zen Buddhist koan — a paradoxical statement or story designed to encourage thought and promote intuitive enlightenment — our paradoxes are meant to be thought upon until our need for them is fulfilled, whereupon we have either solved them at a personal level or come to see them as religious ephemera. The thought process, not the outcome, is the reason for the examination of the paradox.

Like the belief in multiple correct paths and in gods that are both many discrete units and a single unified entity, UPG is an inevitable paradox occurring within Wicca. Because a significant part of Wiccan religious life is dedicated to finding the secrets inside oneself as well as better knowing the divine, it only makes sense that one who lives his or her life in such an introspective and prayerful way will have several moments of epiphany and maybe even *experiences* of the divine. Such experiences may provide a deep knowledge (gnosis) of how the universe works, perhaps even yielding a high degree of certainty in one's beliefs. Without proof, however, this knowledge can never leave the mind of the person who had the experiences as anything but conjecture.

As a rational religion, we know that we cannot expect others to believe what we say simply because we say it. We can have people look upon our other actions and determine the likelihood that we are speaking truth, but once it leaves our brain and comes out of our mouths it is no longer an experience, but a story... and stories can easily be dismissed. Even if we believe the story, how we interpret it may well vary from the storyteller's interpretation. For example, if a mother presents her infant to us as the next Jesus, we may look at what we know about her and decide she's crazy, on drugs or maybe a member of a strange cult. Her UPG does not match our experiences, personal or shared, so we probably dismiss her story as either an outright lie or as some sort of delusion.

We quickly come to the realization that we do not give all UPG the same merit. We develop rules for it fairly quickly as the amount of it in our life builds. We may speak of it very little, or only with those with UPG that matches our own… or we may keep silent about it, developing the quiet wisdom of the sages, speaking about it only when asked. We understand, of course, that UPG is completely out in religious debate: if someone explains that the Bible says, "Thou shalt not kill," we can't say that the vision of Jesus we had last night told us otherwise. Even if it did, we can't well expect someone to disregard the tangible book in his or her hands simply because we said so. Likewise, a Christian cannot well demand that you see the Bible as the word of God simply because his preacher told him so and he agrees with his preacher. The "Word of God" is a quality, not a quantity, and as such, it is subjective and unverifiable. If a quality like the "Word of God" does not match your experiences, and cannot be verified, it is unreasonable for you to be expected to believe it.

As I mentioned earlier, this is a core element of Wicca's theology: If you were meant to believe it, you would not find it impossible to believe. You may need proof, or you may need to do some serious seeking, but it is unlikely that any deity worth following would expect you to believe the things that elicit a visceral negative reaction within you. Contrary to the beliefs of some, being religious does not automatically make you gullible—and being concerned with the spiritual does not mean you must become ignorant of the material. The genuine practice of a reasonable religion requires following it with every ounce of your being. In order to do so, the nagging doubts and internal fears must be explored as well.

UPG and Universalism are inextricably linked. Practiced properly, Universalism allows UPG: all beliefs that people hold are possible, even if not probable, and are treated equally. Restrictive Universalism discounts not just personal gnosis, but communal gnosis as well. It says, quite simply, that any belief that falls outside of the Universalist belief is wrong—a statement contrary to core Universalism.

Communal gnosis is the shared knowledge and understanding (in minds, books, oral traditions, religions, myths and histories) of a people. To explain why blowing off communal gnosis is a bad thing, we're going to stretch our imaginations a little and tell a story. For the purpose of this book, to keep any one group from being singled out, we're going to create a people in our imaginations, influenced (as the Romans, Greeks, Celts and others were) by the Proto-Indo-European (PIE) language migration. We'll call these people the Logosians[25], just for the heck of it, and claim they lived somewhere on an imaginary island in the middle of the Mediterranean, which is still (in our imaginations) there today.

The Logosians had an ancient vibrant religion with wooden tablets explaining their earliest faith that have been carbon-dated at over 7,000 years old. They had a small pantheon of gods headed by Jius, a sky-father god who throws lightning and is also the protector of guests. Jius had many wives, including Eiroo, protector of women and marriage, and the earth goddess Ciris. He had several sons and brothers, including Eoodis, god of the underworld, and Sedin, god of the seas. Their gods, so their legends said, were cast out of the heavens by the other gods and had to build a new home from scratch, a home they built beneath the mountain. The ancient religion also taught that every man and woman on their island was descended from the sexual union of Jius and Ciris, a union that created two people, Leon and Eo. All Logosians, therefore, are direct descendants of the gods.

In the time of Augustus, the island of the Logosians was incorporated into the Roman Empire after a long and brutal war. As time went on, the Logosians eventually conformed to the state religion of the Empire, which eventually became Christianity. A small group of Logosians on the island's sole mountain, however, practiced their traditional religion right up until about eight hundred years ago.

In the year 1941, Marcus Petroski, an eccentric millionaire, found the hidden temple of the last traditional practitioners of the ancient Logosian faith, and was so very

---

[25] I've been asked where this term came from, and it came from my head and the word *logos*. Another imaginary people I discuss elsewhere, the Katru, come from people discussing the Logosians as *my* (Kat's) Asatruar. The Logosians *really* are imaginary. REALLY.

moved that he formed, on the spot, the Logosian Reconstructionist movement: an attempt to recreate the religious
practices of the ancient Logosians through archaeology, the
personal practices of islanders, and the writings of Herodo-
tus, Julius Caesar, the great Doriad (who wrote the first stories of Logosian religion) and Vector, author of three epic
poems set on the island,.

For fifty years or so, the Logosian Reconstructionists, or
"LRs" trucked along happily, finding out all sorts of things
about the ancient Logosians and themselves... fueling ad-
vances in archaeology, genealogy (because their religion
taught that the power of the gods was passed down
through genetic relationship to them) even language. Their
movement was well-established long before any books on
Wicca were translated into their native language.

Then, in 1995, a book on Logosian religion was translated into English. A beautiful history of the fairly mellow
faith, which advocated family unity and personal duty, captured the hearts of thousands of Americans, and whether
one could or could not become an adopted Logosian became a heated debate. It was decided that since the Logosians believed that power translated down through
bloodlines, adoption was impossible.

A few years later, the point was made moot when
equally imaginary Wiccan author JD Conroy wrote his book
"Logosian Majic" which combined the many-welcoming
religion of Wicca, which taught that we all had equal
power, with the deities and mythologies of the Logosians,
and was strangely nearly identical to Conroy's earlier book,
Roman Majic, even down to facts that weren't so. For example, the Logosian god Sedin, the god of the sea, was not
also a god of earthquakes like Neptune, but there it was in
Conroy's listing in the book: Sedin, the earth-shaker, god of
the seas and earthquakes. In another example, Conroy
taught that the Logosians and the Romans had state religions that advocated harming no one and had no slavery or
corruption. History, of course, has taught otherwise. But
since Conroy's book only did well in small metaphysical
circles, it fell under the radar of the Logosian Reconstructionists.

Just a few months later, charismatic and equally imaginary Wiccan author Copper Crowfox wrote her groundbreaking book "Logoscraft" which used the slim facts in Conroy's book as the basis for her tradition, Logosian Wicca, which she claimed to have been practicing for 20 years. Logoscraft was a hit, and sold several hundred thousand copies. Within a year, websites were all over the 'net proclaiming to have the truth about Logosian Wicca, the ancient religion of the Logosians. Like in the real world, most of this information just came from other books.

The High Priest of the LRs, Bela Carmine, who was raised in the US, took exception to this movement, and tried everything to get the truth out. He tried suing Conroy and Crowfox, tried making websites of his own and tried to train more people in his religion. Slowly, but surely, we got to the position we are in today with most Wiccans knowing Crowfox and Conroy's books to be fiction, but with beginners and community newbies repeating their nonsense, often right in the face of Logosian Reconstructionists. Worst of all, with the vast amount of information out there, these newbies would tell the LRs that not only were their gods NOT cast out of the heavens by other gods, but that they were just faces of the other gods and that their belief that they were descended of the gods themselves was only right if it meant every human was.

Logosian belief was recast by these new Wiccans: eight thousand years of practice, of polytheism and tribal religion, blown in about a decade as Wiccans tried to fit a singular people into their "all persons" mold. With wry grins the remaining LRs listened to the new followers of their gods proclaim that the ancient ways were a misinterpretation and that their study and practice was moot even as experienced Wiccans tried to show otherwise. The Reconstructionists called the Logosian Wiccans, quite bluntly, The Borg, as they watched their culture be assimilated and taught to millions of people as something it wasn't, their scholarship and history be damned.

The Logosians would be funny if they weren't practically real. Above, you see elements of what has happened to the Greek, Roman and Celtic Reconstructionists, the Asatruar, the PA Dutch and Indigenous Americans at the hands of careless Wiccan authors. Unlike the Logosians, however, those peoples *are* real and have a lot to say about their faiths. What their communal gnosis states is what we should believe of them. If they say they were all puked up by stars and only people with purple hair can be their priests, so be it, it's their right. If they say their gods are discrete entities that exist side by side with others, that is their right as well, so be it, and who are we to claim otherwise?

Wicca is a new religion. UPG, reinterpretations of ancient mythos and any individual's personal view of how an ancient religion *should* have been mean nothing faced with the weight of the communal gnosis of any culture. In other words, if a culture had eight thousand years of polytheism and the belief that all gods are *not* one God, then one Wiccan, or even thousands of them, cannot change, and should not try to change, those beliefs.

We'll hear more about the Logosians later. Any resemblance to actual authors and events in the story above is probably intentional and is covered under US copyright laws as an act of satire, even though the Logosians, their religion, the names of their gods and the like are not real, and none of the books or authors mentioned above actually exist.

Theisms Part One: Polytheism and Henotheism

[Many people say Wicca is best described as henotheistic, but what does that mean? Henotheism, Polytheism, and Pantheism are just a few of the "theisms" that you'll hear of in Wiccan discussion, and it can be difficult to keep track of them all. The next several paragraphs will give you more discussion of Theisms than you can possibly keep track of. Relax: there will not be a quiz later.]

We're going to take a break from the Logosians, UPG and the like for a little while to go into some basic vocabulary[26] for discussing the varieties of Wiccan belief. "The-

---

[26] If this seems like this is a long list of vocabulary terms, you're right! One of my *favorite* critiques of this section, via email, complained that it was like some kind of list of vocabulary terms...my response then, and now, was "thank you for noticing!"

isms" are ways in which people deal with the concept of divinity. The root word is the Greek word *theos*, or god, which was used in ancient Greek to discuss both masculine and feminine gods, much as we use the word gods today. This makes the study of "Theology," for example, the study of gods of all genders, not just male ones.

The first "theism" you need to know to discuss Wicca is Polytheism. It comes in five flavors: literary, liberal, pantheonic, conservative, and semi-conservative. As long as you understand the word's basic meaning, however, you'll be fine. Polytheism is a term that literally means many gods. Wicca, in its infancy, was polytheistic but not described as such. Even in Gardner and Sander's works we see the Abrahamic god described as "The god of the Christians" and the Wiccan deities described as "The god of the Witches" and "Our goddess." This "us and them" polytheism is often called "weak" polytheism, and is the polytheism found in the Hebrew Bible, for instance when Moses points out that Pharaoh's gods are unable to do anything against his own, but does not claim that his alone exists. This sort of polytheism is also common in a lot of works on Early Modern Wicca and in Western slanted books on comparative theology. In it, a multiplicity of gods is discussed, but only in literary terms.

It is for this reason we also call this form of polytheism "literary polytheism." We also see this form of polytheism in poetry and art, where portrayal of multiple gods does not mean that the author endorses their existence. The personal theology of the author may regard these gods as aspects or facets of their one god, or even see these gods as nothing more than symbols for virtues they endorse. It is easy to make the mistake of taking literary polytheism as genuine Paganism, and this can lead to difficulty. If, for example, you declare that the Statue of Liberty, as a portrayal of the goddess Libertas, is a Pagan holy site, you bring into question whether or not the secular State should maintain her. When you see her instead, as she was designed, as a personification of the secular quality of liberty, the maintenance question is promptly disregarded. She is secular, and for people of all religions.

This brings into question the desires of the creator. We can say, without prejudice, that the adoption of the motto "In God We Trust" was an act of religious and Western imperialism. It was adopted at a time when the government of the United States was in a panic over the perceived threat of "godless communism." It was also at this time that "Under God" was added to the formerly secular Pledge of Allegiance. These were not cases of literary monotheism but genuine attempts to make atheists and people of non-Abrahamic faiths feel unwelcome in the United States. Both acts were shamelessly unconstitutional, as most government scholars will admit when pressed, but that's a topic for a different book.

Liberal polytheism is the most common true polytheism found in Wicca. It is the belief that all gods, of all peoples, exist. It sees deities as discrete units, often considering most pantheons to be full of individual, unrelated entities[27]. Liberal polytheism prefers to take followers of gods at their word, when the Celts say The Morrigan exists, and the Hellenes say Aphrodite exists, they believe them. Liberal polytheists believe that people who claim their god is the only god are incorrect, but generally accept that those individuals believe that, and even that their god may teach it. Often, adherents can point to polytheistic traditions within faiths considered monotheistic today to back up their point of view. Liberal Polytheists often view peoples as having a specific god or a pantheon, such as the tribal gods spoken of in the Bibles.

Pantheonic polytheism is the belief that only one pantheon of deities exists, and that all other deities are misunderstandings or interpretations of this pantheon. A Hellenic pantheonic polytheist, for example, may see Odin as simply an interpretation of the "genuine" god Zeus. So-called Indo-European Reconstructionists often see all the gods of the

---

[27] An exception here is generally made for the unique qualities of the Roman Pantheon. Liberal polytheists sometimes see, for example, Jupiter and Zeus, as one and the same. Whether the Roman Pantheon is separate from the gods it absorbed or not is a debate that has raged since long before the creation of Wicca, and certainly is unlikely to be settled anytime soon

Indo-European diaspora as interpretations of a core group of deities, so that while Aphrodite and Ishtar and Venus are one deity, Athena and Venus, or Freya and Kali, are not. Most Reconstructionists are *not* pantheonic polytheists, but tribal-based liberal polytheists: concerned with their gods alone, but assuming that other peoples have gods as well.

Conservative polytheism, like pantheonic polytheism, is a belief in which some deities do not exist. In conservative polytheism, what deities exist or not is a less exact concept than the pantheonic approach. A conservative polytheist, for example, may believe that all deities that require (or historically required) animal sacrifice are either non-existent or misinterpretations. In general, conservative polytheists have some criteria they use for deciding if they believe in a god or not. This term is generally applied to those people who can list what deities they believe exist and explain why.

Semi-conservative polytheists fall, predictably, somewhere between conservative and liberal polytheists, and in general believe in all gods until one deity or pantheon gives them a reason to think it does not exist. My son, who is pondering becoming an atheist in the future, says presently that he thinks he believes in every god except the Abrahamic one, which could not have allowed the attacks on September 11th, 2001 to occur in his name. As it was a study of the Holocaust that led to my own atheism as a teen, I can understand where he is coming from, but I am personally uncomfortable in ruling out any deity.

Wicca is generally seen as being polytheistic in some sense. The most common exploration of polytheism seen within Wicca is a sort of modified henotheism[28], although monotheistic -and even atheistic[29]- Wicca can exist, since Wicca is unconcerned, in general, with the idea of what the

[28] Both henotheism and kathenotheism were terms coined by Max Müller while trying to accurately explain the differences between Vedic traditions and their contrast with other religions.
[29] While I have no space in my personal worship for gods that are constructs or metaphors, I see no reason why other people can't follow them, unless and until they declare *my* gods don't exist.

divine is comprised of (beyond a balance of genders). Henotheism is a term generally applied to the Vedic Religions, and describes a type of polytheism in which many gods are acknowledged, but only one is worshipped. This is also common to Dianic paganism, in which many gods may be acknowledged, but only The Goddess[30] is worshipped. It is also common to Patron-based (or Cult) Wicca, which may worship the entirety of the divine, but is focused on one deity alone. Modified henotheism is the most common form of polytheism within Wicca, in which a small group of deities, often two, are actively worshipped, while other gods are acknowledged.

There is a resistance to the term henotheism in much of the Wiccan community and I believe it stems from the aforementioned apologetic polytheism that many Western authors express when writing of the Vedic Religions. While the term initially applied strictly to the practice of having many gods but worshipping only one, it has grown to be seen as worshipping only one god because all gods are *really* one God. This is an intellectually dishonest view of henotheism, and—incidentally—is also not a historical view of the Vedic Religions.

The most frequently occurring form of henotheism in Wicca is a modified henotheism best described as the practice of having Patron and Matron Deities: two gods—one female, one male—who are viewed as the most important deities for the individual or worship group. This is where the parallels to the mystery cults of Greece and Rome are the most poignant, because these deities are worshipped in the greater context of the community religion. A Wiccan dedicant of Hestia, for example, may freely go to a Summer Solstice ritual honoring Persephone without a fear that her goddess will find her actions inappropriate. This depends on the deity, of course. We can imagine that a dedicant of a god that declared all other gods false or evil would not be

---

[30] Who may be seen as the sum total of all deities, a significant difference between Wicca and Dianicism. In this form, Goddess is capitalized, just as God is when speaking of the god of the Christians.

so free to move about. The modified henotheism in which a person is dedicated to both a male god and a female one simultaneously is almost exclusively a Wiccan phenomenon, and is sometimes confused with duotheism or ditheism, which will both be explained later.

Related to this is another form of henotheism, kathenotheism, which can be described as the worship of one god at a time. A temple dedicated half of the year to Apollo and the other half to Dionysus would be one such example. Many Wiccans are kathenotheists who honor a goddess as their primary deity during half of the year and a god during the rest of the year. Another strong contingent of Wiccans seem to combine kathenotheism with more traditional Wiccan practice, worshipping a singular goddess all year but having two gods-a winter one and a summer one.

As you can see, describing Wiccan belief with such a large selection of terms can be very confusing, which is one of the reasons why so many people don't even try. As I've tried to explain, no one will quiz you on this, but you should no longer be surprised if Joe Pagan's version of polytheism is quite different from Jane Pagan's, and more importantly you should now begin to understand that unlike monotheism, which basically comes in one style, polytheism represents a plethora of styles.

Theisms Part Two: Monotheism, Atheism, Pantheism & more

Now that you've got the idea of polytheism down, we're going to discuss a few more theisms, and attempt to confuse you further. I've tried to list these in the order of most gods to least, and hopefully we will get through them together without going insane, becoming completely lost or otherwise not understanding.

Duotheism is just what it appears to be: the worship and belief in only two gods. This may be literal, the belief that only a Supreme God and a Supreme Goddess exist, or it may be more figurative, the belief, for example, that all goddesses are one Goddess and all gods are one God. Like our friends the Logosians, however, we know the problems with making claims about the reality or actuality of other people's gods. Duotheism is not uncommon in Wicca, but is often seen as little more than a misunderstanding of true polytheism.

Duotheism is not to be confused with ditheism, however. Ditheism is also the belief in two forces, but rather than a male and female energy, or a God and Goddess, ditheism is the belief in a good entity or force and a bad one. Like the Dark Side of the Force in *Star Wars*, or interpretations of European myths that match every positive deity with a negative one, ditheism teaches that pure good and pure evil both exist and operate simultaneously within the world as counteractive forces. Rather than a true blend of personalities and desires working out for a general balance of neutrality, ditheists teach that any neutrality is merely a result of equal effort by the good and bad gods. Few, if any, Wiccans are ditheists and most Wiccans teach that nearly every action has both its good and bad qualities, but that these qualities originate within the individual, not with some dark and light god.

Pantheism—the belief that all is god—is more encompassing than duotheism in some ways, but in other ways it's similar to monotheism. I make this comparison because a poor understanding of pantheism, just as with Universalism, can lead to the misconception that pantheism is just another way of saying that all gods are really one God. However, that is an oversimplification of the concept. In true pantheism, it is not that all gods are one, but that all things, from every drop of water in the ocean to each molecule of our bodies, are god. In this understanding, the idea of discrete deities is not impossible. Think of it this way: just as you and I are two different beings that are part of the whole, any deities are a part of the whole as well. Whether this whole, sometimes called simply The All, has will or thought is another question entirely, and not all pantheists agree on the answer.

More confusing yet is the idea of panentheism, which differs from pantheism in the belief that god is not all things, but is *in* all things. In Abrahamic mysticism, this is often described using the metaphor of the body and soul: pantheism is the belief that all things are the body and soul (or totality) of god, and panentheism is the belief that god inhabits the world like our soul inhabits our body. In pantheism, god is the world and the world is god. In panentheism, god is the world and more.

Some alleged pantheists or panentheists could also be seen as monotheists in disguise. While they are believers that god is all around them in one form or another, they still see all things as only one God, and all other gods as misunderstandings, facets, or aspects of the Ubergod. Monotheism is not merely the worship of one god, but the belief that there exists but one God and one alone. This belief can include denying the existence of other gods outright or subtly, such as belittling the existence of other deities by claiming they are just interpretations of a reality too big to be understood by mortals. Making these and similar judgments is harder in polytheistic traditions, where the existence of yet another deity is not difficult to comprehend.

One friend once likened this to a math equation. If, in a given algebraic equation, you find that "$X = 1$," you are not offended, or even surprised, when other equations find X equal to a different number. In fact, in some equations, X can be equal to many numbers. As a simple example, $1X = X$, no matter what value X is assigned. In that case, one, three, negative ten, XIV or 42 may well all be valid answers. However, monotheism is a bit like requiring X to equal three, no matter what problem you are trying to solve. This is why monotheists don't deal as well with religious ambiguity in general. Since the polytheistic equation has more answers, ambiguity doesn't present as many problems for polytheists: polytheists realize that their own answers will vary from the next person's.

Last of our theisms, Atheism is the belief that there are no gods, either that there are no deities at all (hard atheism) or the belief that the gods are the thought-forms or unconscious mind of mankind, or mere archetypes he uses to interpret reality (soft atheism.) Related to this is agnosticism, which is best described as the belief that there probably aren't any gods, but there isn't enough information available to state that conclusively.

To make this all a little clearer, I have prepared a chart illustrating the number of gods within each of these forms of theism and the number of gods worshipped by people practicing these forms of theism. Liberal, conservative and various variations on polytheism and the like are not included herein.

Number of gods existing versus number worshipped in theism

\# of gods that exist:

0	1	2 only	2 or more
Atheism	Monotheism Pantheism Panentheism	Duotheism Ditheism	Polytheism Henotheism Kathenotheism

\# gods that are worshipped:

0	1	2 only	2 or more
Atheism	Monotheism Pantheism Panentheism Ditheism Henotheism Kathenotheism*	Duotheism	Polytheism Modified Henotheism

*One god is worshipped at a time

Number of gods existing versus number worshipped in various types of theism: As you can see, while religions with two or more gods (or forces) outnumber monotheistic religions, many people only spend their energy on one god, or one god at a time.

How I and Others Have Made People Even More Confused

And now, a confession...

I, and many other people who've written about Wicca, are probably as responsible as anyone for the confusion regarding what Wiccans believe and what Wiccans don't. I've just spent over two thousand words trying to explain the different forms of theism you may find in Wicca. You'll note I didn't say, anywhere in those thousands of words, which was the "right" form of theism for Wiccans to practice. Put simply, since Wicca is an experiential religion, I can only tell you to believe what you experience.

Unfortunately, your experiences (or lack of experience) may lead you to become confused or even deceived by something that you read unless your author has been very careful. Rather than point any fingers, I'll describe a one of my own failures — this from my first book, *All One Wicca*. In the second chapter, I provided what I thought was a good metaphor for the existence of multiple truths:

> Try the following visualization: Imagine a great sphere, just slightly smaller than infinite. If you zoom close enough to the sphere, you'll notice that it's actually made up of billions of little hexagons, and that each hexagon faces a different direction, like facets of a huge jewel. The sphere is all one thing, but each facet, viewed from close enough, seems to be independent of it.
>
> Truth is that sphere, and those facets all are created by truth, and have an equal portion of truth. There is room for many different truths in the universe, and limiting ourselves to seeing one facet is limiting ourselves to missing the beauty of the whole thing. Personal truth may be merely one facet of this great object, yet it is no more or less important than any other facet. Before you begin looking at the sphere, look at your facet. The sphere will come...[31]

When I wrote this, what I thought I was saying, and, indeed, what my wife thought I was saying, was that truth (not the gods, or a path) is a really big thing that no person can grasp the entirety of, but that any person can eventually (through multiple lives, achieving nirvana, going to heaven, etc.) understand the existence of. However, communication with my readers showed me that I had used such vague terminology that what the metaphor meant to any individual reader depended on their personal facet of the sphere. Here is one of the emails I received, heavily edited:

> Dear Kaatryn-I was reading your webpage (allonewicca.com) and I must say I don't understand. On one page you say that people shouldn't use the rites of other people unless those people agree to it, and then you say that all truth is one big sphere. If it's all the same truth, anyway, aren't all the rites having the same purpose, and then why would it matter who was doing what.
>
> Wicc------79@aol.com

---

[31] *All One Wicca*: Chapter two

The questions that the above person and others wrote me about varied, but all shared the same basic premise: that I had said that all truth was the same truth. As you might imagine, this confused me greatly, as I couldn't imagine at the time where these readers had gotten that idea. Wicc------79@aol.com, unlike many of the others, gave me the clue I needed, because she mentioned truth being "one big sphere," helping me to discover how my metaphor had led some readers astray.

To my mind, and what I thought would be to my reader's minds, another part of what I had meant by the metaphor was that the thing we call truth was so big that we often perceived our individual truths as all alone in the world, and that we could grow to a place where we could see the truths of others, and that they were all interlinked. This linkage, to my mind, was like a giant buckyball[32], or the parts of a soccer ball, with common seams and bonds running through everything. My "sphere of truth" metaphor was not referring to the *One Truth*, because I don't believe in such a thing, but instead to a sphere made up of all the truths.

This led me to what I regarded as a scary conclusion. If my writing, which I thought was painfully clear, even to the point of being boring, could be taken to mean something so different from what I intended, maybe the metaphoric speech that I and many Wiccan authors frequently use was at the heart of the confusion about Wicca. To look outside the Wiccan community, we need only turn to any two Christian churches, or similarly established religious groups, to see the problem. I think most of us are aware that few Christian churches, if any, debate whether or not the Ten Commandments say you shouldn't kill. When it comes to discovering the underlying message of a metaphor, story or parable in the Bible, however, you can get very different answers.

---

[32] A molecule of buckminsterfullerene, a spherical and extremely stable form of pure carbon, C_{60}, which is best described as interconnected pentagons and hexagons similar to the appearance of a geodesic dome.

The Wiccan community at large, not just me, was sending messages that, just like the Christian Bible, could be interpreted using whatever filter was in a reader's head. Simple statements such as "eating people is wrong," for example, were nowhere to be found in most Wiccan books and websites. However, if someone asked a Wiccan if eating people is wrong these four words might be hidden within a long explanation of the innate value in every thing, a story that could be used to defend capitalism, slavery, starvation or being a Jain, depending on how you chose to take it.

The truth is that such metaphors can be easy to use, since authors are presuming people will use good judgment to determine how far they can be taken while still retaining their core meaning. The problem is that it's also easy to assume that "good judgment" in the matter is exactly equal to the author's own judgment. It's much more difficult to depart from metaphor and discuss all or even most of the issues' exigencies.[33] In our example, you would have to also explain that while eating people is, in general, bad, restricting the Logosian natives from their indigenous practice of consuming the hearts of their deceased fathers would be an act of imperialism.[34] And worse, you may even have to address the distasteful question of whether, if you yourself trapped with a corpse and no food, eating people is still wrong. Metaphoric speech can help you avoid such ridiculous (and one hopes) hypothetical extremes.

The solution is that we must, every one of us, own every word we write, whether it be in a book, on a website, in an email, or on a blackboard. We must be concise and exact, and if we use metaphor, we must explain it as completely as possible. Put simply, anyone who writes on the subject of Wicca has the massive responsibility of teaching everyone who reads their materials exactly what they mean by it. We've grown from our infancy where merely saying "whatever works" was enough to a clumsy religious adolescence where we must be strikingly clear. In the past, we

[33] Exigency, noun, the thing that is required in a given specific situation.
[34] As a biologist, I do not recommend eating things on your branch of the evolutionary tree unless you have scales or feathers.

knew that anyone who read those two words would be a part of a greater community that would add the necessary disclaimers, but that is no longer true. Today, Wiccans are a nation of diverse adherents, some of whom may never meet another community member face to face.

Authors (myself included) simply no longer have the luxury of not being precise, historically accurate and mindful of other faiths in our writing. As described in the section on the Wiccan Rede, shoddiness, vagary and expecting that the typical reader comes into the study with a community behind him are things of the past. Admittedly, when we started out, there was no way of knowing this, but it is undeniable now.

As if shoddy writing was not enough, authors on Wicca have to deal with the innate prejudices of their readers. For example, you may've noted that Wicca leaves a lot of questions up to your experience. For some readers, this disqualifies it as a religion altogether. We can't just tell such people they are outright wrong and expect results, but if we are to deal with the prejudices that spawn such claims we have to confront those prejudices up front. That confrontation begins with knowing the prejudices exist. We can't use UPG and our emotions to dictate what another believes, and we must confront the fact that it may well be that to some people, Wicca is not a religion. We must balance the need to be clear and accurate with acceptance of the fact that some people are *not* going to approach our words fairly. Put simply, we have to realize that while we are responsible for the interpretations of our readers, we have no obligation to those who refuse to interpret our words fairly.

Since I brought it up, I'll end this unit with a tangential discussion of the question above, both as an example of understanding both sides of an argument and how to deal with people who don't seem to approach a question fairly. So, without further discussion, I present my answer, verbatim, to when I was asked this question by a reader who objected to Wicca in general and me in particular.

Reader: "If Wicca leaves all these questions up to your experience, how is it a real religion?"

Kat: "Religion is a term that is hard to strictly define. Being of an etymological slant, I like to think of it as the actions and beliefs that bind you to your cultural milieu and your deities, a combination of shared mores, folkways, and a relationship with the divine. This definition holds up well for Eastern and Western religions, and certainly holds up for Wicca. If we use the narrow, predominantly (but not exclusively) Abrahamic concept of a religion as a sort of combination of directions for how to be a member of a specific community, a set of promises about what will happen to you, your friends and enemies after death and a rule book for getting on God's good side, Wicca fails.

"What Wicca teaches instead is the *mechanics* of practice, the development of community, individual growth and knowledge and a relationship with the divine. We are a less specific faith, comparable perhaps to the Religio Roma, the state religion of the Roman Empire: we have our community-wide holy days and practices, basic things that we use to recognize members of the same religion: symbolism, vocabulary, a basic liturgical calendar and the like. We have our local religious entities, with their own sacred days, like Pagan Pride days and Wiccan nights out, and we have our sects and cults that follow specific holidays, gods, and practices. The celebration of the Autumnal equinox, for example, may be celebrated in one way by a coven in Buffalo, another way by a coven in Philadelphia, and a third way by a coven in San Francisco, or even in many different ways within the same location, but it is still recognizably Wiccan, just as a Baptist service and Catholic mass are recognizably Christian.

"We do not teach what happens after death, but give you tools to explore that for yourself. We make no promises, indeed, we teach that if the faith does not work for you it is likely you may do better elsewhere and encourage you to explore other faiths. We do not answer questions, we teach you how to ask them."

Recommended Reading for Topic Two:

Geisler, Norman L. Ph.D., *Primitive Monotheism Christian Apologetics Journal, Volume 1, No.1,* Spring 1998. [Southern Evangelical Seminary]

Starhawk, *Religion From Nature, Not Archaeology (Starhawk Responds to the Atlantic Monthly)* http://www.starhawk.org/pagan/religion-from-nature.html

Discussion Questions for Topic Two:

2.1 (This may require some research on the part of participants.) How did the Society of Inner Light attempt to
divorce itself from Early Modern Wicca? What is, in
your opinion, the end result of this?

2.2 Have you ever had an experience where someone was
insistent that your definition with the divine was
wrong? How did you deal with it?

2.3 The belief that all gods are really one God has been described as a theory that "feels good, but doesn't work
when you think about it," do you agree with this? Why
or why not?

2.4 Universalism is an attempt to resolve the Christian
paradox of an All-Loving God with a hell. What other
methods have been used to approach this paradox?

2.5 What is a theological paradox? Why don't they invali-
date religion when they exist? How are they different
from flaws in a theology?

2.6 If UPG doesn't stand up to debate, but instead is designed for personal use, what is the purpose of it?

2.7 What kind of evidence for another faith would be required for you to contemplate changing faiths?

2.8 Describe your personal religious beliefs: are you monotheistic, henotheistic, what? Explain your answer.

2.9 Why has there been a change in what Wiccan authors
are required to discuss and the way in which they do
so?

Is Wicca an ancient religion? If it's not, is it still relevant? What is Modernism? Reform? Who is Hutton? What is the Tomas Timeline?

Some of the Legends

It was common in the past for Wiccans to believe that their religion was an ancient religion practiced by Paleolithic man and passed down by secret societies to the present. Few Wiccans believe that today, although a search of the Internet can turn up many websites that make this and other claims about Wicca. The claims can range from the misbegotten belief that any cave drawings or ancient artifacts that represent a man with horns or a female figure are depictions of the duotheistic Wiccan "God and Goddess" to the idea that Wicca, and any variations on its spelling, is an ancient Celtic tradition (which will be discussed in the next topic). The problem here is two fold. On the one hand, people are using the bad research of a couple of authors (most notably Margaret Murray) to create a history that isn't there, and on the other, they are using this flawed paradigm to interpret everything they find.

We'll return to our dear, much abused, Logosians. Since they aren't *truly* Western Europeans, they were spared the indignities of falling under Murray's oft-quoted *Witch-cult in Western Europe* thesis, but they still are subject to the idea of the Paleolithic Witch-Cult that runs rampant through Wicca. So, when archeology unearths three ancient female figurines with large breasts and full bellies in the gravel in a cave on the island, the Logosians, whose religion has always figured around a male-led pantheon, are promptly told that their ancient religion was really Wicca, the religion of The Great Mother Goddess, and that these figurines prove it.

The Logosians, as usual, do not take this news quietly. First, they point out that the ancient figurines are at least a few thousand years older than the earliest Logosian ruins, so there is no proof that the people who made those figures were the progenitors of their culture. In addition, those figures might not even have originated on their island, as people moved around a lot in the Mediterranean. Next, they tell their critics that they don't know what these figurines were used for, and claiming they were religious elements without some proof is irresponsible. These figures could, they point out, have been the Paleolithic equivalent of a Barbie doll. In addition, the fact that they are all female could mean nothing at all regarding the leadership of the people's religion, pointing out that in the ancient religion that they have proof of, images of the father god were strictly forbidden and that only gods of lesser power were drawn and sculpted. Lastly, the Logosians quite correctly state that Wicca is a religion with a history less than a century old, and certainly was not responsible for these figures unless the figures are hoaxes.

The fictional example above actually covers the biggest flaws in the idea that Wicca is an ancient religion with evidence of its practice extending into pre-history. There is little evidence to suggest Wicca was in existence 100 years ago, let alone tens or hundreds of thousand years ago, but well-meaning researchers occasionally link evidence for the existence of ancient people (and little else) with the existence of an ancient religion.

This isn't a new practice. Ancient Greeks finding the fossilized bones of mastodons or dinosaurs quickly claimed to have found the bones of the heroes of the Trojan War and the fossilized bones of dinosaurs were used as evidence for the existence of dragons in Asia and Western Europe. We interpret everything we see through the science of our age.

You have to understand that the average, modern "first-world" citizen knows more about science than most ancient cultures put together. The increase in basic scientific knowledge has occurred exponentially throughout human development, and 100, even 50 years ago, the means for interpreting data were not as well developed as they are today. A century from now, our means will no doubt seem backward.

So, put yourself in the place of a young archaeologist many decades ago. The hottest book you've read in years claims there was an ancient religion, and gives archaeological evidence for the existence of that ancient religion. This book was written by someone with numerous degrees, and printed by a respectable university press, and belittles critics of it ruthlessly. Maybe you aren't even sure that the theories about this religion are true, but then, on a dig, right where the author told you they'd be, you find evidence of that religion. Chances are that you believe at once that you've found more proof of that ancient religion, so you promote your find as such.

Murray's *The Witch-Cult in Western Europe* is a book that's been responsible for exactly that kind of "discovery." Murray's claims even led to the establishment of an entirely new religion that followed the liturgical calendar and ritual structure she enumerated. Murray comes with a powerful résumé of degrees and learning, which she makes sure you know about. She uses extensive quotes in French, which (while fine for those who speak French) are certainly muddling to those who don't, especially since where the French is translated, the translation is often poor. She also uses scientific language—without, unfortunately, the scientific method—so the pages veritably explode with quotes and "evidence." All in all, she presents a very good imitation of extraordinary research, which can lead a reader to feel as if a mountain of proof for her theory exists.

However, if we look at *Witch-Cult* through a modern lens, we can see it for what it is: a collection of tangentially related historic incidents being used to "prove" an interesting theory. Like fringe Christian archeologists who see evidence of any flood, no matter how small, as proof of the literal truth of the Bible, Murray had an agenda to push, and a strong desire to win people over to her point of view.

In the early days following the Second World War, many people saw modern religion as having failed utterly to stop the horrors in Germany and elsewhere—so the ideas in *The Witch-Cult* would be attractive to some who thought that the answer lay in the rediscovery of Murray's ancient religion. Modernist scholars of Wicca believe that Early Modern Wicca was created after World War II in part as a reaction to the sociological and psychological research that was being done to explain the Holocaust (and, to a lesser degree, the use of atomics on Japan). If you regard Wicca as a primarily British invention, you quickly become aware of its soothing effect on what one friend who was a teen living through the bombing of London calls "a thoroughly trounced population."

Murray's book took on new life after World War II because it seemed to address some critical questions that WWII had raised. For one, her take on the Witch Hunts struck a new chord in the post-war era because she had framed the historical persecution of witches as the systemic oppression of a real people, a real culture and a real religion. Until Murray, the witch hunts had been seen as a list of several separate atrocities, each fueled by hysteria and driven by various charismatic leaders. But Murray's take on them inadvertently provided a way for Europeans to regard Hitler's rise to power (and Germany's willing submission to him) as an anomaly in the history of modern Europe, something that had never happened before in any scale, and could never happen again in a civilized society. It was an awful nightmare that could only ever happen in Germany, but never elsewhere and never again. So by peopling her tale with a group of people who would stick by their ethics even under torture, Murray provided Early Modern Wicca with an answer to the cultural challenges of fascism and of Stanley Milgram's 1961-2 scientific studies on obedience[35][1], which demonstrated that 65% of the otherwise perfectly average people he tested would administer what they thought were severe, even deadly, electrical shocks to people who had done nothing to deserve such torture. They did it simply because a person they perceived as an authority figure told them to do so.

Whether Wicca solves those challenges or not is a question for future historians.

Purpose of Religion and Why a Modern Religion is Relevant

Religion can help people deal with difficult questions and discomfort with society, but what purpose religion itself has is a subject that elicits pretty heavy debate. Lama Thubten Yeshe[36], giving a talk in Brisbane, Australia in April 1975 said, "The only purpose for the existence of what we call religion is for us to understand the nature of our own psyche, our own mind, our own feelings." When asked what he felt was the purpose of religion in society, Rabbi Jack Moline[37] said that the role of religion was "to be a voice for the ethical use of power." Hinduwebsite.com's mission statement reports, "We believe that the primary purpose of religion is to ennoble man, to make him realize the true purpose of his life and create universal harmony, understanding and brotherhood among people." We are also familiar with the purposes claimed of individual religions: to achieve nirvana or heaven, to avoid hell, to have a relationship with god and do what he wants you to and the like. As we mentioned earlier, because beliefs regarding a religion's purpose are highly subjective, discussing the relevance of a modern religion is doubly so. We must ask not only if it meets the purposes of religion, but if its status as a modern religion cancels out those purposes.

Let's begin with the various purposes of individual religion mentioned above. The first four of these reasons (to achieve nirvana or heaven, to avoid hell and to have a relationship with the divine)

---

[35] Most recently available as *Obedience to Authority: An Experimental View.* (Stanley Milgram) New York: Harper/Collins. 1983
[36] http://www.buddhistinformation.com/tibetan/purpose_of_religion.htm
[37] http://www.interfaithalliance.org/Resources/moline_c.htm

should not be affected by the age of a religion, unless the religion teaches only that the age of the practices is what makes them work. Since we can't address that question directly without turning religion into a quantity that can be proven to work or not in a replicable fashion (which won't work with every purpose listed,) we'll ignore it momentarily. The first three are related, although we have to step away from the religion specific ideas of heaven, hell and nirvana. They say, basically, that the purpose of religion is to attain a particular afterlife. Wicca only succeeds tangentially at this purpose, because the mere practice of Wicca does not assure any sort of afterlife, but hopes to give the practitioner tools to attain the knowledge needed to make a decision regarding the afterlife and how to get that particular one, if applicable. This would be seen as a failing of Wicca as a religion if, and only if, these other faiths had demonstrable proof that they got their afterlife of choice and others did not. Near-death experiences, for example, have happened to members of most religions, including Wicca, without pointing toward the truth of only one, so they are reduced to the level of UPG, and aren't valid for this discussion.

The fourth of these purposes of religion, to have a relationship with the divine, is achieved highly effectively with Wicca, but as another quantity that can only be expressed as UPG, it is difficult to describe fairly. The person with a vibrant working relationship with the gods or other divine energy can only assume other people who claim to have such relationships are truthful, and as these folk exist in all religions, it can only be seen as a success Wicca shares with other religions. Certainly a relationship with the divine is a goal of Wicca, so if it is to be seen as one of the core purposes of religion, success stories show Wicca to be a functional, relevant religion. Of course, some religions limit this "relationship with the divine" to a relationship with their specific god, and by that measure Wicca can fail. For example, while there are a few syncretic Wiccans who have a relationship with Christ, the numbers who make that work are far fewer than the number of non-syncretic Christians (or, as one friend says "Christian Christians") that make it work.

Another example of Wicca failing in a relationship with a specific deity is best described in metaphor. The Logosians, you may recall, are all descended (or believe they are) from a pair of people descended from their gods. These gods require for their worship two things: the relationship by blood to these deities and the practice of specific rites. Wicca does not prevent a relationship with the Logosian deities, but according to the people who follow that religion, certainly does not *create* such a relationship. A Wiccan wishing to follow the Logosian gods would still need to be related by blood and follow the proper rites. Wicca fails in creating the relationship, but it also succeeds for one small minority—a Wiccan of Logosian ethnicity is not *prevented* from performing the rites of his ethnic gods, and, indeed, if called to serve those gods, is *encouraged* to do so.

Of the oversimplified purposes for faith I mentioned earlier, this leaves only one, the idea that religion exists to tell you how to do what any specific god wants you to. Wicca fails in this only if mankind dictates what god wants you to do. If, for example, the Logosian gods *themselves* say that I can only make them happy with me by giving up all my possessions, moving to their island and having 15 children, I know that that's what *they* want me to do. If, however, a book or person tells me that I can only make the Logosian gods happy by doing the above, I am put in a difficult situation of judging who is actually telling me what to do, and I have to use as many tools as possible to make a rational determination, judging everything from the reliability of that book or person to what motives they may have.

Wicca attempts to make the practitioner develop a religious and spiritual lifestyle that allows them direct contact with the divine, a lifestyle that involves self-improvement and trying to make the world an essentially better place. This may result in a relationship with the divine that also tells you how to live your life in accordance with it or shows you the clues you need to act within divine will, if applicable. You'll note that this idea is completely in line with Lama Thubten Yeshe's idea of the purpose of religion, doubly so if you see the divine as an outgrowth of ourselves and self-knowledge as knowledge of the divine or the first steps toward it. Likewise, this actively fulfills how Hinduismwebsite.com defines the purpose of religion, "to ennoble man, to make him realize the true purpose of his life and create universal harmony, understanding and brotherhood among people."

This leaves Rabbi Jack Moline's less generalized purpose of religion in society, which you may recall was "to be a voice for the ethical use of power" and it is in this where Wicca not only succeeds, but succeeds better that many other religions because it is a *modern* religion. By not limiting its discussions to the past, the ideas regarding what power is and how we should promote its ethical use become unlimited. Genetic testing, stem cell research, modern birth control methods, cloning and much more become things discussed in their modern context, taking their history into account, rather than discussed in an ancient context we attempt to graft onto modern life.

For example, imagine that a tragic childhood disease once affected the Logosians, like practitioners of many tribal religions. This disease would come upon their children in the night, seemingly out of nowhere and kill them, leaving them with a blotchy face. The next day, if the child was not removed from the house the moment the body was found, everyone within the house would get it, and all of them would die. To keep everyone from dying, the Logosian religion dictates that any child that should die with a blotchy face should be burned within twelve hours, and the families of such people are to be avoided for one month. In addition, people with blotchy faces (who could be carrying the disease) are not allowed in temples or any public area.

Now, several thousand years later, this condition has been eradicated by hygiene and immunization. Is it fair to tell any family who practices this religion a child that died of, oh, an allergic reaction, must be burned within twelve hours of death? Likewise, can the teen Logosian Reconstructionist with bad skin never attend a rite? By having rules that developed in a modern context, we can make better sense of these types of questions, and be a voice for the ethical use of power (political, scientific, military, etc.) without the historical baggage. We use history as a guide and a valuable tool for learning without allowing it to become a straightjacket.

Modernism: What it is, Where it Came From, and Why it's Gaining Momentum

It is difficult to say when Modernism began in Wicca. Certainly as early as the sixties there were people who wrote from a somewhat modernist perspective. But the idea of Modernism as a movement, as a reaction to the revisionist history presented in many books on Wicca, is really a phenomenon of the last ten years. This is not surprising, as most of the books loathed by the Modernists have been published since the early 1990s. It is a movement without leaders, although Ronald Hutton, author of *Triumph of the Moon*, is well-loved by Modernisms' proponents. It is, in fact, a movement better defined by its causes than by any one person that can be seen as its head.

Modernism is best described as the movement towards an accurate history of Wicca and Paganism by quality secular research. The idea is that such research not only strengthens the community, but also strengthens the religions by making the foundations for them indisputable facts instead of easily dismissed fantasy. The belief is quite simple: if a truth is discovered tomorrow, it is not made truer by claiming it has always been known. We discover new truths all the time, Modern Pagan Religions among them.

My personal journey into Wicca began as a quasi-Modernist one, and parallels the development of Modernism in the community. When I began, I was told that Wicca was a modern religion designed to replicate the ancient religion of The Great Mother Goddess and Father God. This represents the sort of soft Modernism that we see so often today. Authors such as Hutton, as well as various critics of Wicca over the years, to one degree or another have dismantled the idea of Gardner's Wicca as having been anything thing but a creation of his time, if not by him, then by a contemporary. For people invested in the idea of the beliefs as ancient, seeing the practices as reclaimed or reconstructed from ancient rites allows them to practice the Modern Pagan Religions without the sensation of following some British guy's imagination.

As I grew in Wicca, I watched as the community began to move away from this soft Modernism — and it was not just my own teachers, but also the authors I was reading as well as the teachers of my cohorts. Like a lot of young Wiccans I left the community for a while simply because I felt the first few years of my study had been a bunch of lies and misinformation[38], as it had involved reading books like *The Witch-Cult in Western Europe* without the knowledge to see through it. On the other hand, my teachers were struggling with teaching a new Wicca. They'd been given the *Witch-Cult in Western Europe* and *Witchcraft Today* as presenting the actual history of the religion they learned; even though they'd reached a personal place where they no longer believed that Wicca was an ancient religion, the books they recommended — the same ones they studied when they were learning — taught just that.

---

[38]And, in fact, my own hard Modernism is because I don't want another individual to feel like I did then.

The cognitive dissonance that I and others like me felt at reading one thing and being taught another could only be resolved in four ways: by leaving Wicca completely; by ignoring the old, incorrect history; by ignoring the new, correct one; or by coming to grips with the idea of both a mythic history and an actual one. All four of these internal resolutions are apparent in Modern Wicca. Books and websites teach that Wicca is ancient religion, that it is totally new, that is it a complete crock not worth your time, and that it is a completely modern religion with a mythical history in which both the actual past and erroneous ideas of the past are relevant... all are easy to find.

Personally, I am a hard Modernist. I think the only Wiccan past that matters is the actual one, and that our mythic history as an ancient religion is best discarded altogether. I believe that our need for mythic history is fulfilled by the myths of our less immediate ancestors. Of course, I am also a lunatic, horrible at languages, who took a semester of ancient Greek in college *for fun*. So while I think age does not make a myth better, I see Homer and Hesiod as somewhere between old friends and a really fine wine—deep, comfortable pleasures that are utterly incomparable to anything created in the recent past.

So I see the need to avoid throwing out everything that doesn't support the Modernist present. Starhawk's The Spiral Dance, for instance, which never really inspired me, was critical in my wife's journey into Paganism. Many women, who, like her, were coming from sexist, patriarchal religious traditions—especially moderate lesbians put off by the aggressively anti-man slant of other writers[39]—saw this book as the first real framework for the concept of god as a woman. What I feel Modernists must do is move these books that conflict with known history, books that support or appear to support the idea that Wicca or Paganism is a reconstruction or reclaiming of a fictitious past, to higher levels on their must-read lists. In other words, only students familiar with the reasons behind the mythic history and well-versed in the actual history should be reading books that could cause the cognitive dissonance my generation

---

[39] Of course, neither Phoenix nor I would describe her as a "moderate lesbian" during her journey through Feminist Paganism

of Wiccans went through. I understand this is primarily a selfish goal, but it has worked so effectively for me that it is a practice I highly recommend.

Modernism is reactive. It gets louder and stronger when faced with that "new generation" of books on Wicca that describe Wicca's history as irrelevant while clearly supporting the revisionist party line of Wicca as an ancient religion. As the needs of the community continue to grow away from the bulk of what is currently being published, Modernism may become the primary voice of the community, a voice that will hopefully remain rational. Its new goal, above and beyond its primary cause-being a voice for truth, is avoiding militancy while refusing to abandon the truth: a very difficult line to walk.

Thinking Mythically as a Modernist

One of the accusations against Modernism is that it saps the beauty and light out of Wicca. Modernists, of course, object to this accusation, and any one who has attended the rituals of a Modernist group will probably tell you that they are not any less beautiful than the rituals of a revisionist group. What Modernists do that allows them to have the archaic language and fanciful rites with a firm knowledge of reality is realize that there is a time and place for thinking mythically. To understand that idea, we have to deal with several concepts, beginning with a brief understanding of what the definition of a myth is and what purpose, if any, myth has.

First, we'll deal with the term "myth" itself. Contrary to its modern usage (meaning stories that are mistakenly believed to be truth), the word "myth" means a story believed in at one time or another by a group of people. It is easy to see where the modern use comes from, however, in that stories that were once believed to be true by a majority, but which are no longer be believed by the majority of contemporary peoples, are often given the term "mythology" (e.g.: Greek Mythology, Celtic Mythology). On the other hand, the same type of stories that the majority still believes true are termed "religion" (e.g.: Vedic Religion, Christian religion). In reality, myth and religion are two separate but related entities going hand in hand: Christian myth and religion, Greek myth and religion and so forth.

The term myth itself comes from the Greek term for a speech or discourse, the term that would later come to mean a story or fable, and is a little hard to grasp until you recognize the relationship between speaking and stories in ancient Greece and the ancient world in general, but that's a tangential discussion at best. In the study of theology, as in philosophy, the term mythos is contrasted with another term, logos. Mythos refers, for example, to the Adam and Eve creation story in Genesis, while logos refers to the rules and regulations of religion.

A discussion of the meanings of these terms in ancient Greek, coming from a person with as poor an understanding of the language as mine, is silly at best, but I will state, quite firmly, that any dictionary that tells you either term has a singular one word translation is not worth the paper it is printed on. In this work, we'll focus *exclusively* on the theological usage of the terms as defined above, so if you see either term, you can assume it is used in this manner.

To rein in this tangent and get back to the point at hand, you'll find we've now defined any singular myth as a part of a greater mythos. It is a story, or a set of stories, which go hand in hand with the spiritual practices or other beliefs and practices of a culture, or—in cultures with multiple conflicting religions—the set of stories of any one of those conflicting religious traditions, as well as the secular myths of the broader culture itself. "Myth" can refer to an individual tale or the collective body of myth for a group, and can be distinguished from a law or rule, which would be a part of the logos of a culture.

As you can see, this is a fairly unwieldy set of working definitions. As the saying goes, however, if it works, go with it. By using this set of definitions we can move onto the idea of a myth's having a purpose. The concept of a myth's purpose does not refer to why we should create myths, but instead to the theory of why they exist and what they seem to do. This theory is explored by examining the similarity of many myths. In other words, these "mythic purposes" do not indicate that Hesiod, for example, looked up and noticed his people lacked a coherent theogenic myth and wrote Theogony, but rather that Theogony is one of the creations of a culture that answers the theogenic questions of that culture.

Answering questions can be seen to be the essential shared purpose of all myths. These questions can be roughly grouped as questions about history, the gods, nature and our neighbors. The first sort of myth, a creation myth, seeks to answer as many of those questions as possible, by giving beliefs regarding how the world came to be the way it is today. They can be based, like all myths, on observation, speculation or a combination of both. Creation myths range from the two myths of how the world came to be at the beginning of Genesis to the modern myth of the Big Bang[40]. Any discomfort we feel with the discussion of scientific myths and religious ones on equal terms is something we should deal with at the personal level, but suffice it to say that unless you were there, you don't have the news story, the factual account... just the myth.

The second type of myth is related to the creation myth, and sometimes encompassed within it. In simplest terms, it is the nature myth, the explanation of how a natural event happens, based on observations of the event and thoughts about how it could've happened. This is opposed to the actual nature of the phenomena which *can* be witnessed (unlike the Big Bang): the tides, lighting, rain, sun, seasons and so forth. For example, the sun moving across the sky could be Helios upon his chariot, or faeries could be responsible for painting the autumn trees red and yellow... or a sudden curdling in the milk could be caused by nearby witches. Modern nature myths exist as well, such as the belief that thunder and lightning are independent of each other or that all endangered animals had huge thriving populations before mankind came along. These myths are made by a combination of three things: the observation of phenomena, a lack of knowledge about the phenomena and an opinion about why the phenomena should've happened. It is this third factor that the Modernist recognizes in his practice, recognizing the reasons behind why we would like any specific nature myth to be true.

A third type of myth is the etiological myth. It is the myth that explains human nature or creations in terms beyond the strictly rational. Whether this myth is that a religious group came into existence because an angel or space alien appeared to their prophet, that the United States thrives because of the number of Christians it has or that a temple was built at a particular site because a god said so, it has the same principle: that a thing made by man exists with divine sanction.

Another type of myth is the historical myth. These are those myths that explain a historical event or person in ways beyond the news report format. Vietnam, for example, has been called a war

[40] A full justification for this statement, originally designed for the companion website, is included in the follow-up to this book, *Wicca 334: Further Advanced Topics in Wiccan Belief.*

without a myth, because the reporting of it was primarily direct, informative and in full color. Compare this with "news" stories about World War II from the time, in which the public generally got the material after intensive editing. One example of a recurring historical myth is that George Washington (and Augustus, Napoleon and William Wallace, among others) refused to sleep in a warm bed while his men slept on the cold hard ground. The poetic details of the ride of Paul Revere and D-day wax mythological at times, as do stories of battles in The Bible, The Iliad and the Eddas.

The last type of myth, the theogenic myth, tends to answer questions about where the gods come from. They can be a part of a creation or nature myth, or, like Hesiod's Theogony, a compilation of the ideas of the creation of the gods that came into being after many of the stories existed in partial form elsewhere. Similar to these myths are those that explain the creation of empires and countries, like the founding of Rome or the United States.

What a Modernist does with these myths is recognize that they fulfill some internal need for understanding and therefore it is best to allow them to sit side by side with fact, when available, as yet another part of reality worthy of honor and recognition. The Modernist uses the myth not merely as an answer to a question but as a window on the people who created it, and explores the myth to better understand those people, and through them their gods and themselves.

The Tomas Timeline

Whether you are a Modernist or not, discussing Wicca can be a challenge because it has gone through several stages, which are labeled differently by everyone who discusses them. Jayne Tomas, de-facto founder of UEW, tried to make a coherent timeline of Wicca's progress that I have since elaborated upon. It consists of six categories, arranged from Pre-Modern to Post-Modern, and tries to make sense of the growth stages in Wicca. The word "Modern" is used to distinguish the Wicca practiced today from any ancient groups, real or imagined. It is not recognition of Wicca as having an ancient form, but of the modernity of the current form.

*Stage 1:*Pre-Modern Wicca (?-1954): This is a collection of works and people who, while not using the word "Wicca" are seen to be highly influential in its creation (or, if you prefer, its discovery.) Typical books of this time period include the highly influential *The Witch-Cult in Western Europe*, and the works of HP Blavatsky and

Frank Podmore. British Spiritualism, Theosophy and the literary romanticists primarily flavor these works, and they tend to be written for the metaphysical literati.

Stage 2: Early Modern Wicca (1954- early 1970s): This stage, which includes Gerald Gardner, features the foundational works of many traditions. In it, the religion we'd know as Wicca is exclusively called Witchcraft, its practitioners called Witches. While it dwindles to a trickle in the mid-1960s, its death knell comes with the creation of the Principles of Wiccan Belief. It is basically the belief that Witchcraft is a singular religion, "the Religion of The Wica," discovered or promoted by Gerald Gardner. Non-Gardnerian authors at this stage insist that any differences between their practice and Gardner's are a result of distance between the groups or things he hid from the public as oath bound. At this point, the religion of Wicca is a single religion, and the idea of multiple branches is nowhere to be found. Different practices are still considered the same religion.

Stage 3a: Middle Modern Wicca (mid 1960s-1980s): This stage was a reactionary movement to Early Modern Wicca, in which several new "Old Religions" appeared. As a reaction to Gardnerian Witchcraft, these traditions teach that their tradition is the old, true Witchcraft, and that Gardner and his lot are liars or thieves. This is called "Revisionist Wicca" for this reason, and while it was mostly dead by the mid 1980s, it occasionally rears its ugly head to this day. Included in this stage of Wicca's development are numerous works that attach a culture to Wicca and call it the ancient religion of that culture, thus justifying the differences between groups of Wiccans as the differences between, for example, Celts and Romans. The idea here is that multiple traditions of Wicca exist, but that each culture has a "true Witchcraft" of its own.

Stage 3b: Feminist Paganism (Late 1960s-1990): At the same time (or nearly the same time) as Middle Modern and Modern Wicca are spinning off from Early Modern Wicca, Feminist Paganism, which many view as springing from the same sources, was beginning to arise. It was characterized by a female voice that spoke exclusively of goddess Worship or gave mere lip service to a "god" force. At its best, it spoke powerfully to a disenfranchised minority, and helped to give power to women by refuting the notion that, as god was the CEO of heaven, man was the CEO of earth. Feminist Paganism encouraged the exploration of female deity forms and was a powerful force. At its worst, however, it claimed that any god, even the god of

Wicca, was the Christian God. This early Feminist Paganism evolved into Modern Feminist Paganism and even spawned the reactionary "Real Man" movement, in which men were encouraged to explore their god-self. Where Feminist Paganism ends and Wicca begins can be a difficult thing to see, but the subtle differences are real enough to warrant the view of Feminist Paganism as a related offshoot that takes a different direction.

Stage 4: Modern Wicca (1980s-present) Modern Wicca evolved with the knowledge of multiculturalism. It is a reactionary movement that looked at the inter-traditional strife of Middle Modern Wicca and encouraged peace by saying that whatever worked was acceptable. It encompassed the idea that rituals and beliefs could be drawn from many sources as long as certain beliefs were shared amongst Wiccans. Many consider the late Scott Cunningham the "Father" of Modern Wicca. Chief amongst the ideas of Modern Wicca are the beliefs that no one tradition is "better" than the others, and that petty squabbling between traditions does nothing but harm and is therefore "UnWiccan." At the time of Jayne Tomas' death, this was the totality of the evolution of Wicca: the development from a belief in which only one person can be right to one in which everyone can be right. The problem with Modern Wicca, as defined above, is that the belief that you can do whatever you wish and call it Wicca renders the religion nonsensical.

Stage 5: Post-Modern Wicca (late 1990s-present) Concurrent with Modern Wicca is the reaction to the excesses of Modern Wicca. This movement, which I've called by the predictable name Post-Modern Wicca, has seen the "do whatever" practice of Modern Wicca (which was not really do "whatever" but an encouragement to explore many avenues of faith while staying Wiccan) be twisted and mangled by newcomers to the faith. Post-Modern Wiccans see Wicca as a definable thing. It is not just whatever you wish to do, but a core set of beliefs and practices that can be strayed from, but not without justification for the straying and the knowledge of what you're straying from. Post-Modern Wicca is concerned with the cultural imperialism of later Modern Wicca authors (such as those claiming that Wicca is an ancient Celtic Religion when Celts are still around and can show you what their ancient religion was), intellectual integrity and historical accuracy. Post-Modernists understand that the creators of Modern Wicca, in their haste to encourage exploration by many people, stretched the boundaries so far that Wicca began to make no

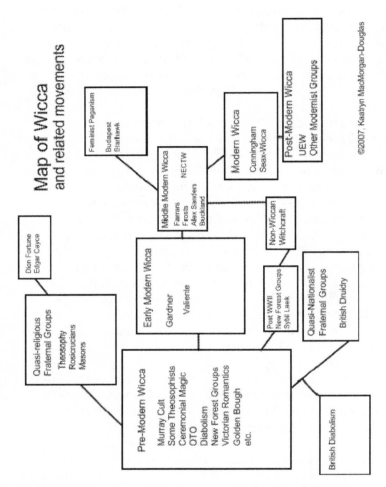

Map of Wicca and Related Movements: From Intro to UEW, 2007. This diagram shows the stages of the Tomas Timeline in the broader context. It is by no means definitive and is provided as an illustration only.

sense. Modern Wicca did not teach that everything was Wiccan, but that a Wiccan could study anything. Post-Modern Wicca agrees with that, but thinks that a Wiccan should study Wicca first.

In addition, Post-Modernists are theological deconstructionists, that is, they examine Modern Wicca by taking it apart and looking at where the parts came from while challenging ideas about polarity and assumptions about what makes a "real Wiccan." In doing so, they are capable of rendering a "purer" form of religious belief. For example, many later Wiccan groups add John Dee's Watchtowers and archangels to their circle. A deconstructionist, recognizing these elements for what they are, and seeing how they were added, may decide the energies or history of such things are best deleted from their personal practice altogether. This is especially true of those few Wiccans who are trained as Ceremonial Magicians, who are fully capable of practicing both Magic and Wicca separately, and often do. One jokes that it is like ice cream and beer; she enjoys both immensely, but has no desire to mix them together.

Recommended Reading for Topic Three:
Hutton, Ronald *Triumph of the Moon: A History of Modern Pagan Witchcraft*, Oxford, 2001
Bulfinch's Mythology: http://www.bulfinch.org/
Comparative Mythology: http://mythus.com/
Excerpts from Max Müller:
http://www.bbk.ac.uk/eh/eng/bahums/pmc/compmyth.htm

Discussion Topics for Topic Three:

3.1. Is Wicca an ancient religion? If so, in what way is it ancient? If not, why do people often claim it is?

3.2. What do artifacts such as figures like the "Venus of Willendorf," knives, cave paintings of horned gods and the like say about Wicca?

3.3. Why do Modernists believe that Wicca came about when it did?

3.4. What is the difference between a Modernist and a Modern Wiccan? A Modernist and a Post-Modern Wiccan?

3.5. Does a Modernist have to be Wiccan?

3.6. What is the purpose of religion? Of mythology?

3.7. What does the author mean by "do whatever"? How does this make Wicca nonsensical? If it does not, explain.

3.8. Karen Armstrong describes fundamentalism using the comparative theology terms "mythos" and "logos." In part, she sees fundamentalism as religions turning from the belief that the logos was the core of their religion to the mythos- believing the literal history of the Bible, for example. Do you disagree with this assessment?

3.9. Each of the "stages" of Wicca are fairly subjective. What is the validity of discussing Wicca in stages?

3.10. One proponent of the Tomas Timeline says that Post- Modern Wicca is just Modern Wicca with maturity. As each stage of Wicca's development is seen as a reaction to the one before, how accurate is that assessment?

Wicca in Practice I: Asking Questions

"What do you mean 'There are no stupid questions?' I could ask you a stupid question every minute for the rest of my life! There are plenty of stupid questions, but you should never be afraid to ask them. More importantly, you should never be afraid to ask how to not ask them."[41]

We are told in kindergarten, maybe earlier, that the best way to get an answer is to ask questions. If you wanted to know the name of a shape drawn on the blackboard, you asked your teacher "What's that shape?" However, even this simple question was an informed one: you understood the nature of a shape. Imagine your teacher's frustration if she explained, "The shape on the blackboard is a circle and its color is red," and you asked "What's a shape?" and "What's a color?"

You need information to ask for data. In the example above, you need to know what a color is, what a shape is... and even what a blackboard is. You picked most of these things up at an intuitive level. You saw a green crayon and heard someone say *this color is green*; you saw a red crayon and heard someone say *this color is red...* and figured out that the color was the difference between the crayons. Maybe you were confused at first. Maybe the green crayon was worn down and the red crayon wasn't, so your first belief was that "green" meant old and "red" meant new. This confusion would probably be solved by the introduction to the third or forth crayon. The neat thing is that you probably never realized you were learning. It all occurred deep inside the brain, and you never even thought about it.

By the time you graduated kindergarten and passed to the higher grades, the amount of intuitive learning you possessed had increased to unimaginable levels. You under-

---

[41]There is a strong debate in the original UEW/Silver Chalice Community about who said this first. Certainly I have said things like it, but I suspect it was originally Jayne Tomas or Tamryn Wyrmstar. Certainly the stupid questions rant is a common one in our house, where challenging common sayings and dogmas like "no such thing as a stupid question" is raised to a high art.

stood cause and effect, colors, shapes, reasons, facts, and, chances are, when your teacher told you there were no stupid questions, he or she was right: you were not going to come up with stupid questions because you knew so much already. If you didn't know enough to ask the questions, you would've been held back.

Now imagine taking calculus in college and a student who speaks English well, and has placed into the class, asks you what the professor means by "adding" and what the "+" on the blackboard is. You probably would be completely shocked; you'd think it was a joke or think the student was having a breakdown. The professor would probably be offended and ask the student how he got into the class. Indeed, contrary to what your old teacher said, there are stupid questions.

So why is it that people with little or no religious experience will ask questions like "What is Wicca?" and not be satisfied with the answers they get? The simple answer is that it is a stupid question — a question without the proper frame of reference. But it has been so long since they've posed such a question that they simply assume it isn't.

So we find ourselves here with what looks like a stupid question of our own: what is the purpose of asking questions?

Clearly, the answer is to get information. The problem is that there is a lot of information you could be seeking. Unfortunately, the person you're seeking it from doesn't know what information you have already from what information you still need.

So let's go back to the question of Wicca. Our newbie asks "What is Wicca?" and I say. "Wicca is a religion" to which the newbie replies "I knew *that*, but what is it?" Perhaps to this I reply, "Wicca is *my* religion," and the newbie still goes "Well, yeah, I knew *that*, but what is it?" In order to answer this newbie's question to his satisfaction, I can keep guessing, throwing out bits of information, until I stumble upon what he lacks. I can ask him "Well, what do you know about Wicca?" in the hopes that he tells me enough to answer his question. If this encounter is face to face, I might guess from body language, but if he's not, I can only guess.

Since this is not the real world, I can imagine I go into the newbie's head. Once I'm in there, I see that he knows a lot about Wicca, and the question he is asking is "Is Wicca a Neo-Pagan Religion?" Since I'm there, I can also see what his definition of Neo-Pagan is, and indeed, that Wicca falls under that definition, so I can answer his question.

Let's step out of his head, though. Neo-Pagan is not a term I regularly use. I think it confuses people, and makes them think that the religions Modern Pagans try to create are new versions of ancient ones. I could go on for several hours answering this guy's question and never get the word Neo-Pagan out. If he's not giving me more data, he's probably not getting his answer.

Worse, if he's not been warned, the fact that I'm likely to wax Socratic is probably going to make him nervous. I won't get past one "I knew that" without going "Well, tell me what you know. What do you think Wicca is?"

The problem with our newbie is that he doesn't know how to ask his question. His definition of Neo-Pagan is a Non-Abrahamic religion that developed in the past 100 years. He could ask me "Is Wicca a Neo-Pagan religion?" which probably would've gotten the answer "It depends on your definition of Neo-Pagan," or, he could've said "Is Wicca a Non-Abrahamic religion that has developed within the past 100 years?" which would've been answered with a simple "yes."

We'll step away from Wicca to bring this point home. You're at a friend's house. She makes awesome margaritas. You hear a whirring noise in her house, and you wonder what it is. It sounds sort of like the blender, so you ask her "Are you making margaritas?" Your hostess, who is recovering from an operation, assumes that you are asking because you want them, and stands up and sets about doing it, answering "Sure" but thinking that you're really a jerk for asking.

Both of you are victims of the stupid question. The smart question version of this conversation works like this: Whirring noise. You: "What is that whirring noise?" Her:

"My husband is sanding the floor, why do you ask?" You: "I thought it was the blender and couldn't figure out why it was running." Her: "Nope, just a belt-sander. It does sound like the blender, though. Hey, maybe I can get Dave to make us margaritas! DAVE!!!"

A smart question assumes nothing. Your hostess is looking at the television, and you ask her "is that the blender?" assuming that she's heard the whirring noise. She looks at the television and says to you "No, it's a television," because the sander's been running for days and she hasn't even thought about it. It can go on like this for hours, but usually it doesn't... body language, experience and more teach you how to ask her questions that get the answers you want. Of course, there is no body language in an email or a chat room, but that's another thing altogether.

How to ask smart questions, give smart answers and defend your position

Asking smart questions involves three things: explaining why you are asking, explaining what you know and defining any terms you use. We'll use a real-life example of a poor unfortunate girl who emailed me, only to get a multiple email lecture on how to ask questions (which is simplified here, obviously):

Her: "Is Wicca devil worship?"

Me: "What do you mean by devil worship?"

Her: "You know, worshipping the devil."

Me: "No, I don't know. What do you mean by devil worship? Give me an example of devil worship. We don't sacrifice cats or anything if that's what you mean."

Her: "You know, worshipping other gods."

Me: "No, I don't know. I don't worship the Christian God, but I don't worship Satan either."

Her: "All other gods are Satan!!!!"

Me: "Then why didn't you ask me if I worshipped gods other than your own?"

Her: "Because all other gods are Satan"

> Me: "And, if all other gods are Satan according to your religion I'm supposed to know this in what way?"
> Her: "You're just being difficult!"
> Me: "Hey, I've answered every question you've asked that made sense."
> Her: "You haven't answered any of my questions!"
> Me: "None of them made any sense."

I followed up the emails with the lecture in how to ask questions, and eventually we really did have a dialog. I admit I was being my usual hard-ass self with her, but one of the things that go with asking smart questions is giving smart answers, and smart answers don't assume. Eventually, we agreed to start all over again, and the revised conversation started like this:

> Her: "My name is Missy. I am a member of a Christian church that teaches that any practice of worshipping gods other than our own is Devil worship. Do Wiccans worship the Christian God?"
> Me: "No, but I don't agree that worshipping other gods is devil worship. In Genesis, chapter 3, we see mankind given the ability to tell good from evil. Certainly in Christianity, people know the difference between good and evil. According to the bible, all mankind does. If we know the difference we can't accidentally follow evil, and I know my gods are good. Perhaps if you showed me where in your holy book the knowledge of good and evil are removed from man I'd understand, or are you saying that devil worship isn't evil?"

My answer addressed questions raised by her statements: She was Christian, so I talked about the Bible. She defined devil worship, so I talked about that definition. I asked questions within her paradigm. If you wish to make a case, this is the level you need to go to. Eventually it all comes back to sloppy thought and sloppy words, but if you can keep five points in mind, you'll be fine:

1. Don't assume you know what another person really means. Don't expect them to know what you really mean.
2. If the words you use have complicated definitions or definitions they might not agree with, explain your definition.
3. If you can't narrow the question you are asked down to yes, no, or simple fact sharing, ask for more data.
4. It *is* valid to answer a question with a list of possible answers and more questions.
5. Always tell someone why you are asking, unless you know they know why.

Practice:
You are writing a series of emails to a person whose website says Wicca is devil worship. The site just says that it is, not why. Practice writing a series of questions to find out why.

A Wiccan friend says in the newspaper that Wicca is not a religion. You disagree. Write a letter to the paper expressing why you think he said that, what you think he means, and why you disagree.

Imagine a campaign selling breakfast cereal that asks "Why not fruity pops?" Write a letter to the marketing agent explaining why this is an effective campaign, or why it is not.

Topic Four: Wicca is not Celtic and Other Simple Truths.

What is "Celtic?" What defines a Celt? What do we know about them? Is Wicca Celtic? What is the ancient religion of the Celts? What's Faerie Wicca? Is it real?

What is a Celt?

The Celts are one of the indigenous peoples of Europe. Historically, their lands ranged from Ireland, though Great Britain, into France, Germany, Spain, Italy and elsewhere. In 387 BCE, a group of them even sacked the city of Rome. In the modern world, they are found in their indigenous lands, as well in most other countries. Large Celtic communities exist around the world, and many of the largest cities in the United States and Canada have huge Celtic communities, particularly Irish, Scottish and Welsh communities. It is commonly estimated that there are two to three times more people of "pure Irish decent" in The United States than in Ireland itself.[42] Even where they have mingled freely with the cultures around them, they've remained visible in distinct ways. For example, my wife's father, born in Italy and clearly of Italian decent, has a last name shared by lords (both ancient and modern) in Lowland Scotland and Wales[43] — a name unpronounceable in Italian.

The problem with so-called Celtic Paganism[44] is multivariate, but is largely the result of three distinct issues. First, the Celts are a hard to define people consisting of several hundred tribes, multiple languages that are roughly divided into two groups (though all descending from one language) and a set of mythologies that can vary from one group to another. This makes it hard (not impossible, though!) to weed out good Celtic materials from bad because any difference may be (but is not necessarily!) the result of a tribal difference, not poor research. Secondly,

---

[42]This is difficult to define. One friend defines it as having all Great Grandparents be from Ireland or the children of people from Ireland. Certainly if we were discussing thoroughbred horses, instead of people, this would be a valid definition.

[43]This is enough information to come up with the actual name within three guesses. I welcome emails with those three guesses.

[44] Referring to Modern Paganism, not pre-Christianity.

scholastic research has often ignored the Celts. They didn't leave the huge edifices of Rome, Egypt or Greece, their conversion to Christianity was accomplished with little bloodshed and, until modern times, they lived in basically the same places they always had. As if this was not bad enough, there was—and, to a lesser degree, still is—horrible prejudice against Celts and their languages amongst English speakers, even among other Celts who are English speakers. For example, on the East Coast of the United States, it was often the Scottish factory owners stating "no Irish need apply."[45]

In addition to the difficulty of research and the lack of good source materials, the Victorian age and its Romantic poets led a rush toward fanciful interpretations of Celtic myth and legend. These were often sterilized for an English public or just plain incorrect. The nasty boggles my relatives warned ill-behaved kiddies of were turned into bedtime stories and fables. The use of the Celtic milieu for these fanciful stories lives on in their name: Fairy Tales.

It's not surprising, then, that Modern Pagans, when creating mystic concepts, often label their fairy-tale-flavored faith as Celtic or "Faerie." The problem with this is that the Celts are still around, and will tell you that Wicca, Witta, Faerie Paganism and the like are not their religions, current or ancient. Worse, it can be difficult to refute the claims of people promoting their non-Celtic faith as Celtic because a mountain of nonsense is out there to back them up. That this material is nonsense is not hard to prove. For example, the claim that there was an ancient Irish Potato Goddess is pretty easy to refute, since the potato plant doesn't get to Europe until the 16th century, but the massive bulk of bad

---

[45] Including factories owned by some of my own distant relations. While I am a mutt at best, I was still reminded fairly regularly as a youth (at the least, on every St. Patrick's day) that my blood included Scottish and other Celtic flavors, but NOT Irish. One distant relative still living in Cornwall insists that despite the high number of Morgans in Wales we are utterly Cornish and not Welsh... Telling other Campbells we're descended from Romans gleans nasty looks... The prejudice now is reduced to jokes and dirty looks, but it is still prejudicial at its heart.

material can make it hard to avoid, and when people don't bother doing any research into the validity of what they are learning, the fact that a lot of other people say it becomes proof enough.

So it's not surprising that there is a lot of anger between the Pagan and Celtic communities. On the one hand, Modern Paganism offers to resurrect ancient religions, but on the other, what they are resurrecting is often completely wrong. With the Celts this is especially tragic, because they've been watching the slow murder of their culture for over a thousand years, and the people doing the *worst* right now do so while claiming to be *helpful* and even *loving* the culture they are damaging.

If you ask people in the Celtic Communities what a Celt is, you'll get a number of different answers, but they all share a common theme: recognition by other Celts of your status amongst them. My own definition is a little strange: I do not recognize any definition that would include myself. I was born in the United States, and was never exposed to anything particularly Celtic as a child, even though my family is predominantly Scottish. My birth names are English and French, more specifically Saxon and French. I was not raised in a Celtic community, nor brought up with a church, let alone a traditionally Celtic one. As far as stereotypes go, I *do* fit many: I enjoy Guinness and have a fairly typical round-cheeked, short, pale skinned, auburn haired Celtic phenotype. I have perfect pitch and have sung in local pubs, where I've also gotten in the occasional verbal spar. I am curmudgeonly at a young age in a thoroughly Scottish manner, and am nearly as happy griping about things I cannot change as I am spinning an utterly false tale to a child, only to say "No, it's not true at all" when asked "Did that really happen?" While I meet stereotypes, which many people do, I'm not a Celt because I live up (or down) to a few stereotypes.

What I am, instead, is a Celtic-American, more American than anything else. A Celt, unlike myself, is a member of a greater Celtic Community, speaks (or tries to speak) a Celtic Language and raises their children with that language in a community invested in the preservation and furtherance of that culture. I'm, at best, a kind-hearted caretaker of my own Celtic culture; my sole investment in it is a quest for better knowledge of myself (as well as, from a biological standpoint, knowing what genetic diseases I'm more susceptible to). At worst, I'm a dilettante, and it's for that reason that I reject any definition of Celt that includes myself. Put simply, in addition to being recognized as a Celt by other Celts, someone must have more invested in the culture than I do in order to be a Celt. That's pretty subjective, all in all, and I don't expect anyone to define Celt as "more Celtic than Kat MacMorgan." Still, it is reasonable to say that the Celts are capable of defining who is and is not Celtic, and don't need any American's help in doing so.

The next unit will explain why Wicca is not Celtic and why Celtic Wicca, Witta and the like aren't either. I had the great fortune to be exploring both Wicca and my Celtic Heritage before McCoy, Conway, Stepanich and the like ever got the idea of combining the two, and was thus spared falling into the trap of accepting their nonsense as true. Like the imaginary Logosians, who had a couple thousand years of belief called incorrect within decades of its rediscover by Neo-Pagans who had claimed their culture (see page 31) the Celts, who are neither imaginary nor extinct, had a culture long before Neo-Pagan authors imagined one and slapped their name upon it, a culture worthy of preservation and interest, and deserving of protection from profiteering.

What is Celtic in Wicca, and how did Things that are not Celtic get stuck with that Label?

There are very few things in Wicca that are inherently Celtic. In general, the entirety of Celtic culture borrowed in Wicca is the *language* used for the non-astronomical holidays (Samhain, for example.) Even the practices that occur on the holidays given these names are rarely Celtic in nature, and whether or not they should be called by these Celtic names is a valid question, especially considering that Early Modern Wicca labeled them August Eve, November Eve and the like. To read the erroneous literature out there, the four elements are Celtic, although Celtic holy numbers tend to come in threes, and more rarely, in fives. The con-

cept of duotheism—having a Great Goddess above goddesses and a Great God above gods is also claimed to be
Celtic—although the early Celts were polytheistic, and are
many religions, most predominantly Christian, in their current culture. And finally, the eight liturgical holidays, enumerated by Murray, are called Celtic, even though they
used a radically different calendar than our own to figure
their holy days.

Surprisingly, it is not about these issues that most Anti-
Wiccan Celtic Reconstructionists criticize Wiccans, and this
may have nearly as large a hand in the lack of corrective literature as the ignorant belief that the Celts have somehow
vanished and therefore no one can say that the new "ancient Celtic traditions" are neither ancient nor Celtic. Instead, the alleged Wiccan belief in harming none is what is
attacked. Since the majority of serious practitioners, as discussed earlier, do not see a universal prohibition of harm as
a Wiccan belief, this myopic attack on one aspect of Wicca—
an incorrect one at that—may have wasted years of valuable dialog. We often cannot even discuss why Wicca is not
Celtic with Modern Celts without first hearing that our belief in harming none (which we don't have) is wrong and
not Celtic.

What should be discussed instead (and has begun to be
covered in the past few years) are the things that some Wiccans are actually claiming about the Celts—for example, the
claim that the Celts had a singular God and Goddess. To
understand the phenomena, you have to understand that
these Wiccans sincerely believe that the Celts are an ancient
culture that went the way of the dinosaur. Their works will
inevitably state things like "we don't know what the Celts
believed, but we can make educated guesses based on archaeology and their legends." That archaeology often includes the relics of pre- and proto- Celtic cultures, as well as
Romans, Saxons and a few dozen other peoples and those
legends are usually fanciful translations of ancient Celtic

Epics, if not entirely new works with a Celtic flavor.[46] The main side effect of this belief is that these Wiccans see any statements about what Celts do and don't believe as completely subjective. Thus, if I were to say "Wicca bears no resemblance to the ancient Celtic religions" these Wiccans would say that I was overstepping my bounds, since no one knows what the Celts believed. That might be followed by the claim that they are correct in saying the Celts practiced Wicca because there is no proof otherwise.

Setting aside, for a moment, the fact that there is, indeed, proof otherwise, this idea that something must be true because you can't prove it is false is a scary concept. It's also a huge divergence from scientific thought, which teaches us that something is not definitely false until proven to be so. The difference can be subtle: one says something is true merely because you can't prove it is not true, the other says that something may or not be true until it is proven to be false. This is a huge distinction in thought, and this shoddy logic should be something we keep an eye out for when evaluating materials.

Convincing these Wiccans that the Celts are still around is the first step towards helping them understand that what they say about Celts and Wicca is incorrect, but inevitably, some of them are going to decide that Modern Celts who disagree with them are somehow less Celtic. Often, the fact that the mass conversion of Celtic cultures to Christianity was nearly bloodless is brought up in some manner. These people see modern Celts as divorced from their distant ancestors because more recent ancestors practiced Christian-

---

[46]Indeed, one of my favorite fantasy authors of all time is Kenneth C. Flint, and I once met a Modern Pagan whose beliefs were entirely modeled on a book of his about Sidhe in New York City. I've heard of similar experiences with Pagans basing their religious beliefs on other Faerie-in-the-Modern-age books as well. While basing your beliefs on a fantasy book is neither new nor bad in and of itself, many of these people will tell you the authors of these books have written the 100% truth and are engaged in a cover-up, which is kind of scary. For my part, I don't think vampires or faeries are employing Rice or Lackey to hide their existence by fictionalizing it. (I admit some doubts about David Bowie, however.)

ity. Strangely, the fact that the ancestors of the Wiccans claiming this are also nearly always Christian is not seen as important. It is as if the person's own family or personal journey from Abrahamic Religions is seen as more valid than the transition of thousands of Celts. On a personal note, I've never understood this point of view, so I can't really explain it. To me, the fact that the Celts exist is enough to trust what individual Celts say about their beliefs until those individuals give me a reason to think they are misled or being deceptive. I just can't grasp what would make an otherwise reasonable person state that the modern people of a culture s/he does not belong to are incapable of understanding their ancestors as well as some outsider does. I've been witness to this behavior enough times to say only that it exists, not why it exists.

Understanding that these people believe that Celts don't exist is key to understanding why they say their Modern beliefs are those of the ancient Celts. For many, it is *not* a case of outright lying, although certainly some people have done some lying, but a case of "fill in the blanks" gone awry. Murray taught that the Witch-Cult of her thesis existed in Western Europe. Gardner claimed the ancient Witch religion is British. Sybil Leek claims it is British and French. And a score of early authors claim it is rooted in what is now England, specifically.

Your average educated person knows a bit about who came and went in Ancient Great Britain. They have knowledge of the Normans, of the Romans, of the Anglo-Saxon diaspora, knowledge that gets less speculative as you approach modern times. They know, from histories, epic poems and plays, that these cultures' beliefs bear little resemblance to Modern Wicca. They also know that another group of people existed in the area—The Celts. For reasons described earlier, this average educated person knows little or nothing about the Celts. When they read, for example, that Wicca is the indigenous religion of Great Britain, they know who *didn't* believe anything like Wicca, and therefore assume that the culture there is little information about is the culture that is being spoken of.

It's not hard to see how in four generations of Wiccan writing the "unknown indigenous people with a religion like Wicca" became the Celts. I would even go on to say that as Celts begin to openly criticize works that credit them with the creation of Wicca, it is likely we shall see the "unknown indigenous people with a religion like Wicca" become the Picts, or another as yet unnamed Paleolithic culture. What is overlooked for some reason is the simple fact that indigenous peoples from the area of what is now England never practiced Wicca. It is probably overlooked because it is a less romantic idea that points to heavier flaws in Murray and Gardner than merely neglecting to name which group of indigenous people they were referring to, and the average person often feels too uneducated or unimportant to argue with the printed word.

With the "they must mean the Celts" mentality, you can see why every minute detail of Wicca is attributed to the Celts on occasion: if someone asks why you stand in a circle and you don't know, you can easily say you do so because the Celts did. If someone asks you why you hold your hand in such a way and you don't know, it can be for the same reason. In fact, it may be your teacher told you that's where the practice derived, because her teacher told her the same thing. Those who see ancientness as the core source of validity in a religion will want to avoid research into the actual fact of the matter. The "teaching chain" probably goes back four generations at most before you reach some progenitor that invented your process, either by taking parts of pre-existing practices, using them in a new way and inventing the rest… or by creating it all. It does not go back to the Celts. It may be inspired by them, or inspired by works inspired by them, but it is not ancient Celtic Practice. Indeed, even the holiday names, the sole thing in Wicca genuinely of Celtic descent, are phonetic spellings in an alphabet the Celts did not have.

Celtic and Faerie47 Wicca: An attempt to merge what should not be merged.

With the knowledge that the only things really Celtic in Wicca are a few words under our belt, it becomes possible to objectively evaluate such things as Celtic and Faerie Wicca. In her fabulous essay *When is a Celt Not a Celt,* Johanna Hautin-Mayer covers in detail the flaws within such well-discussed works as Edain McCoy's thankfully out-of-print "Witta: An Irish Pagan Tradition" and Kisma Stepanich's Faery Wicca books. These books are typical of the early movement to attach Celtic images to Wicca and make rather extreme claims that (it can be argued) would not have been made had their authors realized that very real Celts were going to question what they wrote. Hautin-Mayer attributes many of these mistakes to the authors' apparent lack of research, and certainly any case study of a book about the Celtic-flavored Wicca movement will show huge numbers of historical inaccuracies that can be corrected with little more than an encyclopedia.

Part of the problem here lies in the structure of Wicca itself, which often does not attempt to describe the divine in cultural terms, but in general terms. The young, new Wiccan is encouraged to look to his spiritual and genetic ancestors for an understanding of the divine as he studies. It is almost inevitable that a Wiccan of Celtic descent is going to find his ancestral gods among the Celtic pantheon, and the epics that inspire his soul will be found in Celtic cycles. That is where he will turn during his circle. There is nothing inherently wrong with this, although some Celts would see this as somehow worshipping their gods in ways alien to their culture, often describing it as invoking the divine, most Wiccans do not view the casting of a circle as an invocation of the divine, but instead as what Starhawk calls an

---

[47] I make a distinction here between Faerie Wicca and Feri Paganism. They just aren't one, and refutations of one have no bearing on the other.

enacted meditation[48]." For simplicity, I will discuss the circle in its use as a dynamic meditation, which is a fancy term for things like Tai-Chi and ritual dances that enact a change in mental state. The Wiccan circle is an exercise that promotes the inner stillness that assists in the worship of any god—it is a deliberate walk through mental and physical stages that lead the practitioner to a state that assists in communication with the divine by altering *the Wiccan*, not the gods or even the space in the air around him. To bring this home with silly metaphor, if Joe the Purple God of Daisies and Frogs is traditionally worshipped by his followers by singing the mystical purple flower song and by chanting "wugga wugga" when eating, the Wiccan follower of Joe the purple god would probably sing that song within his circle—but the song would not be altered in any way, and he would still chant "wugga wugga" when he ate, in circle or not.

Thus, the worship act would be the same whether the follower was a Wiccan or a traditional follower of Joe the Purple God, and the difference would lie in the worshipper's preparation and in his community ritual. It is here where Witta, Celtic Wicca and Faerie Wicca fail. They attempt to take the personal worship of individuals (which are, unfortunately, both cast as the worship of a community and as historically accurate practices) as communal worship. The practices outlined take the communal worship of Wicca, which may involve several practitioners doing different things within the Wiccan paradigm, and claim them as practices of all Wiccans, as well as non-Wiccans, despite the fact that they are the practices of individuals.

Individual worship hurts no one. If you think that dancing around a bonfire naked with black chicken feathers on your chest will cause The Morrigan to ride you like a Loa, that's fine. It's when you write or teach that dancing around a bonfire naked will cause this to happen to other people, despite the assurances of her historic followers that this is

---

[48] I admit here, to using the same quote in both of the books I've written on the subject...but it is an AWESOME term, and deserves use and recognition of its author.

not so, or when you write or teach that this is a historic practice, that you touch on dangerous ground. First, whenever you make a statement that is causal (doing X causes Y) you need to have darned good proof of the matter: you must demonstrate that it is replicable and that the effect is what you claim it is. Marie the newbie would be able to pick up your work, do as you say, and have the same effect, with some proof that this Morrigan was the same as the Celtic entity. Second, if you claim it is a historic practice, the onus is on you to prove it is, not on others to prove it is not. Lastly, you have to take responsibility for all the people who do the ritual as outlined by you — their disappointments included.

I'm wandering here a bit in this discussion because I am attempting to avoid painting the authors of these Celtic Wicca materials as nothing more than culturally exploitive imperialists, which there is certainly evidence for. It may be true that the UPG of people like McCoy and Stepanich showed them that their experiences, described in their writings, worked. For all I know, the gods themselves came down and told them to write what they wrote, but they offer no proof of this, so we can only guess at their motives. What we can do is compare their writings to those of the Celts themselves and see which comes out as more believable.

Returning to the concept of Wicca itself, Wicca is best described as a religion of the polis. Like the state religions of Greece and Rome, Wicca represents the baseline practices required for inclusion in the community — in this case, it's not citizenship in an actual nation, but citizenship in the virtual nation of Wiccan practitioners. There are certain things we use to recognize other members of that nation, core beliefs and practices, but like those state religions, individual practices vary from that core. Iule the good Roman might begin everyday with an invocation to his ancestors, Quinta the equally good Roman might begin each day by stoking the sacred fires in a temple... and Septus the nearly-as-good Roman might sleep in and miss his bath, having had a long walk last night from the shrine to Mithras. However, they all stand in the plaza and participate in the sacrifices and prayers that the entire dutiful citizenry are called to.

This idea can be fairly different from those ideas present within the Abrahamic Religions that many Wiccans were raised in. It is easy for those raised with the idea that having practices different from your neighbor means you have a different religion—it is easy for them to see their individual practices as a new and different religion. If Caitlin the Celt casts the circle the same way as most Wiccans, celebrates the eight holidays outlined by Murray, uses the tools and methods of Wicca, and believes in concepts of minimal harm, self-responsibility, and the like, she does not become a practitioner of a new religion when she refines her concept of the divine. She can stand right next to Petros the Wiccan follower of Zeus in a circle and participate as one without affecting her relationship with her gods.

This is perhaps best outlined with what's been called the triarchy of religion: the religions of Family, of Nation and of Heart. Rather than use another fanciful example, I'll stick to the one example I know best: myself. My religion of Nation is Wicca. I am a citizen of the virtual nation of Wiccan practitioners, thankfully born in a country where freedom of association allows religious nationhood to differ from literal citizenship. When a presidential candidate says, for example, that Wicca is not a religion, I am amongst those he is slandering. When a newspaper article says that Wiccans are all 12-year-old girls, I have the right to object. More specifically, my virtual nation is the Universal Eclectic Wicca tradition within Wicca, just as I am a citizen of the United States but more specifically an Upstate New York Yankee. As part of my religion of Nation, I celebrate on the eight days in Murray's liturgical calendar, and have certain techniques of worship I share with other Wiccans.

My religion of Family is two-fold; with my son and my wife I practice a sort of Anabaptist secular humanism. Recently, my son has expressed interest in Wicca (although he is strongly leaning towards atheism) and has participated in a few rituals, but he was raised with the idea that his religion is a decision for him to make when he has gathered information, not something he is by virtue of his birth. In addition, he's been taught that morality transcends religion and that his job is to be a good person, regardless of religion. With my wife alone, I practice both Wicca and Hellenic Reconstructionism. This makes for a busy liturgical calendar, but as we are often required to miss practicing together because of our schedules, we learned long ago that sometimes doing the minimum required on a holiday is just as spiritual as having a huge festival. Together we celebrate a number of festivals that are pan-Hellenic as well as the Wiccan festivals.

My religion of Heart, the most specific religion and the one that speaks most powerfully to me, is what is probably best described as membership in an ecstatic cult of Apollo. As you move from the broadest category to the narrowest, the validity to others of your practices declines, so that while I will often speak on my religion of Nation, I speak considerably less on Hellenic Reconstructionism, and perhaps least on the worship of Apollo. Likewise, I discuss Wicca in general frequently, and do not expect the practices of my tradition to have much bearing on the entire community, nor do I expect the practices of my family to have much bearing on my tradition, nor my personal practices to have much bearing on my family. They are all related, and if any one piece were in conflict, I would need to reconsider the practices of any part of that religious life.

Likewise, our Celt, Caitlin, may have Wicca as one of her distinctions, and traditional Celtic practices as another. She may combine these things when practicing or not, as her faith dictates. To bring the example back to me, my worship of Apollo requires certain things of my behavior and lifestyle, and I'm not ashamed to say that at a particularly clouded and hedonistic time in my life I failed in those things and was promptly both shown the error of my ways and how to be cleansed of the spiritual residue they left behind — information that had nothing to do with Wicca and could not be found within it. Say, for example, that Caitlin followed the imaginary Celtic god Lowena Angus the Black Cow of Happiness (I don't encourage the following of any imaginary gods, but I also don't wish to use a genuine example and have it used by someone to establish their worship techniques).Now we imagine that followers of Lowena Angus are required to consume a bottle of wine once a day at sunset, abstain from sex outside of marriage and avoid consuming beef or anything made from barley. Nothing in this silly collection of rules stops her from entering a circle, participating in communal worship as a Wiccan, or even taking the Catholic Mass (although the rules of the Catholic Mass might stop her).

Again, it is our Abrahamic prejudices at work that prevent us from understanding this concept. Most cultures outside of the Abrahamic ones had levels of worship: participation in state and personal cults, as well as private practices of individuals and families. Put most simply, if you wish to be a Wiccan and a practitioner of traditional Celtic religions, you do so *not* by altering your Wicca or Celtic practices to smush them together unnaturally, as Celtic and Faerie Wicca do, but as separate parts of your spirituality. In no thing other than religion do we attempt to create these monolithic things that are for all people at all times. Even in cooking, we know that garlic tastes good in some things but not all things. The vast majority of gods are not offended by parts of your spiritual regimen that do not include them or are not dictated by them. The vast majority of gods are not jealous or exclusive, and the vast majority of religions do not dictate that their followers have no spiritual life outside of them.

What is an Unethical Religious Practice and why are they Allowed to Exist?

This leads to the question of how the average Joe (not to be confused with the deity of the same name) determines what to blend and not blend in his religious life. In general, Joe is fine as long as the religious practices he is engaging in are ethical. In other words, if Joe's religious practices are not based in lies or otherwise creating some kind of harm, he's free to do as he will.

What is an unethical religious practice is a difficult question because some people see all religious practices that differ from theirs as inherently unethical. For some, unethical is defined by non-religious personal beliefs. An animal rights activist, for example, may find that any religious practice that involves animal sacrifice is unethical, but another person may hold the view that sacrifices that (like the vast majority of animal sacrifices) which provide food for the followers and/or are done humanely are not unethical. This is a fairly subjective question when you deal with very specific concepts, so we're going to return to the Celtic and Faerie Wicca "traditions" to discuss unethical religious practices in the hope that an example makes it clear.

Celtic-flavored Wicca does three distinct things: blending Wicca and Celtic tradition (which is not always inherently unethical), teaching that Wicca is the traditional religion of the Celts (which is unethical because research demonstrates otherwise), and assigning to both Wiccans and Celts various practices and beliefs that one or both may not have at all — which is highly unethical. When this is done completely by accident, it is unethical in that it could've been avoided. If the author or leader owns up to and tries to correct his or her errors, it's utterly forgivable. When this is done out of laziness or greed, however, it is not only unethical, but also unforgivable, for it is the intentional exploitation of one or more cultures for personal fun and profit.

These movements and their affiliated books are unethical because of the grave disservice they do to the religions they are about. Taking the words of other peoples and manipulating them to one's own ends is never correct. If you disagree with the practices of a people, you do not simply ignore that those practices exist when writing about them, but state them and why you disagree with them. You give the reader the chance to make an educated choice rather than follow what you have done. Some of these writings and practices are beautiful, even inspirational, but as long as they are based on lies, they do damage to everyone they touch.

Being inspired by these things is not unethical, but continuing the exploitation is. If, for example, you purchase a book (or recommend purchasing a book) by one of these problematic authors knowing full well that it is full of lies and inaccuracies — an act that tells publishers this type of practice is all right, I might add — you are financially supporting the exploitation, and thus are somewhat morally accountable yourself). If, on the other hand, you read one of these books at the library or purchased it not knowing what you were supporting, the fault lies squarely on the author.

We find ourselves in the difficult position of being required to be smart shoppers in the bookstore, which for bibliophiles like me is almost painful. We can't purchase every title on Wicca just like we can't drive whatever car suits our fancy if we like the environment, or eat whatever we want if we value our health. Like the automakers and people who make bad foods, publishers are held accountable for what they put out. They either publish everyone—in which case the responsibility for writing ethically falls 100% on the author—or they are to be held responsible for what they choose to publish because their choice indicates the presence of standards.

Not surprisingly, it is unlikely that the vast majority of houses would've published the Celtic and Faery Wicca-type books. When a historian, for example, plays hard and fast with the truth in a book by a mainstream publisher and that publisher finds out, the book is pulled and the author is promptly sued. The religious and "new age" publishers are often less concerned with truth because they see the fact that the books are religious in nature as somehow meaning that they can say whatever they want.

This is likely one reason why these unethical practices are published: shortsighted editors that cannot see the difference, for example, between an author that says that they believe that the Celts came from Atlantis and an author who claims the Celts practiced Wicca. One is a belief; the other is a statement of an incorrect fact. Perhaps the belief that there is no truth in religion is to blame here, but simple fact-checking seems so important to the concept of authorship that it would be altogether impossible for many authors, let alone people who worked with them, to avoid it completely without a fairly unique paradigm.

Perhaps, as mentioned earlier, the unethical practices, which really do boil down to practices based on lies about other people, are merely the result of the belief that the authors would not get caught. It may even be that the real practices were just too boring to sell books. At a young age, many children will tell lies because the lies are so much more interesting than the truth. Psychologists encourage parents to respond to such lies by acknowledging that it would be really neat if that were true. For example, I recall asking my son, at four, that "Although it would be really neat if you had seen the papers throw themselves on the floor, wasn't the truth more boring?" They attribute this lying to two things: the sincere belief that the child really thinks that his or her imagined reality would be better than the real one, and the child's lack of understanding that this kind of lie is wrong. We may find ourselves wondering, when authors paint really interesting realities that are patently false, if their parents never encouraged them to tell the boring truth instead.

It would be a less-boring-than-reality untruth to say I knew why authors and editors allowed unethical things to be written. I could say greed, I could say sloppiness, I could say arrested psychological development, and I could even say that it was because they thought they could get away with it. None of these things are completely true, however, and it is likely a combination of these things and more that have allowed the current situation, which, while most severe in the Celtic-flavored community also stretches throughout Wicca. A Celtic friend asked me, quite bluntly, what reason my community had to do this injustice to his people and others and I found myself forced to answer that I simply did not know. What I do know, however, is what to do about it.

An Introduction to Intellectual Integrity

Those familiar with the allonewicca.com website are familiar with the term intellectual integrity. At its core, intellectual integrity consists of making the decision to not lie about persons, places or other facts when writing about your religion. More specifically, it is the decision not only to not engage in those behaviors, but to not sponsor or promote them, nor to stand for those that do. It can be a bit of a scary concept. On the one hand, we don't wish to seem to be splitting the community into two parties-the ones that embrace intellectual integrity and those that don't, and on the other hand, those who are expecting this integrity already (which is not too much to ask) shouldn't have to ask for it, or work toward it. It should already be there.

Intellectual integrity takes the place of the community censure that those originally writing things like "whatever works" expected to be in place. Whatever works and whatever feels good are not the same ideas. A Wiccan doing things that exploit other people, by definition, is not doing what works. Those stating whatever works expect that those that seek their inspiration and practices from other people will respect the people they are learning from. To the authors, there is no purpose in saying "Whatever works does not mean whatever you want," because it's an obvious distinction.

Incidents of persons apparently devoid of intellectual integrity are not hard to find. A person who is a guest at a group's otherwise closed ritual, a guest on the condition that s/he not reveal the ritual, only to write a ritual identical to it in his/her work... an Irish woman with no Native American blood watches a movie on Native American rituals, writes a book called "I am Shaman" and sets up Shaman[49] Workshops where she makes $100 a head performing a ritual that is not genuine, and which neither does what she claims nor comes from where she claims... This lack of integrity can be based on nothing more than greed, but we also see examples of it based on ignorance. The student at that Shaman Workshop paid good money to "become" a shaman; when she writes books as a shaman, she's *not* intentionally fooling someone. She had an experience that was powerful and was told that that experience made her a shaman. If Caitlin the Celt's mom lied, for example, claiming the family had an unbroken line of Wiccans that went back 500 years, Caitlin is not a bad person for repeating it.

So, in addition to asking people to just not lie, intellectual integrity also asks people to research what they learn to

---

[49] The problems with such an idea are many. The fact that shaman only accurately refers to a practitioner of specific Siberian ecstatic rites is just part of the issue.

get all sides of the story. It asks people to explain why they are making their claims. If I pick up a book by imaginary shaman David Spottedpony it might say "David Spotted-pony has been practicing shamanism for 47 years. He began the study with his father, who learned it from his father, etc." If I pick up the book of our imaginary shaman above, it had better say she became a shaman at a Shaman Work-shop run by the author of *I am Shaman*. Both books give me the chance for further research. If I know the author of *I am Shaman* has a questionable background, and if her student covers that, I know the book is more objective than if the book just takes the author of *I am Shaman* at her word. Likewise, I can look into David Spottedpony's practice and even his father's. Forty-seven years is a long time to leave no trace of your practice and with a little footwork, I should be able to learn something.

A few friends of mine are practitioners of a British fa-milial magical tradition (FMT)[50] going back at least 200 years and claiming to go back longer. The family is Chris-tian, so they aren't a precursor of Wicca, but they believe that they are granted power because of their mystical roots and ties with the land. They have authenticated letters be-tween family members that speak of these beliefs dating to just after the American Revolution as well as older docu-ments that are harder to authenticate. In what my research shows to be a fairly typical view of the type of FMT, they believe that blood relation to a particular relative is the source of their power. They also believe in entities that we would probably call household gods or ancestral spirits that have to be appeased and honored in various ways.

Intrinsic to their FMT is blood relatedness, and as such, they are more interested in genealogy than any group but perhaps the Mormons (who they have no nice words for, seeing the practice of posthumous baptism of non-Mormons as nothing other than trying to capture the spirits

---

[50] Any information here not fictionalized was vetted through the matriarch of the FMT noted. It is used with full permissions and her blessings. I used a rare technique called **asking permission**, I use it a lot and recommend it highly.

of other families, a worthless practice with the singular result of disrespecting both living and dead and absolutely no other effect). Part of their FMT involves several other families with similar powers and similar lineage, and they try to keep track of all the current descendants of these people. This research flavors who they'll marry, date and more… and they have long-established rules for dealing with non-related relatives and methods for adoption.

Even if you think this is complete bunk, genetic relatedness is an intrinsic part of their practice. It flavors everything they do. It is in every single part of their learning. Even their "prayers" to their ancestors begin by invoking the blood in their veins. This is poignant in that it is an extreme version of what often occurs in modern ethnic Reconstructionism, but it is vital that you understand that for these people participation in their rites could involve DNA testing. While their beliefs allow non-related people into their circle, the tests to do so are difficult and complicated.

Some of their beliefs involve a sacred site that is on their land–a circle of low, flat stones built within the past 200 years. They believe that this stone circle encases a great power that, if offended, could do horrible things to the surrounding countryside and the rites to quell it would be dark and extreme, and probably involve someone dying. To my skeptical American ears, the rites seem backwards, even outright wrong. However other things they have done have had powerful results that I've been witness to, so I believe that they *believe* their tales regarding this stone circle, even if I'm not prepared to say I believe that evil boggles rest in people's backyards. An ex-wife of this family threatened to do the ritual to awaken this boggle and set it free because she didn't believe in it and was going to prove it was false. She was kept from the circle with physical force: hunting rifles, sticks and strong young men barred her way. This occurred even though their beliefs were that she, as a non-genetically related individual only had a one or two percent chance of having any effect. Within three months, they had done the intense magical and physical labor to move the stone circle and whatever was underneath it, rededicate it, hide it and set up a simple security perimeter. Their local priest even came out and put a blessing on the new area. Like me, he was a skeptic, but their belief in it was enough that he felt it was important to indulge them.

The ex-wife is a good example of a complete lack of intellectual integrity. She was going to do a ritual she didn't have the right to do for her own selfish ends. As if this was not bad enough, a local witch who'd visited the old site with her boyfriend was going to do a Wiccan-type ritual there to appease the old spirits, purify the land and undo the anger she "felt" there, anger she claimed was created by the rituals of this family, which were based pretty much in fear of what would happen if the rituals stopped happening. She intended to do this despite the fact that the land was not hers, the feared entity was Christian and the area was already "pure."

This witch exhibited another kind of lack of intellectual integrity, which was sadly also fairly well demonstrated by Starhawk shortly before the initial release of this book when she and several protesters burned sage and did a purification ritual on a road used by industrialists on Native American land without the permission of the land holders. Notable publicity witches and even Christian "prayer warriors" have done the same thing: trespass on other people's spiritual and physical property. To quote Joseph, the patriarch of the clan detailed above: "If I unleash a nasty force on my land, and it is confined to my land, I put it there for a reason and even though your purification rite is not going to make it go away, you're injuring *me* if you try to send it away." The intellectual integrity here consists of knowing what spaces are not yours to invade. In short, it's about not fooling yourself…not lying to yourself about what you probably know deep down inside to be the wrong thing to do.

This is all that intellectual integrity is really. It's not lying, to yourself or others, about what you are doing. If the Logosians say you have to be a blood relative of theirs to participate in their rituals, then don't participate in their rituals. A minority of polytheistic cultures *do* say you can't worship their gods without certain requirements, so if you choose to do so without meeting those requirements, then have reasons and be willing to explain them. Don't simply claim the culture doesn't care what you're doing. If the Celts say their indigenous religion is not Wicca, then don't say it is. If you make things up, don't be afraid to claim authorship of those things. If you want to do a ritual to purify some land, make sure it's okay with the owners of the land. In short, take responsibility for your actions and words. This includes both acts of inspiration and things you teach. Remember that your rights (and your rites, as well) end where another's nose begins. The moment something leaves your personal domain—your brain, your journal, your land, your private ritual—the whole set of rights and responsibilities regarding that thing changes.

Intellectual integrity is not about getting things right or taking every opinion into account before doing something. It is about is being wise. You must learn to be wise about your motives, your facts, and your rights as well as the feelings, motives, rights and the like of the people around you. It is not, as some have complained, some sort of slippery slope. If you remove elements of other cultures from Wicca, it still stands as a religion. If removing erroneous or stolen elements from your brand of Wicca renders it nonsensical, the problem lies not in Wicca itself but the brand you practice.

Believe it or not, having intellectual integrity is pretty easy. Once you start, not only is it hard to stop but it begins to flavor everything you do. Those who embrace intellectual integrity are generally recognized (even by people who hate them) as really stand-up people. It might not be the way to win large numbers of friends or have the flashiest or trendiest circle, but it certainly improves your reputation as a force for truth in the universe. For those of us who see serving truth as serving the divine, it becomes even more important, because every checked fact or corrected error becomes a sort of prayer.

<u>Recommended Reading for Topic Four:</u>
Imbas.org

When is a Celt not a Celt:
http://www.cyberwitch.com/wychwood/Library/whenIs
ACeltNotACelt.htm

"Why Wicca is not Celtic" can be found here:
http://www.clannada.org/philosophy.htm
*Author's note: This essay is an excellent example of stuff that is
utterly unhelpful. The Celtic beliefs are spot on and much or what
it says about what Wiccans believe is nonsense. Note the lack of
any books on Wiccan belief in the bibliography. The lesson here is
this: If you are going to discuss beliefs comparatively, you need to
do the same amount of research into both sets of beliefs.*

Topic Four Discussion Questions:

4.1. Using the recommended reading, find some elements of Celtic belief. Compare and contrast them to Wicca in general.

4.2. What religions are currently practiced by Celts? Are practicing Celtic traditions necessarily indicative of practicing a traditional Celtic religion?

4.3. Read the essay "When is a Celt not a Celt?" Discuss.

4.4. It has been said that "Wicca practiced by a Celt may be Celtic Wicca, but Celtic Wicca itself is a myth." Can you make heads or tails of this comment? What do you think it means?

4.5. What is meant by a "Triarchy of Religions?" How is this vastly different than Abrahamic thought?

4.6. Give an example of how an ancient person may have many different religions. Does this make one or more of them more valid than the other?

4.7. What is the purpose of a Wiccan circle?

4.8. Why do you think unethical works on Wicca are allowed?

4.9. What would be the ideal "Celtic Wicca" book, if such a book could be ideal at all?

4.10. What is intellectual integrity?

4.11. Intellectual integrity has been called "the stupid thing we should all have already anyways." If you could narrow a definition down to three or four words, what would it be and should we all be doing it already anyways? If we are already doing it, is a discussion of it relevant? If we are not, why aren't we?

Topic Five: The Religion of The Great Mother Goddess and Wicca

What is the "Religion of The Great Goddess?" How is it different from Wicca? Why is it often confused with Wicca? Are there different versions and degrees of it? What is Dianic Paganism? Dianic Wicca? Feminist Paganism? Thealogy? What does Wicca believe about the Goddess?

Why is Feminist Paganism so often confused with Wicca?

In the early days of Feminist Paganism, just as in the early days of Wicca, no distinction was made between types of Witchcraft or types of Pagan religions. The witch, whether Wiccan, Dianic or even Satanic, could use the words "Wicca" and "witch" with impunity. In those early days, such distinctions were less important. Our numbers were small, and the outside community basically considered us all to be freaks and weirdoes.

This has changed significantly in the past twenty years or so, but many of the books we use today date from before the time when these distinctions became important, so it's no wonder that beginners find themselves bewildered and confused. Worse yet, some persons who are victims of this confusion go on to write equally confusing websites or books. Often, their error lies not in confusing Wiccan authors with non-Wiccan ones, but simply in not understanding that such distinctions exist.

Both Modern Wicca and Feminist Paganism are movements that essentially react to the oppressive religious régimes around them. For Wicca, this reaction is primarily to British cultural phenomena. For Feminist Paganism, the reaction is to cultural phenomena in the States. As so often happens in matters of religion, the American version is considerably more extreme and reactionary than the British version — at least at its outset — so it should not seem overly surprising that in their initial forms, the differences between Wicca and Feminist Paganism were more matters of degree than true differences.

For example, while Wicca reacts to Abrahamic patriarchy by having a god and a goddess, Feminist Paganism does so by having a goddess alone. While Wicca describes itself by the gender neutral term "theology," Feminist Paganism uses the female specific term thealogy[51]. Another distinction is that Wicca sees the God of the Christians as a separate entity from the god of Wiccans, while Feminist Paganism sees all goddesses as one and all gods, especially the god of the Christians, as one God. Again, it is extremity of belief drawing the distinctions, especially in the beginning, not the middle ground most practitioners are closer to.

That is not to say that all practitioners of Wicca are moderates and all practitioners of Feminist Paganism are extremists, for any such claim would be highly erroneous. What is observable here instead is a *tendency* towards stronger reactionism on the part of the Feminist Pagan movement as a whole than in Wicca. This isn't so much a problem as it is the inevitable result of the fact that Wicca, as a religion initially practiced by white middle class people and written about by white upper class men, does not speak to the disenfranchised state of women in general. Feminist Paganism is inextricably linked with Feminism, with its completely valid fight for equal rights for women. It is impossible to be a Feminist Pagan and not a Feminist, as opposed to the fact that one may be a Feminist or not and be a Wiccan.

The term "Feminism" has taken on a pejorative slant in the general public, mostly because the term is often linked

---

[51] This may be nothing more or less than Naomi Goldenberg's lack of knowledge-intentional or otherwise-that the Greek word *theos* is often gender neutral. In many languages, including Greek, the gender-neutral word and the masculine word are the same in some of the cases of the word. Theos is a term that means a neutral gender or male god, and is sometimes even used for a female god. It is also the term pluralized to mean a collection of gods, both male and female. Thus theology is the study of all gods, male and female, whereas thealogy is only the study of goddesses, which, while applicable to the study of some forms of Feminist Paganism is hardly applicable to Wicca or all forms of Feminist Paganism. What Goldenberg and people like Mary Daly fail to realize is that in insisting that even demonstrable gender-neutral words are male words, they are making the world more male-centered than it really is. Those of us comfortable with ambiguity are a lot more comfortable in general with such terms, but then again, as a woman, married to a woman, whom I refer to as my wife, I'm no doubt one with the oppressor. That my wife makes twenty times the money I do and has supported me when I've stayed home and played housewife makes me the oppressed, too, so I think it evens out.

with Feminist extremists with no qualifier. I highly doubt any Wiccan, experiencing the divine as male and female or beyond gender, would find him/herself disagreeing with the ideas of true Feminism—complete and utter parity between men and women—but it is likely that many Wiccans would refrain using the term to describe themselves for fear of being associated with extremists. This is part of a wider phenomena moderate Feminists warned of for years before it occurred, and let me take a break from this discussion to present four words that every English-speaking human claims to hate to say but in truth really loves: We told you so.

It is mostly the age of the books recommended by teachers of Wicca that have led to the fuzzy distinctions between types of Feminist Paganism and Wicca itself. As discussed, the early Pagan community was too small to need distinctions between groups. The confusion this causes, while fairly preventable, is also prevalent simply because it is something we don't speak of often. We primarily enter into discussion about it when a modern author fails to make those distinctions. I have the good fortune to be part of two Pagan communities in which Feminist Pagans and Wiccans both participate, so the distinctions are as clear as names and faces…but with solitaries and the book-taught, it is difficult to make a distinction if you don't know it is there. If you don't move about in the community, you'll probably never know it is there. Like many such confusions, the cure is not just reading about the community you are a part of, but going out and experiencing that community. Worse still, if your outside experience is insular and shielded, it is no better than staying home and reading a book. Meeting people who disagree with you is the way to truly learn what you believe…and meeting people for whom distinctions are important is the only way to truly live and breathe those distinctions.

What is Feminist Paganism and does it come in Multiple Forms (as Wicca does)?

Now that we understand in part why Feminist Paganism and Wicca are so often confused and used interchangeably, we have to define them to understand the differences. If you are reading this, I must assume you have *some* background knowledge of what Wicca is, so I'll focus instead on defining Feminist Paganism and its many forms.

Feminist Paganism is generally considered to be both an offshoot of the spiritual movements that created Wicca (or perhaps an offshoot of Wicca itself) and the inevitable result of the combination of Feminism with the archetype-based Jungian paradigm of psychology. This spiritual, feminist Jungian movement, perhaps best typified in Christian thought by Ann Belford Ulanov, and in Neo-Pagan thought by Naomi R. Goldenberg, takes *selected parts* of Jungian psychology and extrapolates it onto religion. Since Jung saw the collective unconscious in the ancient religions of man, it is only predictable that his followers would redefine ancient religions within his paradigm—a logical fallacy, but a predictable one. This fallacy is, namely, that if evidence for Jungian reality is found in ancient religion, then ancient religion can be recreated from Jung's theories.

As a Pagan theologian speaking from the Behavioral/Cognitive Neuroscience school of Psychology, I have to admit a fairly hefty personal bias against this Jungian scavenging. I've had a very rounded education: the classics, biology, neuroscience, classical psychology, modern psychology, mythology, theology and much more...and I've never seen Jung's theories as holding water outside of the world of comparative myth and religion. In these schools of thought, you can acknowledge trends within the myths of the world as speaking to the human condition without trying to attach pseudoscientific reasons for the similarity. Things are seen as similar because of similar sources (as in the PIE expansion), because they speak to some deeper human need (as in myths about food, or love) or because they are logical outgrowths of common thoughts (like flood myths, which answer the question of "what would happen if it never stopped raining," a question few have not wondered about on a rainy day). I see Jungian-based therapies as working because they encourage introspection, and I sincerely think that the positive effects found in such therapies would be more profound and common if led by trained philosophers and clergypersons than psychoanalysts. Indeed, one of the most profound moments in my life came when I was feeling disenfranchised and low, and a philosophy student engaged me in a discussion of Plato's *Phaedo*, sending me home with a stack of readings on the soul, death and life from his textbooks. Reading this stuff, then discussing it changed my life[52] and definitely helped me lose the funk I was in.

I mention this because while I am trying to be objective regarding Jungian-flavored Paganism, it is quite likely that my innate bias against it will flavor what I write and I try to write from a position of full disclosure. In other words, like most people, I have an opinion on what I am explaining, but unlike many other people, I'm not emotionally invested in whether or not you agree with me, only that, if you do agree or not, you understand why. Again, let me stress the need for you to do the research yourself. For example, a search on the Web for "Jungian Psychology" and an observation of the types of works written about it should be very telling in and of itself.

Coming back from that brief tangent, Jungian Feminist Paganism takes Carl Jung's ideas about archetypes and the collective unconscious—but not other parts of his theory—and extrapolates them onto religion. All gods, all beliefs, are defined as a shared psychic phenomena between humans, and all religions are seen as mere methods by which we interpret something too big to grasp on our own. On the one hand, this has the positive effect of giving people a sense of shared confusion, as the agnostic bumper sticker says: "I don't know and neither do you." On the other hand, this indicates that any UPG that consists of revelations about the universe that fall outside the Jungian paradigm is blatantly incorrect. The paradigm is a sweeping one that is inherently atheistic: there are no gods, only archetypes; no heavens, only the collective unconscious. Man is the center of this universe; he creates all things. Taken to its extreme, not only do gods not exist, but they are just extensions of our

---

[52] In his book, *Plato, Not Prozac!*, Marinoff proposes therapies not all that different from what worked for me 10 years before it came out.

wants, needs and desires. The logical outcome of this is clear; if you deal with your wants, needs and desires, then you lose your need for gods.

The Feminist Paganism version of Jung's theory takes the idea of a Great Mother Goddess as a force for positive change in the universe and uses it to power various socio-political agendas. By working within her archetype, women can find the power and wholeness they may have been denied by society and their upbringing, change the goals of government and rid the world of injustice. She represents the qualities of the ideal feminine: nurturing, creative, destructive, powerful. With her, a woman can do anything.

The Great Mother Goddess is seen as lifting up those whom the Abrahamic god drops, namely women. She is also perceived as an underdog entity actively forbidden and hidden by patriarchy and Christianity. The early writings on The Great Mother Goddess are often almost painfully anti-Abrahamic. She is cast in the image of the destroyer of patriarchal society and Christianity, often unforgivably so, not a balancer, but a swing of the pendulum to another extreme. It is not surprising that extremity of belief should come from Jungian Psychology into religion, as Jung saw many of society's faults as a direct result of Abrahamic belief, but there is little doubt he would be disgusted by the creation of a parallel religion with a sex change.

It is to their credit that many Feminist Pagans were capable of separating out the inspirational and empowering parts of what one friend calls by the painfully wordy name "The Neo-Jungian Extremist Radical Feminist quasi-religion of The Great Mother Goddess who will Stomp out Christianity" from the negative parts, and it is because of that ability that Feminist Paganism's followers can be separated into four distinct categories. These categories range from the patently atheistic old-school Jungians who believe that The Great Mother Goddess is little more than a powerful image we can study for self-knowledge to woman-centered ditheists and Dianic Wiccans.

The term "Dianic" comes from Margaret Murray's *Witch-cult in Western Europe,* and refers, essentially, to the great (and fictional) witch-cult whose existence is detailed within that book. In Modern Paganism, Dianic refers to any feminist Pagan branch, but usually to those groups in which The Great Mother Goddess is the singular deity. In most Dianic groups, The Goddess is a real entity, as opposed to the mere archetype she is to Neo-Jungian Feminist Pagans. For this reason, although the Neo-Jungians do refer to themselves as Dianic on occasion, I limit the use of the term to those who experience The Great Goddess as Murray's witch cult would have–as a genuine entity.

Within the Dianic category, I see three distinct groups. The first, which I refer to simply as "Dianic Pagans" see The Goddess as the singular deity of the universe, perhaps even seeing all gods and goddesses as a single entity which they name Goddess. The second group, which I call Dianic Ditheists or woman-centered ditheists see The Goddess as one of two entities in the Universe and equate all male gods with the Abrahamic god and his followers. These are the people who see all of the negative aspects of our culture as the result of focus on the male deity. Some of these Dianic Ditheists even go so far as to see God-centered worship as evil or destructive.

The last group of Dianics, whom I call Dianic Wiccans, sees gods and goddesses as equal entities but focus, for personal and cultural reasons, on the feminine part of the divine. Since some of these Dianics are not Wiccan, they are also sometimes called Dianic Duotheists (easily confused with Dianic Ditheists) or simply Dianic Pagans. For the purposes of this work, however, Dianic Wiccan will refer both to Dianics who are Wiccan and Dianics who are Wiccanesque.

In all four groups—the Neo-Jungians and the three types of Dianics—belief in the myth of The Great Goddess religion of the past is _not_ a prerequisite for membership. Indeed, right at the beginning of the movement, scholars like Goldenberg warned that basing their faith on shoddy research and speculation would make the new Goddess religions just as bad as the old patriarchal ones. Just as Wicca finds itself recuperating after a long sickness brought on by a desire to declare itself ancient, Dianicism is struggling with the idea of being a completely modern religion based on a myth that may have been invented in the past 100 years. Both are stronger for recognizing their modern roots, however, and the directions they take in the near future may reveal them to be truly long lasting religious traditions.

I have discussed the frailty of the concept of all gods being only one God in another chapter, and for that reason, I will refrain from discussing it in any further discussion of The Great Goddess religion. Those criticisms of all gods being one God work equally well for all gods being one Goddess. As I've stated, any time you claim a religious truth that shows other religious truths to be wrong, more than "I believe" must accompany that truth if you expect it to be given more weight than the next person's truth. In all gods being one, the burden is great indeed, for it is the history of all the polytheistic religions, all the Abrahamic Religions and most other religions that one has to weigh against. Again, as I've said, I am highly uncomfortable in saying that all those seeing their gods as discrete entities, throughout all of time, are incorrect.

The Thing Itself: The Myth of The Great Goddess and her Followers.

What follows here is complete fiction. It is an example of the teachings of The Great Goddess Myth based on numerous pseudohistories, legends, faith poems and rituals. After it is given, we'll dissect it and explain how it can be used for good as well as evil. The line numbers will be used in that discussion. In addition, where a "fact" of the myth comes directly from a book, it will be mentioned in a footnote, but the reader should be aware that the majority of the elements in this myth are from websites and discussions with people who believe it.

1. In the time before the coming of the new religions, more than thirty-five thousand years ago[53], mankind knew only two deities: the Goddess who was the birth-giver and the God who was the predator and the prey.
2. She was carved by her people in stone with huge breasts and pregnant belly, and he was drawn on the

[53] Starhawk, *The Spiral Dance*, Page 3

walls of caves as they celebrated their union in their every action.

3.Thousands of years passed, and the people went from being nomads to being farmers.

4. Similarly, their gods went from gods of nomads to gods of the land.

5. Many of the festivals of the followers did not change, however, and the dates of these festivals are those of a pre-agricultural society.[54]

6. As the people became more aware of their effects on the universe — that plants grew from seeds and children grew from intercourse — so did their gods.

7. The all-mother became a goddess of earth, barley and wheat, and the father God became a god of the rain and of the sky to reflect the new knowledge of the people.

8. Slowly, the farms grew into villages and the villages into towns, towns into cities, cities into empires.

9. As the relationships between peoples grew, they interpreted The God and The Goddess in new ways, creating the pantheons, families of the divine, but the followers knew these were just new names for the Mother and Father, who were unchanging.

10. So, in remote villages and towns, The Goddess and Her Consort were worshipped as they always had been.

11. They were honored with shrines, dances and rituals at sacred wells and in the fields.

12. Rituals were performed at sacred circles of stones set up centuries before for that very purpose, and the priestesses who danced and worshipped there, called Witches, knew arts that would go unlearned by the masses for millennia, things like the use of foxglove, mandrake and other herbs, astrology, astronomy and mathematics.

13. For Fertility, they practiced a rite of sexual intercourse that perhaps later degenerated into orgies but was originally a simple act of sympathetic magic.[55]

14. The priestess led the people and was the wise woman, the midwife and the arbiter of disputes for many years.

15. In the early 12th century, persecution began, first slowly, then with great vigor, coming to a head in the 1480s, with the Papal Bull of Innocent VIII and the publi-

---

[54]Murray's The Witch-cult in Western Europe, Page 12

[55] 5. Ibid, 15

cation of the "Malleus Malleficarum." [56] This began decades or horrible persecution and executions that would
last right up to the 18th century, in which more than 9
million[57] people were killed, although it can be argued it
occurs in the current day with the executions of Modern
Witches in Africa.

16. In all the Witch trials, the evidence, often revealed
under torture, was very similar.

17. The fact that this information was very similar points
to the reality of the Religion.[58]

18. The fact that faeries, the number 13 and certain personal names appeared in many confessions is especially
telling.[59]

19. It would be only in the past two-hundred years that
women have reclaimed the word Witch. Those who use
the term stand as one with the nine million people killed
with the purpose of seeing it not happen again.

20. Never again the burning times!

We'll begin with this idea of thirty-five thousand years
ago. Starhawk, in *The Spiral Dance*, attributes this beginning
of Witchcraft to "our legends" but doesn't say where those
legends came from or who "our" refers to. *In our legends* is
her sole disclaimer as to the reality of this statement, but it
should ring huge warning bells in the skeptic's head. We
simply do not know what anyone believed or taught until
we develop the art of writing, in which people state what
they believe. Even oral histories are so fraught with change
that there is no reason to believe that we have any idea
what happened thirty-five thousand years ago!

Line 2 is an example of the Murray flaw we discussed
earlier: using artifacts we *don't* have any written or spoken
evidence for the purpose of in order to "prove" our theory
of choice. One friend who works in advertising has claimed
that "goddess" statuettes were part of an ad campaign by
the first diet invented ("You don't want to look like this!"),
and that the half-man, half-beast figure was created by the

---

[56] Starhawk, 5
[57] Ibid
[58] Murray, 16
[59] Ibid, 17

"Eat More Deer Council." (And look! You can make a nifty hat with the antlers!)

When she said these things, it was in jest, but it illustrated a good point, that our backgrounds and desires often flavor how we interpret things. The artifacts are a sort of inkblot test for the mind: what we see in them is not necessarily what they are. We have to be like Algernon and see them just as what they are without attributing emotions, motives or symbols to them. This is counter-intuitive in a culture that says we must see symbols in everything, but it is a vital skill for scientific thought.

Lines 1 and 2 serve a purpose, however. To those who see religion as better because of its age, this makes duotheistic Paganism inherently better than all other religions. Rather see this myth as good because one can use it to interpret the facts in such a way as to make people with (for lack of a better word) stupid ideas about what makes a religion better than the next see one's religion as good, we can use the myth for good purposes when it is framed as conjecture. A discussion, for example, regarding what we *think* these symbols *may have meant* to their creators is bound to reveal some of our inner prejudices and preferences. Such introspection is often helpful in understanding our religious selves, and goes back to the idea of the inkblot test. We may use the inkblot to reveal our inner selves — what we see in the patterns can be very telling — but it just does not change the fact that an inkblot is an inkblot. In other words, there is a strong difference between seeing a butterfly *within* the inkblot and seeing a butterfly *instead* of an inkblot.

Lines 3 and 4 are another great example of misusing conjecture. We know that people went from nomadic life to cities at some point, although we are not sure why. We also know that, at some point during this extended period of time, the deities followed by people changed. The only problem is that we don't know the exact dates of either. While there is bound to be a relationship between the two, we can't truly know that it was a causal relationship. Again, discussing why we think one thing led to another is a positive thing. We can use these discussions to try to understand something that's probably never going to be understood. For me, multiple discussions of this have led to the belief that it is likely that Europeans got both agricultural technology and new ideas of deity from the PIE expansion. However, this underscores the flaw of this conjecture: it simply does not work outside the European milieu. For example, the gods of nomads who have not become "non-nomadic," especially those people furthest from Europe, do not fall into this mother/father pattern. Indeed, basing the idea of "what our ancestors believed" on surviving non-European indigenous religions is problematic. It is likely the earliest religions were much more animistic than duotheistic, and certainly not matrifocal or matriarchal in nature. This later form of conjecture, basing ideas about the past on peoples who have had less technological development and cultural sharing than most modern Europeans and Eurocentric cultures, provides a less glamorous view of the past that has better science but is still little more than a best guess. I tell my students to ask one question of all literature about the past: would it require a time machine to know for sure, and if so, does the author have one? If the answer is yes, that it would require a time machine, we have to base whether or not be believe what is written on the quality of the evidence and our opinion of the likeliness of the theory. In general, any theory that would strongly characterize any modern religion as ancient and therefore better is darned unlikely, or we'd all be that religion right now.

Line 5 is one of my favorite examples of Murrayite pseudoscience. Few holidays, and certainly none of the Wiccan ones, are neither agricultural nor astronomical, and it is hard to find any historical basis that astronomy is a pre-agricultural science. Indeed, a true nomadic lifestyle, following herds and weather patterns, would make the true study of the motions of the planets and stars impossible, as a strong change in perspective would be apparent. This change was noticeable to me, a modern human, with little knowledge of the stars beyond the locations of five or six constellations at certain times of the year, with the 200-mile difference in latitude between where I grew up and where I went to college. One can argue that these nomads who followed the herds and moved many times further than I did simply did not have the resources to study astronomy with precision. Certainly then, the claim that "many" of Murray's holy days are pre-agricultural is not supported by the facts, especially since her calendar, used by Wiccans today, consists of four astronomical holidays and four holidays that are celebrated between them...either determined by placing them half-way between the astronomical calendar or on the calends of months between them...months named for and by Romans.

Lines 6 through 9 serve much the same purpose as lines 3 and 4, and with the same flaws. We don't know when the people became aware of how agriculture works, nor when exactly people attributed gods to particular crops. There may be no causal link at all, or they may have adopted both from another culture altogether. Again, we can find a lot of inner knowledge by studying *when it is likely* that such things came about, but in describing things as having come about as a result of a particular phenomenon is intellectually dangerous. As humans, we may have a need to understand why a thing has happened, but we cannot use that need as an excuse to draw false inferences... or any inferences, for that matter.

Lines 9 and 10 begin to construct the mythology of the great surviving religions of The Great Goddess and Her Consort. A few groups who embrace this mythology see the consort as a later addition, or as the son of The Goddess, or even as a lesser being, and can be said to be monotheistic– the God exists only because The Goddess wishes to express herself in such a manner. Regardless of the context, there really is no evidence that anyone believed this, let alone practiced these religions in remote locations. This is a frighteningly constructed piece of rhetoric in that, as it is developed, it begins to make excuses for a lack of evidence, the Christians stamped it out, it was hidden, the tools of the trade were common household items...It is a mythology that says that we can't know what was practiced from evidence, so we must assume that what we are to believe is any explanation that includes a reason for having no evidence. Again, this is the pseudoscientific fallacy of a thing being true because we've no proof it is not true.

Line 11 is a classic example of an unrelated fact being used as evidence for other facts. People have worshipped at shrines, wells, fields and sacred sites for millennia, and many of these sites still exist. Often, we have little idea of who built them or why. Even those we identify as sacred sites are often still mysteries, and those we can connect with a specific culture rarely have descriptions of how the site was used. As a result, we have to use archaeological evidence to determine what probably happened. Few sacred sites have descriptions of what they were used for in writing, and it is these sacred sites that are spoken of in this line. To rephrase it in a more acceptable manner, this line might read "In their rites, these proto-pagans probably worshipped at wells and other sacred sites, as others of the time did."

Line 12 is an example of the above fallacy gone one step further. We do not know why most sacred stones circles were set up, and the evidence of an ancient people in Europe that knew mathematics, astronomy, astrology and herbalism centuries before other cultures is sorely lacking. Even the evidence for the knowledge of astronomy and mathematics that we thing must exist by virtue of the stone circles is conjecture. As an example of how such things could be done, my own teacher once had students set up a log circle that was perfectly round and had an archway in it where the first light of the summer solstice could be seen. As was typical of these projects, they had one year and one day from the day it was assigned, the day before the Solstice. They were allowed to use no modern equipment whatsoever (except to place the logs into their locations) and only the knowledge of the date of the solstice, even though they had to set up the eight logs perfectly spaced, and perfectly round.

While I did not participate in the assignment, a friend did, and he told me their methods. First, they marked the position of the sun the following day with a large white rock that took them three people to move. The rock was squarish, and they made sure that one point of the rock was exactly where their eyes all agreed the "center" of the sun was. Then, they took off and came back a few days before the solstice the next year. Using a piece of rope tied in a fixed circular knot; they traced a circle by putting the loop of the rope around a stick and walking in a circle, holding the rope taut. They stopped to the right of the center of the rock and drew a dot on the ground, and then they drew a line on the ground beside the rope, from the dot to the center and made it exactly parallel. Then they took the moving rope and swung it around like the hands of a clock until it was on the other side of the circle and formed one continuous line with the line they had drawn. Four people, standing at either end of the rope and to either side, agreed that it was a straight line, and they marked the line. They did this again at the other side, using two people's perception of a right angle to make the perpendicular lines, and then eyeballed the spaces between these four dots for the placement of the remaining logs, making sure that the second set of dots made right angles to each other. They placed the logs and the log arch, removed the stone, and it worked just as expected. While their methods didn't prove anything about how ancient peoples made stone circles, it sure showed that a low degree of knowledge was needed. After all, even a child can divide a circle into four equal parts with a stick or a string. All they needed was one person to know when the solstice was, and that, too, can be figured out with the most rudimentary of time-keeping methods.

There is one thing we do know: there was a huge technology backslide between the fall of the Western Roman Empire and the Middle Ages, although the cause for this is unknown. In general, three things are blamed: a catastrophic weather change of some sort (for which there is evidence in tree rings), a series of invasions in Rome and the Western Empire (for which there is evidence in writing) and the prevalence of Christianity, which, in its early days, was aggressively anti-scientific. Contemplating how these things are related is an interesting mental exercise that proves nothing...but does reveal a lot about our own prejudices. Could it be that the fall of Rome was the result of the loss of the favor of its natural deities? Was this technology removed from people's knowledge for a lack of faith? Did the crops fail and the sky darken because proper rites were abandoned? Again, thinking about these things teaches you much but proves nothing.

We can state clearly that it is unlikely that this backslide would have happened if there actually were priestesses out in the rural areas who knew these technologies. If their job was, as we are told in these legends, to keep the people safe and healthy, it is unlikely such secrets would be hidden when the people needed them. Indeed, these priestesses would be best served by handing out the secrets to all-comers, for nascent religions like Christianity would've been hard pressed to get a grip on the populace if the existing religions had such awesome scholars behind them.

To return to the myth, lines 15 through 18 establish the persecution of "witches" as a persecution of the followers of The Great Goddess religion, using some pretty awful conclusions. That the witches all said similar things was undoubtedly the result of the leading questions they were asked, and the similarities between what torture victims "confessed to" and what is in the *Malleus Malleficarum* is not lost on anyone who has read the thing. That Murray claims there is no proof that priests were asking the same questions of all their victims is an almost unforgivable offense against the truth. Likewise, the nine million number promoted by Starhawk and others has been roundly shown to be a huge exaggeration—something Starhawk, to her credit, has reportedly admitted. She, like others, was quoting other people with this number. The actual number comes in somewhere in the tens of thousands, if that high.

The last few lines are taken nearly word for word from over one dozen websites. The folly in them is two-fold. First, people are not reclaiming the word Witch. Those few people we can demonstrate to have practiced familial magical traditions predating Gardner, to a one, do not use the term. They may be Pellars, Cunners, Hexfolk, Alchemists, even Sorcerers, but did not use the term "Witch." In fact, in documented writings of many of these peoples—whom I'll call by the collective term "cunningfolk"—witches are the bad guys. One woman's collection of charms and spells

from the early 1700s in Britain and Germany includes numerous charms, incantations and recipes to remove witches
from the immediate area, stop them from coming into one's
house and get them out of one's barn. For this reason, it is
unfair to say that people are reclaiming the term in solidarity with all those "witches" killed, because they are claiming (not *re*claiming) both the term and the solidarity.

Secondly, this claim of solidarity may be the cause of
the persecution complex many Pagans seem to have, judging from the many frivolous persecution complaints that
Pagan defense organizations deal with (making it hard to
help the people with real cases, I might add!). We all feel
sorry for the people who were killed as "witches," but few,
if any of us, have claim to their sorrow or deserve repara-
tions or apologies for it. One friend calls those people who
claim such privileges "stake chasers" and the sort of wanton
disregard for the facts such a term brings to mind makes it a
truly excellent term for the type.

The idea that these "burning times" were about Modern
Pagans and could come back is instructive in some ways. It
warns us to be wary of any attempts to deny, reduce or sub-
jugate our rights. What it does not do is grant us the right to
act as if society is out to get us or expect special attention.
Our religions' minority statuses do not mean we must be
covered in every Halloween story on the news or have our
songs sung in every school in the land. As one friend says,
"There are things in this world that don't include you. Get
over it."

**The Lord, the Lady, Unnamed Gods, Duotheism and the
religion of The Great Goddess**

Much of the confusion between Wicca and The Great
Goddess religions lies in the lack of distinctions in early Pagan literature, but one other source of the confusion is
shared duotheism. The Great Goddess religions speak of
The Goddess and Her Consort, often seeing the consort as
just another part of Herself. Likewise, Early Modern Wicca
speaks of the God and Goddess of the Witches, and sometimes even speaks of The Goddess and her consort. As
Wicca began to mature, some of the epithets used for the
gods are the same as those used by Dianics and their co-

horts. The Goddess is called "She of Many Names," for example, and The Charge of The Goddess certainly seems to promote the idea that all goddesses are one Goddess.[60]

In reality, early Wicca was either truly polytheistic or duotheistic, depending on your point of view. The God and The Goddess were not called Lord and Lady because they were names for all deities, but because the names of the gods were one of the mysteries. It was possible to move through several degrees of learning without coming to know the secret names for the gods, a secret reserved only for the innermost of the inner circle of a coven. One friend, a traditionalist, claims that the entire concept of the gods having no names (or that any name can be used) is a result of many early traditions being spun off from mother covens before their leaders had reached the inner circle. They were "disgruntled-know-it-alls," to use his words, who thought they had figured out all the secrets already.

Regardless of why the idea of specific gods of the Witches became unnamed and unnamable entities, it is easy to see where the confusion lies. A practitioner of an early Wiccan tradition prays to The Goddess with no name, or to the Lord and Lady, because he hasn't learned the secret names of the gods of his circle yet. A Dianic prays to the unnamed and unnamable Goddess, who is called by all names. It's not hard to see the logical conundrum that results when the two meet, especially since the Wiccan may not know that he will learn the names of the gods at a later date. Add to that the fact that most people drop out of a coven before reaching the inner circle and you see the inevitable occur[61]. The half-taught Wiccan teaches that his Goddess and the Dianic's Goddess are one and the same.

If he'd stayed in the circle, he might've found out his god and goddess were Freya and Pan[62] and either that those

---

[60] Which is part of the reason it was never universally adopted into Wicca, in my opinion.

[61] The other result is people coming up with extraordinarily goofy names for the gods.

[62] This is a matter of public record. Other inner circle names are used, but only the names Freya, Pan, Diana, and Herne are commonly attributed to the inner circles of Early Modern Wicca. For what it's worth, those inner

were the patron and matron deities of a group that believed in all gods, or that those were the names given the lord and lady in a duotheistic group. This would be a group in which all deities were equally divided into male and female deities. All masculine ones, he would have discovered, were embodied in the name of his God — in this example Pan — and all feminine gods were embodied within the name of The Goddess — in this example Freya. His group may even have been a sort of melding of the two, in which Freya and Pan represented the polar powers of the universe from which all the other gods sprang.

In reality, it was the rare coven in Early Modern Wicca that did not have names for the gods, even if it seldom used those names. Thus, those claiming that all gods were one and all names were equal was the original Wiccan core theology are not merely incorrect but blatantly so. As my traditionalist friend puts it, "Whenever someone teaches we [Wiccans] do something for no reason whatsoever, it seems the members of the original traditions have had a reason for that very thing for years."

To place it in more objective terms, the idea of the All-Goddess and All-God is new to Wicca and relevant in its own way, but must not be taught as the original teaching. It is likely that the quasi-monotheistic point of view here described will grow into a new faith altogether, and it cannot be given that chance if we insist it is not the new teaching it is!

The Middle Ground: Patron and Matron Gods

Several Wiccan groups, including Universal Eclectic Wicca (the tradition to which I belong), deal with the tangle of ideas surrounding the names of the gods in a slightly more diplomatic way. Patron and Matron gods are generally based in true polytheism, the idea that all gods exist. Rather than keep the true names of the divine away from

circle names I've been privy to simply did not exist in the English language at all and in another trad the names were simply words for Wisdom and Truth. (And I was given permission to say that provided I did not say which trad!)

the individual practitioner, groups based on this idea teach that the only names for the gods are the ones revealed to you by exploration, prayer and research.

The singular downside of this idea is the fact that it does occasionally lead a person away from Wicca. Since Wicca is not a religion that teaches it is made stronger or better by the number of followers, that people would be led into religions where they feel stronger is actually a good thing. It is for this reason that proponents of this way of seeing the divine sometimes refer to it as a *flawless* theology, although in my opinion the fact that some newbies will seem to change patron deities daily indicates a flaw in *their version* of the theology.

Worshipping Patron and Matron gods is a method of taking the deep revelation of who you've actually been worshipping out of the hands of an inner circle and placing it in the hands of the practitioner. It is likely a result of experiences within those inner circles that led to this. Another friend, a UEW practitioner who migrated from another tradition, related her experience with finding Athena as a matron deity. She says her journey began when her car broke down as she drove across country and a "weird" gray-eyed female mechanic fixed it by the side of the road, refusing to take any money. She came to a crisis point when she learned the name of the goddess in her group was Diana. She simply could not take the experiences in her life— mysterious gray-eyed women; two different planes diverted to Greece; a pet cat named Ulysses; winning a trip to Athens, GA, to see her favorite band; dreams and visions—with the idea of Diana as her deity. The wrongness of it, and her former trad's insistence upon it, led her away from that group completely. Had her group had room for her personal revelation about what deity she had a relationship with, she'd probably be there still.

With anecdotes like that—and trust me, I have my own such stories as well—it's easy to see why this idea caught on fast in the Wiccan community. It is based on the idea of personal gnosis. Prayer, experimentation, research and introspection are tools that lead to an understanding of what gods seem to have an interest in you, or perhaps what god you strive to be worthy of. The actual understanding of the relationship between a Patron or Matron god and their followers tend to be poorly understood outside of the follower's head, which is part of the beauty of it, but it makes telling people how to find their gods fairly difficult.

For what it is worth, in my experience as a dedicant of Apollo, there is certainly something about other such dedicants I have met that tells me the relationship is more than a creation of my own brain. On a mailing list for other such followers that cuts through Wiccan and Hellenic Reconstructionist communities, newcomers would relate the exact same chain of events as my own "conversion." These people related the same or similar experiences, occurring in people who had the same or similar backgrounds. These people were mostly women, in their twenties at the time of the first experiences, from highly-educated backgrounds, but undereducated in their estimation of themselves.

To a one these women all describe the same things: contact, disbelief, some form of proof and a difficulty reconciling their otherwise rational existence with the occasional ecstatic experience. Many came out with a new purpose in life as a result of their conversion—a deep knowledge of self, if you will. Freud would no doubt have a field day with us, except that the hesitance to discuss these events and the lack of their occurrence in public places (for the most part[63]) seems to point to a different pathology than his hysteria, despite an obvious similarity in the demographic.

Bringing it back from specifics, Patron and Matron deities seem to come in two distinct flavors: the first flavor being the all-encompassing Patron or Matron deity and an also-ran secondary deity (if one at all), and the second flavor being the deity pair, usually related in some form, as in Zeus and Hera, or Apollo and Artemis. Kathenotheism is also not an uncommon occurrence, the following of one primary deity during one part of the year and another one

---

[63] Except for one friend, who had an epileptic seizure at or near Delphi and was rushed to the hospital. She had never had one before nor had one since but she simply could not have faked that reaction nor the results of various scans they did at the hospital.

during the other. It is this that is quite common to Middle Modern Wicca, and Modern Wicca, and why many see Wicca as henotheistic: one god at a time.

While this collection is a fairly narrow set of practices, what this form of worship *does* seem to broadly include is the idea that all gods exist and should be honored in addition to the specific deities one is dedicated to. This honoring may involve the participation in deity specific rites, even non-Wiccan ones, or even the participation in multiple Wiccan rites. The mechanics of it, as you may expect, are highly individualized, varying both from group to group and individual to individual.

Recommended Reading for Topic Five:

Christ, Carol P., *Laughter of Aphrodite: Reflections on a Journey to The Goddess*. San Francisco: Harper and Row. 1987

Goldenberg, Naomi R., *Changing of The Gods: Feminism and the End of Traditional Religion*. Boston: Beacon. 1979

Marinoff, L., *Plato, Not Prozac! Applying eternal wisdom to everyday problems*. New York: Harper Collins. 1999

Starhawk, *The Spiral Dance: A Rebirth of the Ancient Religion of The Great Goddess*. San Francisco: Harper and Row. 1979

Discussion Questions for Topic Five:

5.1. Define the following terms: Dianic Paganism, Dianic Wicca, Feminist Paganism.

5.2. Radical Feminist Paganism is described by many people as a mixed blessing on women. How is it beneficial to women who follow it? Women who don't? How is it detrimental to them?

5.3. Why are Wicca and Feminist Paganism sometimes used interchangeably?

5.4. How are Wicca and Dianic Paganism different?

5.5. According to the author, why do outer circle Wiccans use the words "god and goddess" instead of names?

5.6. How can people reconcile the myth of The Great Goddess with evidence for that myth? Should it be tossed out altogether? Why or why not?

5.7. Using the internet, research the "origins" of Wicca. Where do you see The Great Goddess myth? Is it cited? How do you feel about the presentation?

5.8. How does the idea of P/Matron gods reconcile the two ideas of following all deities and following the specific deities of a group?

Topic Six: Pagan, pagan, Wiccan, wiccan and other silliness

What is Paganism, really? Why do people try to separate groups of Wiccans? Is it right? What are the two meanings of discriminating? Is it okay to say I don't agree with another Pagan's Paganism? Why do people say Self-Initiation is a myth? Is it? What is Grandfathering-in? Can I say someone isn't Wiccan?

Neo-Pagan vs. Pagan and how Pagan is Defined.

You may've noticed that I refrain from using the term "Neo-Pagan" in most of my writing while other people use the term extensively. These actions are not personal preferences but matters of definition. To those who use the term Neo-Pagan, literally "new pagan," the distinction they are making is between ancient Pagan Religions and the new Paganism. To those of us who reject the term Neo-Pagan, the distinction is even clearer. "Paganism" refers to those religions that identify themselves as Pagan Religions. Thus the modern religions and those ancient religions are called by their proper names, by the term "indigenous religions" or by other expressions that distinguish them from the present day, such as referring to the "pagan" Rome before Christianity as "Pre-Christian Roman religion."

Much ado has been made of the origins of the word Pagan, which probably meant little more than hayseed or hick to the peoples who first used it as a pejorative. The problem with this line of thought is that any word, taken to its root words and cognates can be manipulated to support one's point of view. Just as the terms heathen and pagan have been manipulated by modern authors to indicate religions that are like those practiced on heaths and in the countryside, one can similarly state that since bands of thieves regularly lived in the countryside and on heaths, pagans and heathens are historically highwaymen and thieves. Etymological evidence for both uses exists, and the point I'm trying to make here is that etymological evidence proves nothing but the origin of a word. Be skeptical whenever someone uses etymology to prove anything beyond word origins.

Having explained the term Neo-Pagan, the term Pagan itself still wants definition. Recently on a mailing list, a young Pagan, facing dissent from her definitions for the first time, lamented the fact that the word Pagan seemed to mean nothing at all. Worse yet, the general reaction to her lament was agreement that the term *was* largely meaningless. Who is a Pagan is a question that results in many conflicting answers, and whenever we try to define who belongs under the umbrella term, we end up constantly redefining the term. As anyone who has learned a discipline requiring knowledge of set theory or how to construct an operational definition will assure you, any term that needs constant redefinition is a poor descriptive term. In short, Pagan may well mean nothing at all.

As I use the term Pagan, it's reasonable to assume I have an operational definition of the term, and like many such definitions it inevitably has the sensation of not really being quite fulfilling. At its simplest level, my definition of Pagan is any person, thing or religious group that defines itself as Pagan. Self-definition is a difficult definition to refute, because you have to claim that certain people are being mendacious about themselves when you define Pagan in such a way that any self-identified Pagan is left out. Put simply, to refute the idea of self-definition you have to say someone using the term in a way you disagree with is lying. Although perhaps the most diplomatic of definitions, using self-identification as a definition is incredibly frustrating to the litigious amongst us, because when we disagree with the actions of any particular Pagan we can't say they are not Pagan for their actions.

It is inevitable that a word like Pagan would have multiple definitions, and it is likely that we don't agree with every definition, but the rational Pagan acknowledges their existence and their right to that existence. In general, there are two groups of definitions of the term Pagan: self-appellation definitions and pejorative ones. Although being offended when a person uses the latter and you use the former seems to be a sport amongst certain Pagans, the terms and their users tend to be separated by enough space that this rarely comes to actual dispute, save when a particularly querulent self-identified Pagan decides to look the term up in the dictionary.

The pejorative uses of the term pagan, perhaps described by some folk as the "name calling" uses, are those that have historically been used on people other than the speaker. They are words of contrast, in which the speaker represents one thing and the pagan represents the other. Perhaps the most common of the pejorative uses is use of pagan to mean those religions that are not Abrahamic Religions, although various subgroups of the Abrahamic tradition have periodically described their Abrahamic brethren as pagan. (e.g.: Christians calling Muslims pagan, Baptists calling Catholics pagan, etc.). We see this use commonly in discussion of cultures or places that converted *en masse* to Christianity, as in "pagan and Christian Rome" or "pagan and Christian Ireland." The more scholastic term for this usage is simply "pre-Christian," a term which carries no indication whatsoever of the quality of the pre-Christian culture, simply that it is the pre-Christian culture.

The second of the pejorative uses is not so easily dealt with. I speak here of the definition of pagan found in the second entry of many dictionaries, the use of the term to mean "corrupted" or "hedonistic." I don't wish to claim nothing can be done about this use of the term, but it is a usage that we can hope would not be found regularly in modern text. In other words, it is a term we should find only in the literature of the past and in the dictionary in that context.

The final pejorative use is the use of the term to mean polytheistic. The flaw in this term is that it largely overlaps the first usage despite the fact that many of the cultures in the first usage *aren't* polytheistic. The simple solution here, one beginning to take effect long before the emergence of Modern Pagan religions, is to use the term "polytheistic" for cultures and people that are. The problem with all three of these pejorative uses is that groups that fall under the uses often don't call themselves pagan, and are thus insulted by the use of the term, which may or may not have been being used as an insult.

Conversely, there are flaws in the self-appellation uses of the term Pagan, uses that individuals and groups *do* use on themselves. For example, some Pagans define as Pagan those groups with an environmental agenda of some sort, thus excluding many Wiccans — and all the Wiccans before environmentalism was added to the faith in the past twenty years — as well as Pagans for whom caring for the earth is a result of their religious beliefs but not something enumerated within their beliefs. Likewise, this definition of Pagan includes many Christians, including environmentally active evangelicals who neither wish to be called Pagans nor wish Pagans to exist.

Similarly, groups that define Pagan as those religions that teach "harm none" are not only excluding the vast majority of Wiccans (who do not reinterpret the Rede as saying "harm none") but all of the warrior traditions, as well as numerous Reconstructionist and Nativist traditions that have been active in the greater Pagan community for years. As with the above use, numerous groups not affiliated in any way with the greater Pagan community, such as the Jains, fall under this usage.

As in the pejorative uses of the term, such narrow definitions inevitably include those who do not use the term at all. This is part of the reason for my own definition's reliance upon self-appellation. Put simply, my definition of Pagan is: *"A person, group of people or religious tradition that describes itself as Pagan (or perhaps Neo-Pagan), primarily those such traditions which are not better described by a non-syncretic Abrahamic term and are based, however loosely, on real or imagined Pre-Christian indigenous religions, especially Pre-Christian European religions."*

What you'll notice first about the definition above is that only one of the three criteria is a requirement: that the group or person refers to itself as Pagan. Some people *do* use the term Neo-Pagan and I include them in the definition. The second criterion, that they are not better described as non-syncretic Abrahamicists, is actually related to the first. No Jew, Christian or Muslim who did not mix their faith practices with other faith practices (syncreticism) would be right in calling him or herself a Pagan. I wish I could say it did not happen, but I have encountered bait-and-switch type Christians who promote themselves as Pagans (because they live in the countryside) in an attempt to infiltrate Pagan groups and bring individual Pagans into their flock. This small minority is not enough to instill paranoia, but my experiences with them require that my definition remove them from the running by indicating that self-appellation is not enough.

The last criterion — that they are based, even very loosely, on real or imagined Pre-Christian indigenous religions — gives the reader an idea of the groups within the definition, but is the least important factor of the three. I add European to the mix here because I've yet to meet a group calling *itself* Pagan that was not based in some form of European tradition, but this is more a clarification than a true exclusion.

This clarification is especially unimportant in light of certain Pagan groups that base their beliefs on completely modern things — novels, modern philosophies and personal revelations — and these groups may still fall under the definition of Pagan used above. At its heart, the definition above is just a start. Tools beyond that definition are developed by trial and error. Like a fine wine, you can be told roughly what makes it right, but in the end you know one when you encounter one.

The Reasons for Distance and the Wrong Way to Differentiate.

It is inevitable, with definitions like the one above, that we will *not* want to include everyone within our definition of Pagan. There is nothing wrong with this desire; we discriminate on a fairly regular basis between one thing and the other. We choose babysitters, where to eat, whom we associate with and much more on the basis of what we hope are fair criteria. It is amusing that the term "discriminate" has come to mean so much more than being choosy. The distinction between discriminating on fair and unfair bases should be made much clearer in our discourses lest we come to the conclusion that we have to accept all people as equals.

To those uninitiated to higher thought, the simple fact that not all people are equals sounds harsh, even wrong. Certainly, those discriminating on *unfair* bases have abused the fact that not all people are equals. To these people, the people who are their lessers are lesser because of skin color or their religion. To the person thinking beyond such terms, it is actions that determine who is greater or lesser. At birth, *we are all equal*, equally capable of growing into good or bad people, and are changed by our experiences and situations, maybe even our genetics…those things do not make a person greater or lesser. What makes a person greater or lesser is the choices people make in dealing with each other.

To bring this idea most seriously home, think of one of the choices that were mentioned earlier: picking a babysitter. No one in their right mind will tell a parent that all people are equal babysitters. No one will say that a convicted child molester deserves the same right to watch your child and earn money as a highly recommended nanny. There are people who, for whatever reason, you will not consider safe to be around or associate with. Likewise, there will be people in this world that you will not like, that will not like you, and that will not give you the respect you deserve as a human being. It is utterly fair to discriminate *on fair bases* against these people.

A person is your lesser if he or she will not give you at least the level of respect you give to that person. I am not speaking of being "nice" and getting niceness in return. I am referring to true respect: the right to your thoughts, feelings and emotions, and the right to not have them challenged unreasonably[64]. As an adult, you have a right to avoid involving such people in your life, whether they are family, friends or coven mates, and you probably already avoid including such people in your life. What you are doing is assigning levels, usually with yourself as a yardstick, to the people around you. Joe is bad, Fred is Good, George is a better person than I, etc.

We do this in other things without blinking. I am a better writer than my wife; she is better in engineering and math. I am better at doing dishes than my son, and way worse at tennis than Venus Williams. I am a worse driver than my mom, and I hold my liquor better than my friend Steve. Such categorization is a natural process of human

---

[64] This is different from reasonable challenge. If I believe the moon is made of cheese, I warrant challenging and you can provide proof I am wrong.

thought, and we are often taught to keep it inside and are so scared of being labeled as discriminating we won't even verbalize why we won't associate with a person, we just don't. Compare this to 3rd or 4th grade, where you could probably list your best friends in order of "bestness;" Betty is my best-best friend, Sarah is my next-best friend, Tommy is my next-next-best friend and so forth.

For whatever reason, society gives us this great big chip on our shoulder about making such distinctions even though we already do. As Pagans, and therefore outsiders, we are faced with an even bigger chip. We don't want to discriminate against fellow Pagans because it is likely some people already discriminate against those same Pagans. We don't want to add insult to injury, so we allow all comers into our lives… which inevitably results in the occasional difficulty. Afterwards, we ask ourselves why we didn't seem to know any better.

It is a larger version of this idea that Pagan communities are embracing when they make distinctions between types of Pagans. I can honestly say that, save for some common terminology, my religion has nothing in common with Silver Ravenwolf's religion, nor the Wicca of some of her cohorts. Do I then say that what she writes of is not Pagan or Wiccan? If I was a different Wiccan, I might, and certainly there are Pagans and Wiccans who will distinguish their religion from what other people write by saying those others write "lower-case w wicca" or "lower-case p paganism" and that their faith, the alleged real thing, deserves capital letters. They may even use derogatory names for the other forms of Paganism, calling it things like The Kraft (like the pasteurized, processed cheese food), Fake-n-ism, and wi$hcraft. Certainly I've been known to refer to something as fluffy or as schmicca[65] on occasion, but there is a difference between using a sneering term in particular company and making a distinction that those who don't follow what you do are lesser people because their beliefs differ from yours. Their beliefs may even be "lesser" than

[65] Schmicca: Wicca that takes a smidgen of this and a smidgen of that without any care what havoc they may be creating.

yours—silly, unsubstantiated, abusive, derogatory—but their beliefs are still valid and it changes nothing about how they may have treated you or their community. Again, it is *actions*, not beliefs, by which we judge a person, if we are judging them fairly.

So it is fair to say that there is a reason for distinguishing between groups of Pagans, and a huge difference between making distinctions and unfairly discriminating. These distinctions help us communicate clearly about our beliefs. I can say that I am a Wiccan, distinguishing myself from non-Wiccan Pagans, and also I can say I am a UEW Wiccan, distinguishing myself from non-UEW Wiccans. These are examples of reasonable ways to differentiate between others and myself. Saying that those that don't believe as I do are not really Wiccan or that they are something other than Wiccan merely because their beliefs aren't the same as mine is not a reasonable way to differentiate.

This isn't to say these distinctions aren't important. When my local Media Witch attacked a local arts guild for having a Witch contest at Halloween because it was defamatory to Wiccans, there were a number of people who objected, some louder than others. It was vital to us that the greater community not lump us all in with the nonsense. The distinctions are vital in this example because one Witch was quoted in the paper as saying it was equivalent to lampooning Jews at Hanukkah, which most of us found nonsensical or even offensive, even as another local Pagan group was trying to do some interfaith work with a local synagogue that thankfully had very understanding leadership that wrote off such comments as those of an extremist fringe.

This is two sided, unfortunately. We cannot expect people to disassociate rational and mature pagans with the lunatic fringe while we equate our local Christian Churches with Swaggart, Falwell and Phelps. We must recognize extremism and ask that the greater communities make distinctions between us while doing the same with other groups. That's not to say we don't hold people responsible for their actions. Certainly when Fred Phelps comes into town to protest the funeral of an AIDS victim, we must fault every Christian minister in the area who does not come out to counter that protest because silence in such a situation is tantamount to agreement with the lunatic fringe of their faith. Likewise, when a self-styled High Priest of all Witches comes into town to promote his agenda, silence from the community is equal to agreement with that agenda, and if we don't wish to send that message we need to be active in our disagreement with it. This especially hard for those of us who'd just as soon stay in bed and cuddle our significant others.

Self-initiation and other Myths.

A significant portion of the perceived need for distinction between Pagan groups comes from the abusive use of group-specific rituals by non-members. A good example of this is the idea of self-initiation[66]. Used originally as a descriptive term for a Wiccan ritual properly called a Dedication, a self-initiation is an erroneous term for a solitary practitioner's commencement or dedication ritual. It seems as if forcing groups to accept their "self-initiations" as valid entries into a group is the major goal of a few scattered Pagans. In my experience, those who do not find that one group bows to their demands move on to another group, so while it may be a few scattered folk, many of us experience these few folk repeatedly, making it feel like a bigger movement than it is.

An examination of the term itself demonstrates the flaw. There are two reasonable definitions of an initiation ritual: the addition of a person to a group and the revelation of the core mythos of a group to a person. The former is called an initiation ritual or rite, the latter is called an "initiation to the mysteries." A Pagan group may include one, both or neither in its practice. It's easy to see the flaw in a self-initiation ritual that purports to add a person to a group: you cannot add yourself to a group of one. It's just not possible. You can initiate another person and make a group of two, but you can't add yourself to a group. You

---

[66] This is discussed *ad nauseum* in *All One Wicca*.

certainly cannot add yourself to a group that has an established initiation rite by doing a mocking, disrespectful or stolen version of that rite.

Initiation to the Mysteries is similarly impossible on an individual basis. In such an initiation, you are shown the core mythos of your faith by a person who knows the core mythos. It involves a dichotomy—revealer and neophyte, elder and newbie—which you cannot recreate on your own. You can be initiated to the Mysteries by The Divine, an act that shouldn't be termed self-initiation. However, it doesn't mean you were initiated to the same Mysteries as someone who was initiated by a person. With your divine initiation, you can then initiate others to your mysteries, but you weren't initiated by your hand.

In a similar vein, since the greater Pagan communities require no initiation rituals to join them, those initiation rites which purport to add you to the "greater Pagan community" should be eyed very skeptically, especially ones which involve purchasing the rite or the items for it from the person promoting it. You were "initiated" into the Greater Pagan community the second you called yourself a Pagan. No rite was needed, and any rite you did was gravy—a bonus, not a requirement.

It is difficult to say that any self-initiation rite is not valid, even if the term itself is nonsensical. This is one of the reasons Pagan groups are so strict about distinctions between each other. A member of the Celestial Grove of Butterfly Loving Druids (CGBLD) does not have the same requirements for entry as the Coven of the Big Fat Frog, and a person who performs a ritual in his bedroom, alone, is not granted membership in either, let alone in both, by virtue of his rite. The rite may be intensely personally valid, but it has no standing outside of that guy's bedroom save perhaps with his deities.

Another example, specifically Wiccan, comes from my own experience. I met a girl, seventeen years old, who had read the First Circle sections of *Coven of the Far Flung Net* and *Buckland's Complete Book of Witchcraft* and informed me that if I needed help with teens applying to CFFN, she, a third degree high priestess of UEW, was there to help. I can see the reactions on my friends' faces when I mention this. She was, perhaps, every nightmare I have had about teeny-boppers rolled into one. I informed her, quite politely, that if she'd been practicing UEW for a minimum of 10 years (our requirement for High Priestess), as I was then approaching my current status of UEW's youngest High Priestess, I needed to change my stationary—something that would cost me a few dollars. Before I changed my alleged stationary, I asked that she at least inform me which teacher had scooped UEW's founder in the youth ordination department.

I expected that I'd never hear back from her, and saved the email for a rainy day chuckle. Of course, there was no stationary. Stationary that proclaimed me UEW's youngest High Priestess would be way too tacky, but it amused me that I'd managed to not just reply to her email with the single word response "liar," which always gets a response, but not usually a pleasant one. Imagine my surprise then, when, hours later, she responded that perhaps she was confused about her position in Wicca. The book she had read, you see, had indicated that she would be a third degree priestess when she completed it, and when she had, she had gone online, read some stuff on UEW and decided that that was her tradition, the tradition in which she was a third circle member.

She'd reread the things she'd been studying and came to the realization that she may've met the requirements for the book, but this didn't mean she met any one else's requirements. To her credit, this was her realization, not anything I'd said, but it illustrates the vital point I'm trying to make here: that not all traditions are equal nor do they all translate well amongst each other. This girl, having completed the lessons in the book, did not have the experience of a third circle UEW member, let alone a High Priestess.

If I had taken her in and had expected her to do what a member of UEW's third circle does, she would probably fail at it. Her expectation of being placed at a high level was a result of a simple lack of knowledge. She felt Wicca was Wicca, and one group was the same as another. In short, she demonstrated the exact naïveté that makes making distinctions between groups so very important.

Grandfathering-in

The fact that you cannot use degree in one group as predictive of degree in another creates a conundrum. It isn't fair that a student may spend 2-4 years in one tradition then come to discard it, for whatever reason, and have to start at day one of training in their new tradition, especially if both traditions have similarity of some sort. (Of course, training for years in a druid tradition doesn't help much for training in a Wiccan tradition, so for simplicity's sake, I'll limit this discussion to Wiccan traditions.)

Grandfathering-in members is one method for dealing with the conundrum. The term comes from the practice, in zoning boards, in city councils and in law, of continuing to permit something technically no longer allowed because it existed before the new restriction came into account. The use of the term is more liberal here, because the skills and knowledge of the person being grandfathered-in to a tradition are what is being permitted, and their entry to the tradition is the date of the "restriction."

For simplicity's sake, grandfathering-in generally says that you cannot be placed into a position that you could not have earned in the time you've had. For example, in UEW, becoming a High Priest would take a minimum of 12 years. That, in and of itself, would be highly impressive. Thus, a High Priest of a tradition taking only 5 years to become a High Priest could only come in as a Priest, perhaps with 3 years of experience toward his ten years needed as Priest to become a High Priest. It also says that you can't grandfather-in at a higher level than the highest level of the organization. If the Head of a group has 50 years of experience in that group, and you have 51 years of experience in Wicca, you shouldn't outrank them by a year. In general, groups take your experience with some kind of modifier. For example, in UEW, some traditions are considered nearly at parity—we think you'd learn as much, or nearly as much, in that tradition as you would in UEW. Thus your experience is considered mostly equivalent. By a similar note, there are some traditions whose teachings don't help a student at all, and many years of study in those groups may mean you know very little.

Knowledge is another aspect of grandfathering-in. A group with three degrees, for example, could prepare a comprehensive list of basic questions a member of the first and second degree would know and expect that a person wanting to come into their group at the beginning of the third degree answer them. If the "test" showed one or two holes in the prospective member's knowledge, they could be filled. If the test showed big gaps, a decision to not put the person in the third degree might be made.

This sounds very complicated and hierarchical, especially to a solitary. In fact, it's about being prepared to fulfill the duties of an organization's level. To use a metaphor, if your house was on fire, you would hope that the firemen knew how to use the hose, had the right equipment and training, etc. A member of a tradition with a high degree is generally expected to have a baseline of knowledge for answering questions, may have the right to marry or perform funerals and similar things. If they don't even know their state marriage laws, they can't responsibly perform a marriage rite.

Likewise, it is easier to work in a group if you know what is going on in that group. I don't know about anyone else, but if I'm doing a ritual in a non-teaching group, I don't want to be interrupted and asked what I am doing. Similarly, if I am doing a ritual in a teaching group, I'm likely to explain why each thing is done and what each thing means, something an advanced group would find annoying, maybe even patronizing. Obviously, this wouldn't be a problem if the ritual was my own, performed alone. Those traditions that have solitary members don't expect the solitaries to act a certain way because of their "rank," but instead consider it vital when those solitaries get together to work and learn with others.

How a group grandfathers-in people varies from group to group. Some groups accept no training except their own as valid for learning, while others consider degrees in any tradition to be equal, and still others (the majority) have guidelines and bases, but still essentially grandfather-in members on a case by case basis. It does solve one major problem of the Wiccan learning curve, however, in that the tradition you find first is *not* always the best or the best for you. The knowledge that you won't be penalized for having made a hasty decision should make us all more comfortable in not sticking with things we find to be substandard.

Why even Wiccans we dislike are probably Wiccan

The whole of the problem with noticing and strengthening differences between Wiccans boils down to the fact that many people, in some senses, are not comfortable with the practices of other Wiccans. I understand this, because I have a personal, visceral reaction to a minority of Wiccans that I meet, people with whom I am actually embarrassed to be associated. These range from a gentleman (and I use the term loosely) who calls me names because I don't consider his self-initiation rite as having any bearing outside of his UPG, to the girl I met on the train as I was reading Jack Miles' book *Christ: A Crisis in the Life of God* who told me Christians like me were wrecking the world, to the teenager a professor asked me to speak with when she decided her Pagan point of view, not her horrible writing, was why she was failing his class.

While I may consider these people bad examples of Wicca (and I do), it is intellectually disingenuous to say these people are not Wiccan. People can have no grasp of basic concepts like the Rede, can be nasty, dishonest, ignorant and bigoted and still be Wiccan. People can lie, cheat, steal, publish lies and disrespect other Wiccans and still be Wiccan. They just aren't any good at being Wiccan.

In a way, this is the fault of people like Gardner, Sanders and Leek, who would constantly indicate that it is likely that there are other unknown groups of witches out there in their writings. If Gardner's new religion had been upfront about its newness, it could've called similarly new Witch groups the johnny-come-latelies they were. If the first persons to use the terms Wicca and Wiccan in the modern sense had made a claim to the terms, they could've dictated who could and could not use it. You may consider the idea of excommunicating bad Wiccans a negative thing or a positive thing, but it will never be possible.

What is possible, however, is for traditions to say who is and who isn't a member, and to set rules for membership. Joe, the founder of Butterfly Wicca, may say that Butterfly Wiccans who commit even victimless crimes can no longer associate with the group. Stephanie, the founder of Glitterbell Wiccans can say that people who eat meat aren't members, etc. The problem comes when Joe expects Stephanie to follow his rules, and she expects Joe to follow hers, or either expects their rules to be followed by non-Butterfly, non-Glitterbell people like you and me.

Christians have a similar problem. Their messiah defined his people as whoever believed in him. He didn't say that people who believed in him and were nice people were his followers, or that people who he liked were his followers, but "whosoever" believed in him. When Christian groups call other Christians fake Christians, or that they are not "true" Christians, or the term of choice, they are being as dishonest as any Wiccan who says that the silly, crazy or mean Wiccans they meet aren't real Wiccans.

This is why it is vital for the traditions to exist and to allow multiple vectors of membership. A solitary member of a Wiccan tradition means something when they say they are a Glitterbell Wiccan, or a Butterfly Wiccan, or a UEWiccan. A person who just says they are Wiccan really means nothing more than they are a person who has laid claim to the term. It's not easy, and it may have moral repercussions we dislike, but the fact remains that people we don't like aren't made non-Wiccan by our dislike of them, no matter how tempting it is to write them off.

With Paganism, it's even worse, because the term has so many meanings and so many subgroups that it really is a nonsense term when not modified in some manner. If people say they are Pagans, you really have no idea what they mean by it. If a person says he is a Classical pagan, a Wiccan Pagan or a Celtic Pagan, he's at least narrowed the field of what he believes. Narrowing the field, and narrowing it again and again, as often as possible, is the only way to speak coherently about one's religion. It's not about making boxes and putting people into them, but about not allowing people to put you into the boxes they've designed as if one size fits all.

Recommended Reading for Topic Six:

Witchvox trads page:
http://www.witchvox.com/xtrads.html

Discussion Questions for Topic Six:

6.1. What are the basic definitions of Pagan? Which are pejorative? Which are not?

6.2. Why does the author reject the term Neo-Pagan?

6.3. What are some of the names practitioners of Pre-Christian religions called their faiths?

6.4. Why is it important to make distinctions between groups of Wiccans and Pagans?

6.5. What is meant by the myth of "self-initiation?" What have rituals called "Self-Initiations" historically been called?

6.6. Are the objections to Self-initiation objections to the rites themselves or to their content?

6.7. What is an example of a bad way to differentiate between groups of Wiccans or Pagans?

6.8. What is grandfathering-in? What is its purpose?

6.9. Why does the author say that Wiccans we dislike are probably Wiccan?

Wicca in Practice II: Gleaning Good Source Material

Not only are all sources not equal, some sources are just plain wrong. Just as your 5th grade teacher didn't consider your dog a reliable interview subject, you must learn to evaluate the reliability of every book, website and teacher you encounter. The best will react to your asking for references or sources with a beatific look.

In college, and hopefully much sooner, we are usually taught to distinguish the good source material from the bad. By the time we go to study Wicca, we may have forgotten this vital skill, or we may think that, since it is religion, all source materials are equal. The end result of this is a mountain of source material that is inaccurate, plagiarized and even outright false. If you go forth into the world of research with the idea that all writings are equal, you will be quickly led astray.

The knowledge that all material is not created equal is the first tool to gleaning good source material. If you think it is true because it is in a book, on the web, radio or television, you may already be too lost to do anything useful. Surely you don't, however, believe everything you read or see! We use the tools around us already to make objective decisions about politics, what to eat and who to hang out with, but often just discard them when evaluating source material.

Books are one good example. A publish-on-demand publisher who will accept anyone who has the start-up money published the first edition of book. Members of the pagan community contributed to this edition, pointing out where they felt this work needed clarification. This is one in a long line of Pagan books published in this and similar manners. For the longest time, the only way to get decent information was to get self-published and in-house published books, and I have the bookshelves of stapled, spiral bound and thermal bound tomes to prove it. **That this book is in print bears no relevance to its worthiness as a source, positive or negative.** Publish-on-demand books on Paganism are as good as their authors, who range from some of the best in the business to some of the worst.

Standard publishers are almost as difficult to evaluate. Oxford University press, publishers of Hutton's *Triumph of the Moon* can generally be trusted to put out information that is factually correct, and if a new work is published by them, you can generally accept it to be decent, although publisher alone is never enough information to make such judgments. Books like McCoy's *Witta*, however, show that Pagan-oriented publishers often lack the capacity or desire to fact check what they are publishing, which puts all works in the genre on an even footing, with responsibility for the quality and integrity of the work ultimately falling on the author. While this is a good thing, it's contrary to the way other genres work, in which self-published works are often the bottom rung and publishing house works are at the top, having been edited with a fine-toothed comb for factual and textual errors. You can't even trust the largest Pagan publishers to turn out material that has few typos, let alone no unchecked facts.

In addition, some of my favorite authors have been clearly blackballed for refusing to toe a party line in their works and have gone from lucrative relationships with larger publishers to exclusive work with small and publish-on-demand ones. Discussions and anecdotes about these events are prevalent in most of the independent author study groups and mailing lists, and horror stories about things coming out drastically different from the way they went in are not uncommon either. While I've never had such an experience with a book (since my first book was designed to be an in-house textbook and was never really expected to have the broader appeal it seems to have) I can understand the frustration of these authors from my journalism days, where I had several stories gutted or had parts removed and pasted into the works of other people on the same staff.

The publication situation leaves the Wiccan, especially the Wiccan studying with no teacher to help sort the bad from the good, in a precarious situation. The book, once considered second only to the journal article in its accuracy, can be as fickle as a website or a fanzine article. The Wiccan finds himself not only having to use the fine-toothed comb that the publishers should've used, but often morally responsible if he doesn't. One of the most loathed authors in Wicca is published simply because her books sell large numbers. A Wiccan who purchases them, even if he discards them, tells the publisher that he doesn't mind bad material in the only language the publisher understands: money. It is no wonder some, like one friend of mine, won't buy any books on Wicca at all without making a journey to his local upscale bookstore, purchasing an extra large latte and sitting there for a few hours screening it.

How to Glean the Good from the Bad

In general, we screen material differently depending on the type of material. When it is not the world of Paganism, those materials, from best to worst are:

1. Textbooks
2. Expert Testimony (interviews with the people involved)
3. Professional or Scholastic Journal
4. Non-fiction book (not counting opinion books)
5. Encyclopedia entries
6. Newspaper articles
7. Magazine articles
8. Websites
9. Opinion pieces, fanzines and in-house materials.

The above may vary from researcher to researcher, but journal articles and textbooks are generally near the top, encyclopedias somewhere in the middle and websites near or at the bottom. In Paganism, however, this list is skewed and warped, with websites that are better than many books, books that are little more than fanzines and encyclopedia entries that may be missing or years out of date. In normal research, the form of the material is the first thing you evaluate, but in Pagan research, it's practically useless.

Susan E. Beck, the head of the Reference & Research Services Department of New Mexico State University Library has prepared an excellent website on evaluating web resources that gives techniques that relate to sorting through the web but also work incredibly well for sorting through the massive amount of Pagan media. She lists five criteria for evaluating resources, and they work nearly as well for Paganism as a whole as for material found on the net. These form the next five criteria I will list, although the descriptions and examples come from my own practice and experiences.

The first of Beck's criteria is accuracy. Accuracy refers to both factual and textual accuracy. Material that is grossly misspelled, especially material from a publishing house that *should* be employing proofreaders, should be looked at skeptically. That's not to say it should be discarded; one of my favorite books on Paganism has horrible typos and sections where it seems entire lines were omitted. Why and how regularly these errors happen should be examined, however. Fifty or 60 minor textual errors in a 500-page book that was self-published or put out by a church or non-profit group is not a sign of neglect. Five in a 100-page book that's been professionally proofread *are* signs of neglect, and if those errors are particularly bad, it is reasonable to wonder what else the publisher neglected. Likewise, if you see a poem or similar thing you know to be by one author listed as being by another or without an author name, you should ask yourself what else in the resource is misrepresented or plagiarized. One colleague and reviewer of numerous books says that he knows five or six facts about Paganism that are wrong and easily proven so, and if that any one of them appears in a resource, he doesn't bother with it. Both his method and the plagiarism example expect you to know something before you evaluate; we'll cover using multiple resources in a bit.

The second of Beck's criteria is authority. Is the resource anonymous? If so, why? Is the author alive or dead, and if alive, does that author make himself available for discussing his work? Does the author or creator of the resource you are using have a good knowledge of what he or she is writing about? What are the author's credentials, experiences and affiliations? A young Pagan with almost a decade of experience doesn't have many, though when we had one or two years of experience that may've seemed impressive. If years of practice are the thing the author claims as their authority, it should at least be enough years to span several lifestyle changes, especially if the author is claiming to be giving you vital life advice. Likewise, do a little research on the organizations and credentials the author presents. This can be difficult with pen names, but a little snooping will turn up a lot of information. Finding out if the resource is produced or paid for by a non-profit group or a commercial one is another thing that may help, although none of these criteria will rule out any resource alone.

The third of Beck's criteria, objectivity, is sometimes difficult to evaluate. Is the material opinion or fact, or, if a combination of both, does the author make it clear where his opinion begins and fact ends? Does the author admit any bias? Materials in which the author not only makes it clear when he has an opinion but also where his bias may be affecting his presentation of the facts are often particularly helpful, especially if he offers alternative resources for those facts. If strong feelings are evoked inside you by reading the material, ask yourself if those feelings are the result of inspiration, of having your beliefs challenged or instead because of emotional words in the work. Is the material designed to make you emotional, to sway your opinions? If so, it may not be the best material to use for real learning.

The fourth of Beck's criteria, currency, was touched on a little in the discussion of Starhawk's *The Spiral Dance*. While Beck is discussing the age of web materials, things like whether or not they've been updated and whether or not the links have moved, the fast-paced growth of Paganism makes this criterion also apply to things like books. If a book is older, it must be read in the context of its creation. If a revised or anniversary edition is available, it should include updates and indicate where facts have changed.

The last of Beck's criteria is coverage. What is covered in the resource that is not covered elsewhere, or, conversely, what does this resource have that is common knowledge? In Wicca, we have a phenomenon called "cookie cutter websites," in which hundreds, maybe even thousands of websites have the exact same material, often plagiarized, in a similar structure, with the extent of the differences lying in the graphics and the brief "about me" statement, which usually includes a brief story of how the person found paganism, how her parents misunderstand her and how mean

Christians are. Ask yourself how in-depth a resource is. Is it a resource designed for the least common denominator or does it teach you something?

Beck's website is one example of a really good set of criteria for the evaluation of resources, but not the only one. In addition to her criteria, I find reviews to be a vital source. Not the reviews on book selling website; those are often little more than contests between frequent visitors to see who posts the most reviews, with little proof that these folk actually *read* the books. I refer to the reviews in Pagan magazines and in online and offline communities. If a vast number of people dislike an author or resource, find out why. If it's that they don't like the way the author dresses or what they eat, you can tell that these feelings are probably not genuine critiques. Be aware when many people say the same thing, however. Contrary to the opinions of a few, if a bunch of people point out the same flaw, it is unlikely that they are all part of a trend or a clique... that flaw is probably *really* there.

The last helpful technique in evaluating material is not really a technique so much as something you'll learn with experience. Locate the primary texts mentioned in any resource. For example, I mention Murray's *Witch-Cult* on a regular basis. Don't take my word for it that she says something, if you can avoid it. Look it up. Become hyperaware of often quoted primary texts, like *Rede of the Wiccae*, so you can recognize where they are misquoted. Be aware of the authors and publishers of these texts, and keep an eye out for self-reference and attempts in one book to sell another. I'm not speaking of authors who gloss over a topic because they've covered it in-depth elsewhere, but authors who suggest things like "This candle spell works especially well with the altar cloths from my book *101 Altars for Samhain* and the ritual oil in my book *The Quintessential Book of Oil Magick, Volume Two*," or who cite their previous works as their source for their materials.

The good news is that these techniques really come to life when you start using them regularly. You'll find with practice that salesmen and proselytes seem to have no effect on you and that you become really good at defending your position. If you are still a student, use these techniques in the library and on your next paper. They may seem obvious, but we forget to use them when we've never actively studied how to use them. Once you have, you may find you never stop, as my own wife found out when we had a verbal spat and my response to her witty comeback was "Could you cite a source for that statement?"

Practice:

Pick five topics in Paganism and look at the first five resources that appear in a websearch of each of the topics. Compare and contrast the reviews, accuracy, authority, objectivity, coverage and currency of these websites. Are any of them good sources, why or why not?

Recommended Reading:

Beck, Susan. *The Good, The Bad & The Ugly: or, Why It's a Good Idea to Evaluate Web Sources.* 1997. http://lib.nmsu.edu/instruction/eval.html

Topic Seven: Rational Wicca and Irrational Magic.

What is Rational Wicca? Is Magic rational? Does any of this stuff work? Do I have to be Wiccan to practice Magic? How do rationalists deal with Magic? Is Wicca inherently magical? I am familiar with both Magic and Wicca- do I always have to blend them?

A field guide to Rational Wicca and irrational Magic

In the course of this work, you have been introduced to the concept of Modernism in Wicca. You have also seen the use of the terms rational Wicca and Rationalism. Rationalism is a larger idea than Modernism, although Modernism is a part of Rationalism. You've already seen the core belief of rational Wicca discussed — the belief that no gods would expect you to believe in things that were impossible for you to believe. This core is at the heart of a greater idea, which literally scares the worst of the New Age Wiccans: that you can be Wiccan without abandoning your senses of morality, integrity and skepticism.

Rational Wicca is not at the heart of any one established tradition or group, although I, *personally*, like to think of UEW as a highly rational tradition. It can be said that Wicca began with a fairly healthy dose of rationalism but poor history. In the present day, however, it has two distinct types, rational Wicca and irrational Wicca. As often happens in field-guides, it's far easier to recognize the creature by describing it than by defining it, so I'll cease attempts to define it at this point.

The first thing you notice about rational Wicca is its attempts to embrace history as best understood at the time. In other words, groups that embraced the Murrayesque histories when they were contemporary aren't necessarily irrational groups. If those histories were shown to be false (and they were) and the groups continued to embrace them despite strong evidence to the contrary, they would not be accurately described as rational groups. The rational groups may have moved the pseudohistories from the position of logos to the position of mythos, or dropped them altogether, but they don't teach them as truth, or expect members to believe them as facts. Thus the level of Modernism is unimportant in judging a group as rational or irrational, but the existence of Modernism is.

The second important aspect of rationalism is honesty in practice, which I refer to as "intellectual integrity." If you cannot affect the weather, do not claim you can. Likewise, if you invented your tradition last year, do not claim it is ancient or practiced for years. This is fairly basic, but valuable in that it demonstrates that we should speak only of those things we know unless we make our lack of knowledge explicit. For example, on the websites of many young Wiccans, they write things like "Christians think we eat babies and kill puppies," even though they've never met a Christian who claimed to think these things. A more honest phrase could say "I have heard that some Christians think we eat babies and kill puppies," or even "Some Wiccans have faced Christians who made false claims about their religion, though I never have." The first phrase is an example of teaching your audience something as fact, even though it is not. A webpage that states what Christians think is claiming some intimate knowledge of the thoughts of Christians, knowledge that may be supported or not by the author. If the author used to be a Christian, and thought that as one, he needs to say so. If he thinks that is what Christians think because a friend told him that, he needs to say that as well.

With honesty comes skepticism. A group claiming to affect the weather or that their tradition is ancient should be prepared to deliver evidence of such claims and shouldn't be surprised or offended if asked to do so. A rational Wiccan can believe things that don't hold up to skepticism or have experiences that don't translate outside of his personal experience, but he doesn't expect these things to be believed automatically by other people. His decision to share them or not with others is a personal one, and having his version of the event accepted automatically as the whole truth should not be his goal in any such sharing. Rationally, he should expect to get a range of different reactions, from alternate interpretations to outright disbelief, and none of those reactions should be disregarded.

This focus on the personal, the belief that an interaction with the divine or a revelatory experience might not apply to the greater group is another key factor of rational Wicca. Rational Wicca realizes that as experience, emotion and devotion vary, so will personal interpretation of stimuli, and that it simply makes no sense to expect that what worked for one person will work the same way for another. For this reason, rationalist groups expect members to be doing religious searching and experimentation outside of the group as well as within it, they compare and contrast what worked between members and rather than reach a consensus about what works and why they try to find what works at the individual level.

This is seen in another factor of rational Wicca, the ability of the rationalist to separate his experiences and practices. Practiced best, a rationalist can use tarot, ceremonial magic, astral projection and other things outside the celebratory circle without expecting other members of the celebratory circle to believe in or find personal value in them. He can use these things and more at will because he finds them important without expecting that all members of his group or all members of the greater Wiccan community find them equally so. Ideally, all he studies is studied in its natural context, and he finds the Wiccan and personal context on his own. Thus, an interest in Celtic gods would be pursued by studying them, and adding them to his personal Wicca would *only* be practiced if his study showed it to be suitable. This is drastically different than the current technique many employ of adding things to their Wicca by finding a book or teacher that teaches a Wiccan version of these things, a book on Celtic Wicca, or Wiccan Magic, or Tarot for Wiccans. Just as in learning medicine where you need to know the basics before you start learning the "good stuff," so it works in adding things to your Wicca. Trust me, though… getting through a secular discussion of astral projection is much easier than getting through two semesters of Organic Chemistry!

This focus on learning causes another factor of rationalism—the explanatory nature of its rituals. In other words, no rational group does a ritual because they are supposed to do the ritual; they explain why they are doing it and what its goals are, even if this explanation isn't vocalized.

This may happen in the actual words of the liturgy, as in the oft-repeated line within the section of the celebratory ritual called "cakes and ale" or the "simple feast": "Here I partake of your bounty that I better appreciate my own." No ritual occurs merely because it is expected, has history or is required. All rituals have some stated goal. For this reason, a rationalist group may even forgo a ritual altogether because it serves no purpose at that time.

This ability to not do what has become purposeless comes to its highest point in what I consider the most important aspect of rational Wicca. Rationalism is what my son calls non-clingy, or more directly, it does not expect you to continue to participate if it is not working for you. You may take a sabbatical, or quit altogether, without fear that other members will hold it against you. You may chose to not participate in a particular ritual, or to drop Wicca as a whole because it means nothing to you at a certain point in your life. The door in such cases is always open, and the idea is that no one can participate in a circle "in perfect love and perfect trust" if they feel uncomfortable with the stated purpose of the ritual.

Compare these rational ideas with the irrational ones of some forms of Magic and Wicca: the belief that you have to do a ritual because it is in a book, the teaching that if a ritual doesn't work for you it is because you did it wrong, the chanting of long streams of nonsense words because they are supposed to do something, that number of rituals makes a better Wiccan and similar nonsense. Some of these beliefs are little more than the Emperor's new clothes—that a spell didn't work or the tarot reading was nonsense is because you lack ability or you did it wrong. The rationalist recognizes these claims as the nonsense they are, and notes that Randi's million dollar challenge for proof of metaphysical ability has never been claimed, nor a similar challenge of Harry Houdini's for proof of contact with the afterlife. If large sums of money aren't enough to motivate people into doing spells right, perhaps the answer is that magic doesn't work like that at all.

Magic as transformation or How Rationalists deal with Magic, Part One

Magic is a difficult pill for the rationalist to swallow at times. People within Wicca and the greater Pagan community often make extreme claims about what they can do with magic, and those claims always go unproven. For the rationalist, these claims may be the last thing they hear of in Wicca or Paganism. As soon as you discuss your amazing magical abilities, the rationalist ceases to hear you as anything other than a prattling loon.

One way that rationalists deal with magic is by viewing it within the broader context spoken of in Hermeticism. Magic in this mindset is illumination, what we might call inner and outer knowledge. This illumination is at the heart of the myth of the philosopher's stone, which the unenlightened might think transforms lead to gold but in reality transforms people from lead to gold, from the unenlightened, unknowing state to one of higher knowledge.

From this position, it is easy to see the division between the magic that the unenlightened claim and the magic the illumined ones have. One simply does not work, save for the psychosomatic effects of believing that what they've done works. The other does not merely work but is instantly recognizable in those who have embraced it. They are transformed from powerless people to the people that we feel compelled to look up to—bright, strong, moral and honest. Even if we dislike them intensely we can't deny their awesomeness.

Magic as transformation can be viewed from a purely scientific point of view or a metaphysical one. The scientific view may see illumined people as having great self-esteem, being self-actualized, confident and the like. The metaphysical one may see such people as highly evolved, even seeing such high mental evolution as the reasons behind such leaders as Christ and Gandhi, and such similar evolution used towards darker ends in society's great murderers and evil geniuses.

This transformation may be viewed as something that happens in one lifetime or in many; something that gives you intense abilities, like flying or breathing underwater; or something that gives you nothing more than the charisma to make people believe what you want them to believe. Regardless of the exact nature of the belief, the practice of magical acts is seen either as the result of this enlightenment or as a step toward it. In this enlightened state, your very thoughts or words may be spells.

The level of belief in this type of magic varies amongst rationalists; they may see the entire idea of magic as nothing more than a metaphor for higher knowledge. Or perhaps they see the transformation as a physical event... or they may even disregard this idea for entire alternate sets of explanations. In magic as transformation, however, the inability of anyone to fulfill the criteria to win any of the numerous money-for-proof challenges is not a condemnation of its existence. This is because the higher mind, if capable of the types of proofs required, is unwilling to exhibit them for reasons only those evolved at that level are willing to understand. This is an uncomfortable conclusion, and does sound, once again, like the Emperor's new clothes: you would only understand it if you were more highly evolved. Since no one wishes to admit to he or she is not evolved to a higher level, it seems as if skepticism is frowned upon and skeptics are seen as less evolved persons.

I am more comfortable with explanations in which the person's transformation would only be apparent to those seeking it or who are themselves transformed. I have met individuals for whom things I find incredibly thorny are easy, and I can apply this to the metaphysical realm with little difficulty. I am less ready, however, to believe we are all equally capable of all things, because if will alone were enough to get past inability, I would speak many languages well and be able to spin out a trigonometric proof as easily as a rhetorical one. I prefer, instead, to see those inabilities and difficulties as vital distinctions between individuals. Because no one person can do all things, man is required to be a social animal.

Magic as UPG or How Rationalists deal with Magic, Part Two

The second way rationalists deal with magic is by seeing it as UPG. Mystical events and practices may produce dramatic results, but, for whatever reason, are not replicable. Since these dramatic results are not replicable, they must exist in the quasi-logical world of personal knowledge and experience. In other words, it may well be that the individual alone is expected to perceive the metaphysical event, and it does not replicate or translate outside of the individual (or small group) because it was not designed to be experienced by the larger group.

I am exceedingly uncomfortable with this idea, as it seems to indicate that there is a force controlling who sees what magic at what time, and I cannot perceive of the gods as that interested in the minutia of reality. Nor do I believe a great bureaucracy (perhaps the ministry of magic?) is out there preventing magic from being seen by all and allowing it to be doled out only in small amounts. I think there is likely another reason altogether for the lack of replicability in magic.

Another explanation for the lack of replicability, and another return to the Emperor's new clothes I'm afraid, is the belief that the only people who can see magic are people who believe in it. While I believe in the power of denial—I have, after all, seen parents whose daughter has been a lesbian for over twenty years convinced it was a phase, and I have personally have seen the hole in the New York City skyline as a surprise every time I see it in reality instead of on television—I am not quite ready to believe that millions of people simply refuse to see magic when it occurs. That's not to say there have not been times when my disbelief in this explanation has been shaken, however.

A good example came from three very dear and rational friends, one a psychologist, were driving back from a conference in the dark evening of midwinter. The psychologist was drifting off to sleep when he heard both the people in the front seat gasp at the same time. He woke up, and of course asked what was wrong. The driver asked the passenger, "Did you just see that?" and the passenger nodded. The passenger said, "Was that what I think it was?"

and the driver said it couldn't be. The psychologist, who had missed the sight altogether asked what it had been, and his two friends simultaneously burst out with these stories about a unicorn at the side of the road.

What impressed him the most, as they drove back, was the lack of corroboration between their stories and the fact that they had called it a unicorn at the same time. When they got back to the field where they had seen it, there were no hoof prints in the snow to indicate that perhaps, instead, they had seen a white horse and tired brains added the horn. Since these friends were reliable people—one in law enforcement, the other an educator—the psychologist asked that they not speak any more of what they had seen until they got to a restaurant to get some coffee and warm up. He carefully wrote down what they had said initially, and once they were at the restaurant, had them each write, without looking at the other's paper, or speaking, what they had seen.

The two stories were identical in some ways, where the unicorn had been and what it had been doing, and that could've been something they'd gotten from discussing it and going to the field, but the similarity ended there. The driver's story was short. He'd been looking for deer, and having seen one off to the right, when he saw a light colored flash to the left, he expected it was a deer, and once they got close enough to see it, he saw what he was sure was a white horse. As they came close, however, the running lights of the car cast a yellowish glow on what was definitely a spiraling horn of some grayish, reflective material. He remembered thinking that gray was an odd color for a unicorn horn, and then suddenly realizing that he'd seen a unicorn and gasping. He described its color as off-white, and said its eyes seemed to meet his and he felt like he was going to lose control of his car even though he didn't even swerve.

In the passenger seat, the story was even briefer. The passenger had been glancing at the stars, the moon, the clouds, farm animals on the rural road, the river that darted out of forest and occasionally along the road when he saw, up ahead, a unicorn. He thought, at once, that he must be tired and imagining things, so he rubbed his eyes and glanced behind him as they passed it. What he saw, a pure white unicorn, with a white spiraling horn coming out of its head made him gasp, and the driver gasped at the same time he did.

The psychologist read these papers and was stunned. There was no simple explanation for what they both had seen. They'd just spent three days at a boring conference with no reference to unicorns, and the three of them had been together the whole time, finding it cheaper to share a three-room motel cabin then stay at the conference's hotel. They'd known each other since college, and none of them was really a trickster, and it was very unlikely any of them was going to team up with another to fool the third. The psychologist realized, as they drove the rest of the way home in silence, that he could find no rational explanation, and when he awoke the next morning, he called several friends he knew to be skeptical types, and all of them agreed that it didn't sound like your typical shared delusion.

He filed it away in his mental file of the unexplained, and noticed that both of the men who'd seen the unicorn never spoke of it to him or each other again, but that they had fairly major changes in their lives soon after the event: a car accident for one, and the loss of a family member for the other. Both of them seemed to have a great sense of hope that seemed uncharacteristic for both of them, and the psychologist attributed it to that night, regardless of the cause.

I come into the story as a friend of the psychologist. I had been discussing the ideas of UPG, and the fact that it may be that metaphysical events occur in our lives for our personal benefit and aren't supposed to be believed by other people. He thought this was a good explanation for the unicorn encounter, and that rather than analyze the mechanism by which it occurred, something that had proven impossible, what should be examined was the effect of the encounter.

Seeing magic as UPG does not mean we see it as real or metaphysical, but is the desire to turn the examination of it away from the mechanism behind it (in part, because we may never understand that) and instead examine the effect of the event. When used to describe why a thing happens it is a highly uncomfortable theory, but when used instead as the idea that the reasons why a thing happens or the mechanisms behind a thing are less important that the effect of perceiving that thing upon the person, it becomes a more useable theory. True, it doesn't help resolve the questions a naturally skeptical human being should have, but it will show us that perhaps other questions are in order.

Magic as meditative or mental or How Rationalists deal with Magic, Part Three

Perhaps the most common way rationalists deal with magic is to see it as meditative or mental. Meditative magic is, perhaps, better described as a branch of transformative magic, because it is the transformation of the mind from a confused or hectic state to a meditative one. In this meditative state, it becomes possible to subject the body to various stimuli that would normally beget a dramatic negative response with no response whatsoever. We have all seen images of swamis piercing their tongues or cheeks with nails while the reporter held out the wounded flesh to show the gaping, bloody hole, and while some of these demonstrations (like fire walking and lying on a bed of nails) are applications of science, others can only be described as the ability to separate the body from its pain sensors.

To the imaginative but irrational person, these events are proof of magical ability, but to the skeptic and the scientist, they are marks of the ability to deal with pain in a way different from the usual methods. Using force of will, training and practice, people are able to shut off the reflexive pulling away from painful stimuli as easily as you and I can hold our leg steady when the doctor taps it with a hammer. We know the brain is a powerful thing, with amazing untapped capacity. Even though statistics that say we use only 20-30% of our brains capacity are misleading, we certainly are capable of using it at deeper and more complex levels than we commonly do.

We are, essentially, fragile naked apes, and like other apes we have this huge chunk of neocortex that seems capable of overriding the lower parts of the brain. We can hold our breath easily to go underwater, or just because we feel like it. We can run into a fire to save a child. Or we can eat things that would make us vomit because a sick and twisted game show is giving us money to do so (something I find morally reprehensible, but something we are all capable of to some degree.) We can even do these things when they don't have readily apparent benefits—jumping between a gun and a crowd when we don't know anyone in that crowd, or trying to save a drowning stranger even though it puts us at risk, and even when we don't know if the stranger is good, bad, or going to kill us for interfering.

This is already a sign of the difference between our brain and the brain of other animals, and we know that amongst our animal brethren, huge differences exist between the capacities of individual members of a species. Look at it even in terms of the animals in your house or in the houses of your neighbors. There are dumb dogs and smart ones, dumb cats and smart ones. I had a cat with a vocabulary of a few dozen words, she knew down, up, come here, catnip, chicken, food, water, and more. If you said these words when speaking to other people she'd react (even if you were ordering pizza and added chicken wings). Her littermate, on the other hand, had to have the catnip toy pressed to her nose before she figured out what it was and would regularly run into walls when her sister banked sharply in a game of chase, occasionally knocking herself out in the process[67].

Even now, I have an incredibly smart hunter cat, who plays very complicated games like "I saw a bird, so now I must yell and run a lap around the house, chase the left foot and meow when you call me until you at last locate me," and another cat who is, essentially, a warm, fuzzy pillow

---

[67] In fact, she died as a result of a v-shaped skull fracture. The vet, who had seen her do this at our house, attributed it to her running across the linoleum floor of the kitchen and sliding into the corner of a refrigerator. When she passed, he examined her and found signs of repeated, long term head trauma and now counsels patients with cats that often slide into walls when playing to gate off rooms without carpeted floors.

that moves from kitchen floor to bed several times a day, eats, belches and moans, but does nothing else deserving of the title cat. These animals demonstrate a huge difference in intelligence and reactivity. One will run away when you flush the toilet, the other doesn't even react to being tripped over, vacuumed around or dripped upon by a person fresh out of the shower. If animals can be so different, surely people can be that different at an animal level?

So it may be that magic is actually nothing more than using your mind at a higher level. ESP, psionic ability, mental energy or whatever you call it may be nothing more or less than a factor of using your brain in a way that other members of your species cannot or have not learned to do. A rationalist realizes that we don't understand the whole of the brain, how it works and why and admits that perhaps these things are feasible. Again, such things warrant the same testing as anything else, but unlike the ideas above, they offer a more rational explanation than the divine or some metaphysical agent determining when and how the most minor of secular metaphysics will work.

Wicca without Magic

The explosion of Wicca in the past twenty years has allowed people who probably wouldn't have ever discovered it to do so. As a result of this, a number of classically trained Ceremonial Magi have begun to make their mark on Wicca. Perhaps the most interesting effect of this is *not* the combination of Wicca with Ceremonial Magic, because that has always been there, but the ability of these magi to separate the two. As one friend puts it, since he knows the full method of casting a true protective circle, he feels no reason to create more than a celebratory one when honoring the gods. He knows where things like watchtowers and elementals come from, and is capable of using them to their full capacity. Thus he feels no need to add them to the purely celebratory nature of his Wicca.

For him, and many others like him, Wicca is a lifestyle punctuated by acts of pure worship. The casting of the circle is not a metaphysical rite but steps taken to prepare the mind for communion with the divine. The energy raised and released to the gods in a high circle is purely personal energy, held and released not by a metaphysical boundary but by sheer will. Spells and the like are not used in their Wiccan practice, but instead in their magical one, each inevitably flavoring each, but still separate.

For people trained in that manner, Wicca without magic is not an act of removing things from a long-established practice but the act of removing elements that have been added to lend credibility to something that is completely credible without them. Tracing a circle upon the ground, marking it as separate space from the area around it, contemplating one's relationship to earth, air, fire and water... and, finally, asking the gods to listen to your prayers if it be their will, is not only *not* supernatural but it's as completely natural as is sharing one's meals with them, singing, praying, dancing to them and reveling in the sheer pleasure of communion with them.

Trained in Ceremonial Magic, these people know that their words, spoken clearly and with will behind them are as powerful as any chants and dances. Sometimes merely the act of looking at the moon and saying thank you to the world for life itself can be more powerful than following any ritual as outlined in a book. These people are not, as their critics would make you think, incapable of doing magic, but are so capable of doing magic that they see no need to do it in ritual.

A parallel in my own life that you might understand is the fact that in our secular lives my wife and I are both trained in high-level decontamination. She has worked in the creation of medical devices that could be ruined by a single fingerprint or piece of hair, and I have worked with similar devices in biological research. We each have taken air showers, worn decontamination suits, masks and gloves and have had to scrub with anti-microbial detergents at times in our lives. We also both cook on occasion. While the experience with decontamination may make us more sensitive to things involving cooking (for example, we have separate cutting surfaces for meat and vegetables, and special cleaners for these surfaces) we certainly don't combine cooking with high level decontamination techniques. In part, this is because we understand that most minor contamination in food is not a big deal. In fact, "guess the hair in the spaghetti sauce" has been elevated to a game here. Thin, auburn and wavy means mine, while thick, black and straight means hers. Gray could be anybody's. But this lack of performing high-level decontamination is also because we understand that it is not necessary to do all things all the time. This is a good thing, especially since it is unlikely my kitchen would pass any form of industrial inspection, even when the dishes are all clean and the floor has been mopped.

For Ceremonial Magi, the choice is similar. They don't wish to do more than is needed for the event. Worshipping the gods does not require a full-scale containment circle with a diameter of nine feet, Theban script around the circumference, imported sand from one's homeland, a dagger of exactly six inches with a triangular blade, imported incense and a wand made of virgin hawthorn. In fact, knowing the uses of these things, adding them may even be worse than excessive. It may be distractive, focusing the caster on the things that they are using instead of the gods they are worshipping. These tools have their place, and if, for whatever reason, a person feels the desire for them he can use them, but he doesn't *need* them.

The easy comparison here is the difference between early Protestants and Catholics. At the time of the reformation, every bit of Christian worship had been placed into a box. Even the prayer of a child at night or around the dinner table had a proper form, as they often do now regardless of denomination. I remember the shocked look of the Christian who asked me as a child to lead a prayer and got "Hey, God, awesome job on the sunrise this morning, really top notch!" It resulted in my being told I did not "know how to pray." It's inevitable in this sort of situation that people who can see the goodness of their god in things like a sunrise or their child's smile would begin to wonder if the proper form of a prayer is as important as the devotion.

It is from these Ceremonial Magi, who can show us where the apparently meaningless aspects of ritual come from, that we get the gift of purer worship. You simply cannot find a more holy communion with the divine that the sudden inspiration to pray, weep, dance or sing at the sight of a sunset, or to whisper a praise at the breath of inspiration or in the face of glory. Simple, ecstatic worship is utterly possible, utterly Wiccan and perhaps even better than worship with magic.

Like the abstract artists who create works that we might see as simple and childlike, and who have the ability to do the more concrete work, but make the decision not to, most ecstatic Wiccans are trained in the formal circle and the typical metaphysical techniques, but make the choice to use them only when they see fit. I am uncomfortable in telling anyone they should just disregard learning a thing altogether, but certainly, once you know the basics and the reason for them, the decision to not use a thing takes on an entirely new meaning. Therefore, though I find Wicca without magic purer and inherently closer to the divine, I find incredible value in teaching people the basics before telling them they are unimportant.

Recommended Reading for Topic Seven:

Crowley, A. *Magick in Theory and Practice*, aka *Magick book IV*; various publishers.

Discussion Questions for Topic Seven:

7.1. What is meant by rationalism?

7.2. Is magic inherently irrational? Why or Why not?

7.3. Describe how Magic can be seen as transformative.

7.4. What is meant by the metaphor of the Philosopher's stone?

7.5. What is meant by "magic as UPG?"

7.6. Are ESP and similar things the same as Magic? What do you think?

7.7. What is meant by Wicca without Magic?

Topic Eight: Wicca and Creationism

How do Wiccans deal with creationists? What is creationism?
Creation Science? The ages of Man? A Creation myth? How does
evolution work? What is a scientific theory? Is evolution a reli-
gious belief? How do we reconcile Creation myths and reality?

What is Creationism?

Creationism is the belief that the world was created by
the divine and is generally a term used to describe only
those methods of creation that are *contrary* to the findings of
science. In general, creationism is a Christian phenomenon,
but it can occur in other religions. Like most fundamentalist
beliefs, Creationism insists that the mythos of a religion be
taken as seriously as the practices of it. Creationists who believe that Sunday is a sacred day reserved for rest and worship, for example, see the acceptance of their creation myth
as literal truth (rather than parable, metaphor or an ancient
people's attempt to explain what was unexplainable) as important to their faith as not working on Sunday. In other
words, they see belief in their creation myth of choice as
having equal importance to their religion's rules. To these
people, right belief is as important, perhaps more important, that right action.

This idea of taking a non-scientific creation myth as literal truth is a fairly modern invention. In ancient religions,
it was common for people to assume that their creation
story was a parable or at the least that it was incomplete.
The stories were often believed to have been revealed by
muses or similar spirits—beings less perfect than true
gods—and then given to mortal men—beings even less perfect. It was always likely that errors and what we'll call
creative truth-telling crept into these myths, and for that
reason, discrepancies within them could be noted without
its being seen as an attack on the faith or an offense to the
divine. Only the gods around since the start of creation
were aware of the actual story, and if they wished it told in
a certain way, they would do so.

Seen in this light, the fact that two separate accounts of
the creation of the universe occur in Genesis makes it similar in most ways to other creation stories. The two accounts

are never resolved. How individuals can declare both to be the literal truth astounds me, but as a Pagan—and therefore as someone comfortable with ambiguity—I understand that these stories are no more right or wrong than the creation stories of Hesiod or those found on clay tablets or ancient tomb walls. I don't suggest that such creation stories are incorrect, just that they are not literally so.

Similar to creationism, "creation science" is the name of an equally illogical attempt to fuse strict adherence to a non-scientific mythos with scientific knowledge. In this pseudoscience, evidence that supports the Bible is called scientific evidence and evidence which fails to support the Bible is called false or erroneous. This type of selective truth-telling is a highly dangerous intellectual exercise. Knowledge of the real "science" behind the creation science claims shows it to be nothing more than the use of complex terms to make fiction sound real. Just as the idea that "Wicca is devil worship" sounds stupid to those who have experienced Wicca, those who've taken a secular biology course—even at the freshman or AP level—can see through the claims of creation "science." You don't need to take biology to do this—just any basic science.

Examples of creation "science" claims include that dinosaur bones are 10,000 years old because scientists have found red blood cells in them and that there are 200 forms of carbon dating, all but a handful of which date dinosaur bones to the past 10,000 years. To those who know absolutely nothing about science, this can sound really convincing, but to those with even a dabbler's knowledge, it is just nonsense. Asked to support their claims, creation "scientists" will regularly throw out facts with little to do with their claims and cite completely false evidence along side those facts. My son, at 10, discussing an unrelated event, came up with the ideal metaphor for their claims: Imagine that I see a woman wearing a red dress, and I describe her as blond haired, blue eyed, tall, mean, stupid and wearing a red dress… when she was, in fact, wearing a red dress—but was short, sweet, had black hair and brown eyes and was the smartest and nicest person I'd ever met. That I correctly said she had a red dress doesn't mean I described her accurately!

Two new forms of creation science include the division of evolution into what is termed "Micro" and "Macro" Evolution[68] (which is merely an attempt to be anti-evolution in the face of evidence for it), and the equally flawed concept of "intelligent design," which supposes that genetic and phylogenic research demonstrates an intelligence that was creating the world and man towards certain ends. Again, it's a lovely theory that lacks only one thing: evidence. Evolutionary dead-ends and extinctions, the fragility of the genetic code itself and the trend toward diversity all refute the claims of intelligent design. The tragic thing here is that there is an absolute beauty in the genetic code. Allowed to stand on its own, it can teach us wonderful things about how life creates itself. Intelligent design takes the wonderful idea that randomness is the tool of the divine and couples it with bad science, bad theology and ridiculous claims of knowing the "why" behind the intelligence.

As with all things, I ask that you *not* take my word for it. While it is true I formally studied biology, I am not making claims that cannot be easily demonstrated. Web-searches on what creationists believe will result in a mountain of evidence for you to evaluate on your own, and I ask only that you check the veracity of any claims they make, look up the terms they use and ask yourself how true their evidence sounds. Don't be told what to believe!

Creationism is a very important thing for Wiccans to be aware of because as practitioners of a religion that values study and skepticism, and teaches that the answers we need can be seen in the universe around us, we are particularly susceptible to falling into the logical traps of Creationism. It is a foot in the door that we should not allow proselytes to get on us. Perhaps by examining their misconceptions we

---

[68] Actually, Macroevolution and Microevolution are terms used in evolutionary biology, however, the creationist term "Macroevolution" means a completely different thing than the evolutionary term. "Speciation" is probably the closest the evolutionary biologists come to the term Macroevolution as used by creationists.

can formulate better ideas about how the universe works. It may well be that the genetic code, the patterns of the stars and our relationship to every living thing are facts with vast amounts of information to impart to us about the divine, but the flaw lies in claiming that this information is the same as fact. Religious knowledge, remember, is its own type of information, not really opinion but also not really fact. It is inherently and unforgivably personal, from the mouths of the gods to our individual ears.

Creation Stories and Myths

When we do not attempt to paste science to our unscientific creation myths, they can reveal vast amounts of information about our cultures. The similarities between our creation myths speak volumes, although just what they are speaking of is a question that can probably never be answered. As discussed previously, just because a question has no definitive answer doesn't mean that asking it, and brainstorming possible answers to it, is futile. Indeed, pondering why we think the world began they way it did and why others think the way they do may be one of the most rewarding mental exercises of all.

In general, our creation myths can be roughly divided into two groups: those in which man is there from the beginning (or nearly from the beginning), and those in which man arrives late on the scene. Interestingly, both of these are featured in the Abrahamic creation myths. In the first chapter of Genesis God creates man as part of the ongoing creation of the world, during the sixth day of the creation process. But in chapter two of Genesis, God creates man out of dust when the fields are unplowed and the creation is going, well, unappreciated. Why both of these stories occur within the same mythos is an interesting discussion for another time. For now we can see them as two different but accessible tribal accounts of the beginning of mankind.

Even in those stories in which man is there at the beginning, he is no longer the same man who was there at the beginning of the world at this point in time. He may be a man of iron coming long after the golden age has passed, or an imperfect man, fallen from the divine's original prototype. He may be, as in the Prometheus myth, a second try by the gods... or even a third or fourth try. He may be, as in the story of Noah and even some new age and science-fiction tales, the child of a handful of survivors of a race who destroyed themselves or were destroyed. He may even be the current survivor of an evolutionary process with dozens of dead ends and branches, the "man" at creation unrecognizable as human, maybe even unrecognizable as an animal.

Of course, the beginning of mankind is not the only start of a creation myth, and the Abrahamic myth, as well as the Sumerian, Greek and most other myths generally begin with the idea that in the absolute beginning, the time before time, if you will, there was nothing but chaos, ether or emptiness. These beliefs, fused into an underlying story, might read something like this:

In the beginning, the world was an empty void. There were no planets, no stars, no light... just chaos, a gaseous jumble of elements bouncing into each other without thought or need. At some point, maybe at the beginning, or maybe billions of years after the first speck of dust made itself, this void realized it was empty and chaotic, and did something about it.

In an instant, this great thing, this thing called All That Is, or I Am, or God, or The Divine, or The Goddess, or The Universe began to create by rending things out of chaos. It/She/He/They separated the dust from the vacuum, matter from antimatter, light from a lack of light. Once the spark of the first separation took hold, the thing realized It/She/He/They had created a new thing altogether — the concept of non-unity, of being one thing and not the other.

The Creation, or maybe the thing that created it (for distinction itself was new to the world) saw that things that now existed, or at least that they now existed as separate things, and watched as they grew and expanded. With the concept of separation came the ability to distinguish, so as things grew further apart, they became more complicated and more and more distinct. Everything became a thing and a combination of things. Matter was molecules, molecules were elements, elements were atoms, atoms were sub atomic particles... and when viewed at their most separate levels they were still the chaos, the equal parts that had existed at the beginning.

Perhaps the best part of the story that is above is the fun you can have reading it to people. My wife, then an engineering student, commented that the movement force in the story could be gravity, and indeed, the story is an anthropomorphized "big bang" (or perhaps theomorphized would be most accurate.) Yet, for all the science she perceived, another friend reading it said that the next line should be "and God looked upon it, and it was good," and another mentioned the rivers of chaos in the Sumerian myth. I, myself, am reminded of the Hellenic creation myths. This fundamental feeling of similarity between the most scientific of peers (who felt the story too spiritual) and the most spiritual (who felt the story too scientific) certainly points to a shared something that, if not indicative of a shared ancient faith (and I do not feel it is) is indicative of the questions we ask as humans.

A koan a friend once told me states only the following nine words: Mankind is the only thing that contemplates his creation. It is an unusual one, not truly a fable, nor a riddle. It doesn't ask a question, merely makes a simple observation that we can't actually prove is true. Of course, the first time I meditated upon it that was the direction my mind took... *Is it the only thing that contemplates his creation? Do we really know if whales think about whale gods or if sea monkeys wonder who opened the first packet?* It was only the second or third time I really thought about it that I understood part of what it was saying. In the creation story above, it is the Divine that makes the distinctions about things, and in our reality, it is mankind.

Man creates languages and distinctions and gives things names, something that occurs not just in creation myths but in reality. Contemplating why we do these things reveals powerful information about ourselves. We can use that realization as a key to understanding the divine, and use creation myths to interpret reality without seeing the myths as utterly true. Perhaps the most interesting aspect of this is that naming things, categorizing them and separating them is most practiced by those studying evolution. Just as realizing that we have something in common with the creative force in the universe can bring us closer to understanding it, so can trying to distinguish things on the most fundamental levels, levels a divine entity would see without microscopes or spectroscopy. Evolution, then, becomes a creation myth of its own, like the earlier ones based on the science of their day, and perhaps closer to the way the Divine works than anything thought of in the past. It becomes a scientific creation myth, as opposed to a theological one: science did it, not any god.

So we find ourselves *not* modifying science to benefit our creation myths, but modifying our myths to benefit our understanding of the world around us. Such processes are surely admirable ones, whether they prove fruitful in the end or not. They cause, at the least, the best kind of questions to be asked: not those questions that give you answers but questions that teach you to refine the question and show you new questions you never thought of before.

Why Wiccans should Know about Evolution

Belief or perceived belief in evolution is something certain critics of Wicca use as a vector for attacking the faith. According to these misinformed critiques, since most Wiccans express a belief in some form of evolution, evolution is seen as a Wiccan teaching and therefore attacks upon it are attacks upon Wicca. The problem here is bigger than a simple misunderstanding, because by claiming evolution is a spiritual belief and not a scientific one, they may remove the status of evolution as a scientific theory and request it not be discussed in secular settings, like the classroom.

Of course, when not discussed, people will still wonder how the world got to be the way it is. I can assure you that if discussions of evolution were removed from the secular setting, we would hear no decrease in the constant hum of creationism. The ramifications of teaching our children that it is okay to reject anything scientific if there is an emotional response by some against it are quite grave, but we should be much more concerned with the idea of teaching them that the only explanation acceptable for them to learn is a non- or anti- scientific one. Strangely, the people shouting the loudest for the removal of evolution (and earth day, recycling and ecology) from the classroom on the basis that it is a Pagan religious belief are often the same screaming that it is their right to have their Christian prayers in that very classroom.

While I want to discuss what you should know about evolution, because it is inevitable that an open Wiccan will be accused of having an "evolution agenda" at some point, I would like to relate an experience of my own in the classroom growing up to give you an idea of the nature of the anti-evolution people. I went to a public high school at the edge of Syracuse, New York. At the time I went to this school it predominantly served the children of its affluent Jewish neighborhood and the neighborhoods surrounding Syracuse University, two miles away. As a result, most of my friends were the children of professors or graduate students, what we called ivory tower babies, or Jewish suburbanites who lived mere feet outside of the Fayetteville-Manlius and Jamesville-Dewitt school districts. The parents of most of the people I knew went to Temple Beth-El or May Memorial Universalist Unitarian.

For whatever reason, children who wished to study things like auto shop and cosmetology were bussed to a school twenty minutes away for those classes, so for the bulk of the day, the school was populated by the college bound and the literati who took things like drama and journalism to fill electives. I did not consider myself college bound, but I was certainly amongst the literati, so when it came to science, I took regents biology instead of general science. This was difficult for me because in my first two years of High School I usually only shared by choice those classes in which I considered myself superior to the college bound kids, things like Gifted English and Drama, preferring to take the easiest courses possible whenever given the choice so that I could sit in the back, read a book and earn a B for showing up and being just a little smarter than your average bear.

Truth be told, regents biology was very easy for me. I was the daughter of a microbiologist, and any question I had could be answered far better by my mom than my teacher, whose real name I forget but who I called Mr. Witless. I regularly did not show up for class, I did no work and I earned a grade of 40%. However, I scored an 85 on the state-wide final and thus, by the miraculous power of the New York State Board of Regents, got an 85% for the class. I do not recommend this technique to other young people, as my guidance counselor called me into her office to ask that I please not tell other students that I averaged 35 points better on my state exams than I did in my classes because, unlike me, they failed when they tried it. In addition, in retrospect, I ended up entering college with horrible study skills, doing well in classes in which the whole of the score was based on two exams... and poorly in classes with weekly exams.

I was in one particular class with students whom I didn't want to be around unless it was as a superior, students who were taking classes like Calculus and Latin (courses I would find difficult but enjoyable in college) and who saw me, I thought, as an ignoramus. After the obligatory lecture in basic evolutionary biology, a lecture I slept through, or at least pretended to sleep through, we left the class and another one of the outsiders began to pitch a fit about how wrong evolution was to anyone who could hear. She ranted about Old Testament this, and Old Testament that, and I took her on. (This was undoubtedly a mistake because I was an atheist with a gripe against all theists at the time.) I removed a side-by-side Bible from my backpack which I was carrying for a friend, and asked this young lady to cite the places where the Old Testament said evolution was against god's will, or that natural selection was not the tool god used. At some point in my angry but not screaming debate of this girl's nonsense, I literally started to cry because I was so frustrated not with what she was shouting but the illogic of it: that it was an offense against god for us to be learning about evolution.

Most of the class had left, though a few students who didn't know us gathered around expecting punches to fly. Although neither of us was likely to do that, this was rapidly becoming nothing more than a theological bully attacking the girl who was probably the school's worst intellectual bully. The theology was winning, not because she had a better argument than I, but because she was arguing on grounds I did not understand. I thought she was making no sense because I didn't understand her religion, but in reality, it was just that she did not understand how to rationally argue. She was all but battering me with her ability to quote verses, but then she made a vital theological error, claiming that god told her, as a member of his chosen people, to beware of people like me, who would use my satanic intellectualism to try to sway her from the true path.

This error was, like Joseph's telling his brothers his dreams in Genesis, not just bad policy—the revelation of personal info from the Divine—but also bad arithmetic. She'd just claimed to be a member of god's chosen people, and that god's chosen people hated intellectualism... in a hallway with a statistically high number of college-preparatory students who happened to be Jewish. To borrow a phrase from the book of Andrew (Lloyd Webber) not only was she thoughtless, she was also rather dim.

At some point the bible was removed from my clenched hands. Hebrew phrases traded places with my snide rejection of her verses, and in about two minutes, this girl who had so obliterated my defense of evolution was not merely on the run verbally, but physically. The book was handed back to me, and the student who had theologically disemboweled her helped me clean up my face, pick up the papers I'd scattered during the debacle and offered to walk me to the art class we shared. Had I been thinking clearly, I would've probably avoided this as a likely proselytization attempt, but I agreed. On our way there he told me he appreciated that I, an atheist, was trying to demonstrate that she was flawed according to her own alleged holy book, rather than write her off as another crazy theist spouting nonsense. That discussion turned into a longer one during art, a discussion that was probably the first chink in my atheist armor.

What he told me—with the bizarre wisdom we sometimes have as children and then abandon years later—was that I needed to realize that every theist out there was not a crazy girl outside a biology classroom foaming at the mouth. I had been in a class of 30 in which a few were active members of the same synagogue as he was, a class full of theists who knew the same material as that girl, some in two different languages, and not a one of them drew the same conclusions she had. They were conclusions, he added, that probably hadn't even been hers but the words of her minister.

As stupid as it sounds now to say it, it took me years to fully understand the complete extent of what he was saying. I took it then to mean that all theists were not stupid or anti-intellectual and those that were obviously misinterpreted their holy works. The real wisdom in what he was saying, though, were the words behind the words: don't believe it when people claim to know what god says, and if they claim the words are in a book, look and see how many followers of that book draw the same conclusions.

This story doesn't show that the Jews in my class were right and a Christian was wrong, but it reminds us that the words a person uses are not always interpreted the same way. She claimed that the book of Genesis was why we should reject evolution, but millions of people read those words and don't reach the same conclusion. The reason is simple: anti-evolution is not in Genesis. It was a teaching of her faith, not a teaching of the Abrahamic mythos as a whole. The problem was not theists, because here were theists that were as vigorous as I in their defense of evolution. The problem was not in Genesis, for surely this young man, who'd formally studied the original form of it, would not have tried to defend Genesis if it was the source of the problem. It wasn't even a flaw in Christianity, or the girl's church, for later another member of her church would apologize for her behavior and point out that her anti-evolution came from her parents, not their minister.

The moral of this tangential anecdote is that we all need to avoid the mental leaps that are easy to make when we deal with anti-Wiccan and anti-evolution people. We need to avoid writing them all off as foaming at the mouth, and realize that their stances are not the fault of their holy books. They may come from new books, and from fringe ministers, and they may even be in small groups, but we have to be clear about where the stance originates. Again, the flaw is not in theism, or the Abrahamic mythos, or the

Bible, or Christianity, but in specific offshoots of these things.

Anti-Evolutionism is not Christianity; it is its own religion. This does not make evolution a religious belief, as they would have you believe, but it does make any religion that does not reject evolution a theological enemy. To these people, a religion like Wicca, which says that the divine can be observed in the natural world, is especially dangerous because it is observation of the natural world that led to the theory of evolution.

Wiccans need to know about evolution because people attempt to claim Wicca is wrong by making claims about evolution. Taking a lesson from my experience in high school, the right way to argue this point is not to simply explain that evolution is a secular theory many Wiccans believe—and that it is not Wiccan Theology. It is also important to male sure their claims about evolution are legitimate. This is an unfortunate circumstance, because we can't be expected to be experts in whatever thing the anti-Wiccans connect us to at any given moment. However we also can't let ignorance go unchallenged. We simply say "You're wrong about Wicca; evolution is a secular theory and Wicca is a religion," or "You're wrong about Wicca; you're wrong about evolution—are you ever right?!!" But most of us don't feel comfortable with half-truths or outright lies and expecting us to leave them on the table without trying to correct them is often too much to ask. We are uncomfortable with being told we are wrong and therefore uncomfortable with telling people they are wrong, preferring to show them where they made a mistake, instead of simply answering their accusation with "No, you are wrong."

An evolution primer

Since we need to know a bit about evolution in order to defend ourselves from people who assume it is holy writ to us—and since, as a theory based on natural observation, it should closely mirror some of our observations—it's best to know a little bit about it. We'll begin with the fundy's first method of attack, proclaiming it is "only a theory."

The ignorance of this mode of attack is apparent if you understand what a scientific theory is. Like the word myth, which means completely different things when speaking of things like Hesiod's Theogony and the materials of urban legends, the word "theory" has two distinct meanings. The first meaning, the one used by creationists, is that a theory is a guess. This demotes things like the Theory of Evolution (and also the Theory of Gravity, Big Bang Theory) to some scientists guessing about things, maybe even making educated guesses. The problem is that scientists have a name for these educated guesses, and they aren't called theories but hypotheses.

A hypothesis is often the first step in the development of a theory, but it is not a theory in and of itself. A scientific theory is an interesting phenomena in that while definitions of it very slightly, it's generally assumed that a student or scientist with a firm basis in the scientific method will know one when they see one, leaving the common defense to the claim that a theory is a best guess to be simply stating "no it's not." My own definition of the term combines elements from Steven Hawking, stacks of biology and statistics textbooks I was forced to read over the years, scientists I've met and my personal experiments, but is right in line with these other theories. Briefly, a scientific theory is an explanation of a large quantity of data that is shown to be predictive of future actions by that data, and that makes a fairly broad claim, but not so broad as to become nonsense.

For example, I may theorize, based on my observations, that the moon grows and shrinks as the month goes by (a theory that could easily be proven false). A good version of this theory would be fairly broad: I'd say all moons do this, and thus if I found even one moon that didn't, my theory would be proven false and I'd have to create a new one. My theory's level of falsifiability would be equal to the number of every moon in existence, and thus, if we had discovered a billion moons, that would be a billion chances for my theory to be false. With a billion chances, if my theory was never shown false, it would be a pretty strong indicator that it was true. If I made a theory just about *our* moon, there would be only one chance to prove it false. This can seem complicated unless you imagine it in less stellar (or lunar) terms.

Imagine you have an 8-year-old son, or brother. Imagine he is the most annoying child in the world. Your boss is wondering why you are constantly being called away from work, and goes to meet this child. In the 5 minutes your boss meets him, he is gracious, sweet and pleasant. You wouldn't think it fair for your boss to consider him sweet and pleasant based on those five minutes, and you wouldn't find my theory on moons that convincing if it was based on only one moon.

A good theory has had many opportunities to be proven wrong but has not been proven wrong. The absence of proof of a theory being wrong doesn't prove it to be true, but it proves it to be much more likely than unlikely. This is the basic difference between unscientific and scientific thought: scientific thought deals in terms of likely and unlikely, possible and impossible. Unscientific thought accepts without questioning, and scientific thought promotes questioning.

So, now that we understand that the Theory of Evolution is no more invalid than the Theory of Gravity for the use of the term theory, we can move onto the evolution part of the idea. The vast majority of antievolution material focuses on Darwin's *Origin of Species*, a work in which, strangely enough, the word evolution never appears. *Origin of Species* is a quick read, even if the language seems old fashioned and difficult, so there is little reason to believe that the antievolutionists have never read it, but certainly their assumptions about it are incorrect enough to warrant wondering.

Origin of Species introduces the concept of variation by natural selection. By "origin of species," Darwin refers to the creation of divergent groups of organisms, groups that cannot produce fertile young when they breed together, like horses, zebras and donkeys—all equines; or pigeons, chickens and blue jays—all birds. Just as in the creation story we discussed earlier, the divine separated matter from antimatter and earth from sky, Darwin wonders what separates one species from another. His theory is that just as mankind can introduce variation in domestic animals with selective breeding, events in nature can cause a type of selective breeding. Put another way, since there is already evidence, from breeders of pigeons, dogs, sheep and cattle, that causing some groups to breed with specific members of their group and not others results in new varieties, it is likely that nature, god or sheer luck causes this to happen in the animal world. After long periods of separation, the difference is enough that these mere varieties become discrete species. It should be noted that Darwin avoids discussing mankind at all in the work, although he discusses it in a later one, using quite different terms than those he used for dogs or pigeons.

That's all that natural selection is: the belief that, since we can do experiments that result in variation in the controlled setting of the lab or farm, it is likely that variation in nature comes from a similar technique. What this natural technique is, what god or nature or chaos does that causes it, is something Darwin dances around. It is likely there is no single answer. We know geographic isolation can influence speciation, we know conditions that favor a recessive phenotype can cause it to be more likely. The exact why will probably never be known because the reasons are far subtler than the techniques of our farmer friends. There is little proof, for example, that some god is out there castrating wild rabbits with a color pattern he dislikes.

That's the core error anti-evolutionists make about natural selection. Natural selection is not something that demonstrates intelligence. In fact, evidence that creatures are selected for breeding at the expense of long lives is commonplace. The peacock's huge tail, which makes him attractive to females, results in his flying slowly and being easy prey. However, since he usually lives long enough to mate, sexual selection results in tails that are bigger and bigger. It's not really survival of the fittest, but survival of the fittest to breed. If the male can live long enough to pass on his genetic material, selection works. His life could be miserable, short and painful, but as long as he passes on his seed, it's "fit."

Another misconception is that a characteristic must develop because it is beneficial to the species. As demonstrated above, the tail is not beneficial to the male except in getting him a female, and we can say that the female's desire or apparent desire for bigger and brighter tails is not beneficial to her male offspring, unless having fewer males is seen as a benefit. This is the problem with anthropomorphizing selection; you begin to have to pass judgment on what is a truly beneficial trait. Rabbits, for example, have fairly fragile immune systems. As anyone who has raised them will tell you, viruses and bacteria that might give us a runny nose and a cough will kill them, or at least make them miserable for quite a while. They also have very breakable bones, as anyone who raises them for game will attest. They can be killed with a stone, or even when they are spooked and dash into a large object. They also are capable of getting pregnant before they are fully-grown and are prolific breeders, resulting in their being nearly everywhere in the world, often as a pest. Which of these traits is beneficial? Large predators find them exceptionally tasty, especially simmered slowly with white wine and butter. Is this good for their continued existence as a species?

The truth is that a bundle of things evolve in each creature. Those with the traits that work in their environment live, and those that develop traits that don't work die. The traits they develop are not necessarily the best way to adapt to an environment (look at our waistlines… fat was good for early man, and now it's our culture's public enemy #1) but they work to some degree. To see a grand design, a careful plan to make things in a certain order by a divine force with perfect knowledge of how things will turn out is illogical. If a god does dictate evolution, he either likes to watch things die off or he's muddling through like a toddler with clay. Certainly there are straighter pathways between prehistoric life and modern life than those we find. Twists, turns and die offs don't indicate a god who has lined up life like dominos, all falling into place. If it speaks to a creator at all, it's one who uses random chance to achieve the desired effect, working much as my friend who had no major in college did, taking a little bit from here, and a little bit from there with the assumption that eventually she'd have enough of the right classes to graduate with some degree.

Two Common Arguments of Creationists and their Counter-Arguments

There are two common arguments that Wiccans who move in interfaith circles hear from Creationists and people with similar beliefs. One is a critique of reincarnation, which some but not all Wiccans believe in, and the other is a critique of the perceived beliefs of Wiccans regarding the creator of the universe. These beliefs are tangential to the discussion of evolution and creationism, but as they both represent a sort of snide anti-Wiccan hysteria, which any attack on Wicca as evolution certainly is, they warrant a discussion here.

The first of these arguments is that, since many Wiccans believe in reincarnation, Wicca is a lie because there are too many people in the world now for them all to be reincarnated souls. Just as in evolution, pointing out that some Wiccans believe in reincarnation whilst others believe in a paradisiacal Summerland or a combination of those ideas is not enough. Ethically, a Wiccan in tune with his beliefs has issues with letting ignorance about his fellow Wiccans' beliefs be misrepresented, even if he doesn't share them, and while he may not believe in reincarnation, it's not fair to his brethren to simply state that all Wiccans don't believe in reincarnation and therefore critiques of it are invalid critiques of Wicca.

The flaw in the "where did all the souls come from" argument is two-fold. On the one hand, few beliefs in reincarnation actually teach that there are a finite number of souls. Most teach that new souls are created, according to the reincarnation mythos of choice, and therefore it would be unlikely that at any time we would run out of souls, regardless of how many people are born and how many people achieved transcendence. The second flaw is in the assumption that reincarnation must be temporally linear. It may be that only a few hundred (or maybe even less) souls exist and have billions of incarnations moving throughout time. This belief, non-linear reincarnation, accounts for things like psychics with alleged visions of the future, who may be remembering "past" lives that have taken place in the future. This belief even accounts for the fact that thousands of people believe that they were Cleopatra or other famous individuals in a past life. Since non-linear reincarnation teaches that you may have existed at any point in time, a stadium could be filled with people, all of them Cleopatra in the past, who each represent the thousands of incarnations between her and transcendence, reincarnations that apparently needed to learn lessons best learned in this part of time. I think it most likely that the vast majority of them have not been Cleopatra but believe that they were, but this is a most generous way of looking at it. Of course, one friend who is a non-linear reincarnationist believes all mankind and god is but one soul at different points in its knowledge, but that belief has ramifications I am uncomfortable discussing in detail.

This is a bit obscure and complicated for the average anti-Wiccan to grasp, but a knowing look and asking them why they think reincarnation is limited to a linear motion in time is often a way to defuse them. Remember, alleged religious educators often teach such questions to these "challengers." These are not questions they've come up with on their own, and they don't seek to glean information about your beliefs in the asking of them. Rather, they've been told that those who believe in reincarnation and Wicca have never pondered such things—which is nonsense, since our religion is one of pondering as much as possible—and that by asking these questions they can win you to their side. Don't discount the asker the second you hear the question, mind you, as it may be an honest search for answers, but be aware of the fact that some folk have asked this question to seek to change your faith. There's no flaw in asking a person why they ask a question.

The second question is more a catchphrase than a question. It's the statement that Wiccans worship the Creation not the Creator. This question is a matter of theological ignorance. To Wiccans, the distinction between Creation and Creator (or Creatrix) is a fuzzy one at best. Saying that Wiccans worship the Creation instead of the Creator is like saying Christians are cannibals who eat their god, a statement based on a shoddy understanding of the theology behind the rites. Wiccans see the Creation and the Creator as inextricably linked and therefore the worship—or, if you prefer, the honoring—of one is worship or honoring of the other. We do not look at a glorious painting and not think of the artist who was responsible for it, nor do we look at an artist, and, without judging his work, and think him a genius. We must see both sides of the coin, not one. Claiming we see one alone is nonsense. We could just as soon come back to this statement with a snide remark of our own but it does no good. Ask the questioner why the question is asked, why they would think such a thing or what they mean by it, and the nonsense of the catchphrase becomes apparent.

There is a vast body of "official" questions out there, handbooks even, with directions on how to challenge Pagans. Many of these are available on the net. I have read them, shared them… and have been the attempted victim of people who believed in them. You have the right to ask, as a human, to be dealt with logically and fairly. Be suspicious of questions that make no sense, ask the questioner what s/he thinks s/he means and why s/he asks those questions. Try to research beliefs you are connected to, even erroneously so, so that you do no harm when you counter theological attacks upon you regarding those beliefs. While we are primarily peaceful, the people who promote such tactics refer to them as spiritual warfare, attacking the enemy and fighting the powers of darkness. By virtue of mere disagreement, you have become the enemy of these people, and even if you do not understand this (and trust me, those peaceful members of the religions these "spiritual warriors" come from don't understand it either) they will not refrain from making attacks on you.

It does not matter if the attacks are silly, ignorant or pointless (and they are). These people take them seriously. Being prepared to deal with the attacks, even if you never have to, is an honorable venture. Our job as Wiccans, if we can be said to have any job, is to be a force for the positive in the universe. We cannot go about the world defending ourselves from these "attacks" in such a manner that we do more harm. For example, Satanists (which Wiccans are not) do not eat babies. If we are called Satanists and told we eat babies, the answer that falls within the tenets of out faith is "We are not Satanists and neither Wiccans nor Satanists eat babies." It harms the next guy over, the Satanist at the house next door, when we imply that he does eat babies. If we do not know what the group we are being associated with does, better we should say so than implicate them for what they have not done, but in the best situations all our answered are educated ones.

Recommended Reading for Topic Eight:

Root-Bernstein, Robert "*On Defining a Scientific Theory: Creationism Considered,*" Science and Creationism (Montagu, 1984),

Hawking, Stephen A Brief History of Time (Bantam, 1988)

Darwin, Charles Origin of The Species:
http://www.literature.org/authors/darwin-charles/the-origin-of-species/

Discussions Questions for Topic Eight:

8.1. What is creationism? Creation science? Intelligent design?

8.2. How is this relevant to a study of Wicca?

8.3. What is a creation myth?

8.4. A common critique of Darwin's natural selection is that it is something he pulled out of his hat. Did he have a basis for his theory? What was it? Is it observable?

8.5. What is the difference between a theory and a hypothesis?

8.6. Can you prove a theory? Can you prove a theory false?

8.7. What is a better theory, one which makes a narrow claim or one that makes a broad claim? Defend your answer.

8.8. What is meant by the statement "A good theory has many chances to be proven false."

Topic Nine: The Science of Belief

Why do we believe? What is a belief? Is there a physiological component to belief or morality? Is it, instead, sociological or psychological? What is a "benefit to society?" Are there healthy and unhealthy reasons to believe?

What is a Belief?

Up until now our discussion has focused on what people believe rather than why. In part, this is because why people believe is something that we've been discussing for years without any conclusive results. The problem here lies in the fundamental definition of terms. To some, religious belief is about faith, which they define as belief in that which cannot be proven. To other people, faith is simply the best explanation for what they perceive, and proof or lack thereof does not enter into the equation. We find ourselves grinding to a halt every time we try to discuss the reasons why people believe because we have to take a break and define our terms. We cannot simply seem to take the terms at their worth, but we have to redefine them. In my mind, this definition is often little more than an attempt to one-up the next believer over because we can very carefully manipulate the definitions of belief and nonbelief to exclude not those who don't believe but those who don't believe as we do.

As English speakers, we probably see this most often in non-sacred Abrahamic writings, common to all three of the main divisions of Abrahamic Religion, in which those that do not believe the way those who wrote the materials do are not "believers in other things," but instead "unbelievers" or "nonbelievers." The idea that they may be, in fact, believers in completely different things, rarely enters into the equation, although it does in the *religious* texts that the Abrahamic religious are based on. Pharaoh is assumed to believe in his god when Moses tells him the god of his people is the more powerful. Pilate and the various other characters in the Greek and Hebrew bibles are not called unbelievers, they just are assumed to believe something else altogether. The idea of unbelief is utterly modern, propagandistic and *not* based on any actual sacred myths, but on the words of people who cannot grasp the fact that those others can possibly not agree with them.

Even atheists have a belief: a belief in the lack of a god. This is not demoted from the status of belief because it is a belief in a non-existence instead of an existence. For the entirety of this discussion, belief will be defined in the broadest of possible terms: a belief is a hypothesis or expectation based on the sum total of the experience and existence of the individual. It may be a rational belief, based on logical conclusions or actual experiences, or it may be an irrational belief, based on nothing at all. It may be a true belief, like the belief that I have breathed air in the past. It may be an untrue belief, like the belief that I have existed in this body without breathing, ever. It may be a hopeful and likely belief, like the belief that I will continue to breathe, or an equally hopeful but perhaps less likely belief, like the belief that I will breathe longer and better and in more comfort than a younger and stronger person.

Beliefs can be described as true, false, likely, unlikely, rational, irrational, provable, impossible to prove, possible to prove incorrect, possible, impossible and most similar adjectives. What they all have in common is that they are some kind of assumption, based on some sort of information… experience, imagination, even sensation. In order to discuss religion, what we need to avoid is the demotion of beliefs about religious subjects to some sort of special status. They have the same status as do beliefs about what will happen in the next moment, or what happened in the past. They are assumptions, based on information.

That's not to say they are made lesser by their status as assumptions. Most assumptions we make throughout the day, assumptions like "the ground will not become liquid under my feet" and "the air in my house can be breathed" are correct assumptions. Those who bemoan assumptions we make about reality are being intentionally ignorant of what an assumption is, or lowering all assumptions to the level of the irrational ones, assumptions about other people's thoughts, for example. Again, we see the redefinition monster rear its ugly head. All thinking things have beliefs and all make assumptions, whether it is a fish assuming that swimming away from a bigger fish will have some effect on the distance between them or a squirrel assuming a branch will hold its weight.

The almost instinctual reaction we have as rational beings is to chalk those beliefs up to instinct or nature, but that shows the prejudice of our own beliefs about belief. An infant's reflex to seek a nipple or to suck on what is placed in its mouth is based on an assumption, either by the infant or, if you'd prefer, by nature, that this will result in the infant's continued survival. A cat, running from a loud noise, runs because it assumes running is somehow preferable to staying put. We may try to limit the idea of belief to those things that occur in the highest parts of our brain, but that's really a disservice to reality. We believe because it is our nature to do so.

As confusing as that all sounds, it's really nothing more than affirming a definition of belief that makes no qualification as to the source or validity of the belief, something that is required to discuss why we believe what we believe about certain things. Only when we first see a belief as a unit of assumption that makes no claim as to the validity of the assumption can we discuss beliefs about anything. We can't, for example, have a discussion about beliefs regarding deity that includes all persons if we define beliefs regarding deity as belief in Jesus Christ, or define beliefs regarding deity as beliefs in the existence of any *particular* deity. We must keep our options open or the entire conversation becomes pointless.

Having therefore discussed the word belief in absurd detail, the actual reason for belief in god, religion, or other things should become obvious: beliefs exist because they have some benefit at some level of our existence. Wicca regularly plays with the notions of religious belief many people have been taught, so I feel it is likely expanding upon why we humans *might* believe can clarify both Wiccan belief and our interactions with the rest of humanity. If nothing else, discussion of the topic may allow us to make educated guesses regarding why we believe something and the next guy over does not.

Physiological Belief

The inevitable result of the current direction of science is the interpretation of belief as something inherent to human physiology, not something developed as a result of society or mental need but something within our physical bodies. Belief or non-belief are difficult to measure, and as a result of this, each physiological study focuses on some aspect of what we might consider the vast field of belief, such as morality or atheism.

Morality is, in some ways, fairly easy to study by examining case studies of frontal brain damage. We can observe the case of Phineas Gage, a railway foreman who, in 1848, had an iron tamping rod enter his skull after an explosion. This rod destroyed a good chunk of his pre-frontal cortex but left him otherwise unharmed, resulting in a sort of moral lobotomy. He went from a responsible man who was viewed by friends and family to be highly moral to what can probably be described as an obnoxious bore. Viewed alone we could easily chalk this change up to post-traumatic stress disorder and a reaction to the way persons in the 19th century viewed deformity, but Gage was just the Ripley's Believe it Or Not of pre-frontal cortex destruction. Hundreds of people with similar injuries from less spectacular cases have had similar results, but let's face it, freshman psychology students don't want to hear about the popular kid who whacked his head on the windshield and turned his prefrontal cortex into a mass of goop when we can instead study a guy who was doing something none of us is likely to ever do and is safely enough in the past that we don't have to worry about the effect of his injury on his family and friends.

People with damage to the pre-frontal cortex are as capable as you and I of telling you all the morality they learned in their life. They can quote passages from sacred books, rules for polite behavior, even tell you the results of negative behavior in the past, but somewhere in their brain that knowledge misses when it translates itself into actual behavior. This factoid is a pretty damaging blow to people whose morality says that if you know it you will use it. The science on people born with this damage is sketchier, as it seems to indicate that this moral center will move, but if you are familiar at all with the localization of brain structures this should not be surprising. Before a certain age, huge chunks of the brain can be removed and the remaining parts of the brain will control areas of the body we know to be controlled by the missing parts of the brain.

Still, if there is a localized brain area for morality, we can say that there is a human tendency for it. Or can we? Certainly there are localized areas in the brain we never use if we don't encounter the stimuli needed to turn them on, but the space doesn't go to waste. For example, MRIs of blind persons result in images of activity in the areas generally reserved for sight, images that simply would not be there if the area could only be used for one thing. While it is likely some sort of evolutionary tendency landed functional morality in one spot in our brain, it isn't impossible that it's just by chance that morality (or, perhaps it is better to say 'polite behavior') clusters in this one spot. Just because there is this spot doesn't prove that we inherit morality from our ancestors, especially when you realize that there is no proof our most evil villains had brain damage — as well as no ethical way to prove that a person raised without any form of morality wouldn't use that part of the brain for something else altogether.

There is, unfortunately, no Phineas Gage of atheism, no person who was struck in a phenomenal accident and lost only his belief in any god. We've seen atheism in people who've had trauma, people who were religious before their trauma and after their trauma were not, but their belief in a god was not the sole thing about them that changed. This is where the stickiness of redefining belief catches up with us. How can we say there is a physiological component unless we can point to the removal of the component as removing the redefined quantity we call belief? No study can show that we stop believing a certain way after a removal of a body part. To even begin discussing belief in this manner we first have to qualify it in a way that makes it nonsensical for a religious discussion. Belief must become quantifiable; it must be something for which you can demonstrate its lack has an effect.

This all sounds very confusing, so I will try to explain with an anecdote. In her senior level psychological statistics class, a friend of mine was trying to find out if there was a hereditary indicator for religious fervor. As her research material, she was using a database of biographical information on separated families and a similar general biographical database. The entries included brief autobiographical sections, and she categorized "highly religious" those people who mentioned things like "God" and "Jesus" in that brief statement. Bear in mind most of these things read like a singles ad: "Hi, my name is John Doe; I'm a divorced father of four who likes to play golf." With the brevity of the statement, as it was under a paragraph in length, religion was probably very important to people who included it.

She was trucking along fine, actually finding a mild statistical correlation, when she came to a set of scores she didn't know how to interpret. On three of the matched pairs, one person was aggressively religious, and the other would probably be seen as equally aggressively nonreligious. She decided to do a statistical analysis of the data with and without these three pairs (that her sample was very small was a known flaw of her study, but a correlation in a small sample can be used to justify a larger study, so most people who are formally trained in such things have experience with large and small samples) and discuss the results in her paper. The professor's reaction was a bit surprising, in that he felt that under her operational definition of religious fervor (bringing it up during the autobiographical lines) these three pairs represented persons being fervently religious, even though the religion varied. For the three "aggressive non-religionists" the religion (as defined by the study) of choice was atheism, but the behavior was identical to the religionists. Since she was studying behavior, he suggested she should avoid rating the quality of content of their statement, when claiming to be rating only the presence of content.

For what it's worth her study only demonstrated that more research was needed. However, it also demonstrates the flaw in trying to study "belief" in such a context. What we are really studying is behavior regarding those beliefs.

Whether or not that is a valid indicator of the reality of those beliefs is a really good question. It is possible that we currently lack the tools to accurately research anything beyond behavior and what we think it indicates about belief. This doesn't make this discussion of belief as a physiological quantity pointless, but does render it highly esoteric. At best, it cannot be truly discussed beyond the theoretical, but, again, that doesn't make it not worth discussing.

The Sociological Benefits of Belief

One of the main benefits of discussing belief from a sociological point of view is that we understand that the social nature of man is beneficial to him. Therefore, we can discuss the sociological aspects of belief in terms of their *benefit* to man. This changes the parameters of the discussion significantly. No longer are we discussing the *presence* of belief, because as a society we can see them in churches, temples, rites and practices. Whether the individual holds the belief or not is insignificant, because enough of the society, or enough of the important members of society, hold the belief for it to be a perceptible thing in the society.

Perceptibility aids study a lot, because when we are discussing what we feel or suspect is present we are in a completely different boat than when discussing the number of churches or faith groups in a town. The first is something we can't necessarily quantify; we can only study behavior or language and make assumptions. The second can be counted and discussed in terms of literal numbers. This makes it easy to study, but requires an assumption on our part that the presence of buildings and faith groups is indicative of belief. Note the distinction: not only may we perceive a thing in a society because of percentage of society or numbers, we may also perceive a thing because enough important people—or at least loud people—promote the thing.

Digressing for a second, Wicca is a good example of the loud people phenomena. It is something that is small enough in society that without the loud people, general society would probably have no knowledge of it at all, but also large enough that the loud people aren't necessarily the best representatives of Wicca as a whole. This is a strong indication of the problem with using visible things as proof of belief—it can slant our view toward the noisiest beliefs, not those that are most commonly held. For example, if you travel outside of the United States, you often find a perception of us as aggressive Christian evangelicals, which is a minority by far of our citizens, but those that fit that description are so loud and so aggressive that those who haven't experienced the reality of life outside that subculture have no clue that we really aren't all like that by a long shot.

Putting that digression behind us, when we see mankind's social nature as beneficial to him, the social effects of religious belief become beneficial enough that it explains why they exist. Put less obscurely, mankind develops religious beliefs because it provides him with a social benefit—and that it provides a social benefit is reason enough for its existence and development. Religious belief, however, has a lot to say about what is and is not good, so it is inevitable that we should ask ourselves if social benefit is always the best thing, from a moral standpoint.

To give you an idea of the distinction I'm making here, I want you to imagine a gruesome culture with an institutionalized system of rape and factory-like child rearing. In this imaginary culture, men and children do all of the work, most of which is related to warfare, and women of childbearing age are put to work entertaining the men and having babies, regardless of how they feel about the situation. Women who can't have children are put to death. This culture's stated goal is to create as many people as possible, as fast as possible, to become soldiers so they can take over all the countries around them. Viewing their stated goal, their disgusting system is highly beneficial: all persons are engaged in the production of weapons or soldiers or the care of the soldiers. From a moral standpoint, however, I hope none of us see this culture as anything but atrocious and extreme.

So, from a sociological standpoint, we have to view the concept of "benefit" without moral qualities before we discuss the benefits—and thus reasons for existence—of religious belief. This is a good thought exercise for any purpose, because the hairs of wariness should be pricking up whenever we hear someone say that something is "good" merely because it is "beneficial." Just as in our discussion of evolution in which we mentioned that the development of large fat deposits was beneficial to humankind—despite the fact that obesity is correlated with numerous diseases, we need to see benefits as relative quantities. A thing may be beneficial to one of society's goals while being detrimental to another. If, for example, the gruesome imaginary culture above also had the goal of having every individual be a self-actualized, content being they are failing miserably in that goal with their current institutions.

So having beaten the redefinition dragon back into its den once again, we can tackle the basic sociological benefits of religious belief. The first should seem obvious using the example above: religious belief can illustrate the stated goals of a community. Some people assign divine creation to religious beliefs, and out of deference to them I will refrain from stating that religious beliefs are designed to promote the goals of the community around them... but neither will I claim that the goals of the community are created around some pre-existing religious belief. Both happen in modern cultures, so it is better to not discuss which came first but merely to discuss that they are interlinked. This linkage can allow a culture to point to a tangible thing—the written documents of its faith, for example—and say "We believe *this*, and we do what we do to achieve what it claims we will achieve."

For most of written Western history, this goal was the creation on earth of a kingdom that worked in the same way the realm of the gods worked. We tend to mistakenly view this as a Christian thing, but even Augustus was viewed as one of a number of pre-Christian rulers with a kingdom that was a mirror of the Kingdom above. He ruled Rome, his cronies claimed, as Jupiter ruled the Universe.

It wasn't just rulers that were the mirror of heaven. Cities, from Babylon to Jerusalem, as well as some castles and citadels throughout the world, were said to have divine counterparts or to be reflections of things above. While it is somewhat likely that this idea comes from the known effect of reflection—few regular sailors have not seen the occasional upside down lighthouse, or my personal favorite, a fish leaping down from (and back into) the sky—the fact remains that by seeing the way things are on earth as a reflection of the way things are in the divine hereafter, you stumble upon the second sociological benefit of religious belief: the justification of the status quo.

I find myself relieved that we've discussed the idea of a benefit not necessarily being a good thing at this point. Few people will agree that claiming something is right because it has been that way for a long time is always a moral claim. It's more often that justifying the status quo allows society to resist change. While having a negative effect on some things, this can also be seen as having some positive effect, as well. If you believe that your king rules because he is chosen by a god to do so, you are resistant to revolution and talk of his overthrow. Regardless of the fairness, or lack thereof, of monarchy, a well run one is generally preferable to a country in the throes of revolution. The end result of revolution may be bad or good (and our world has certainly seen both!) but the state of revolution is, well, revolting. During a revolution nearly everything that makes society preferable to living alone is disrupted, whether it be shipping lanes or the ability to leave your house and have a reasonable assumption of its safety. When you see the status quo without blinders, you can see why it is good for society to maintain it, or at least maintain parts of it.

A similar benefit to society is that religious belief creates an illusion of conformity. If you think that the next guy over believes what you believe, you're less afraid of him, and more willing to put at least a small amount of trust in him. An illusion of conformity is not the same as a desire for everyone to act the same way; rather it is the belief that you and all of your neighbors share some fundamental similarities that, in reality, you probably don't. Truth be told, it is unlikely that the same things that bring you to tears will get your neighbors crying. The joke you find amusing may be quite insipid to them, all things considered. If there was genuine conformity of belief, we'd only need one type of cuisine, and one type of television station. As boring as that seems to you and me, it would not be boring to a people who only wanted one thing. Nonetheless, the illusion of conformity lends strength to our points of view and our actions. We do nothing alone when we assume the next guy over does the same thing.

Another pair of benefits to society found in religious belief is that religious beliefs can justify the laws of the land and dictate codes of behavior. Not killing, for example, is found both in the religious laws and secular laws of the vast majority of societies. By having this one-two punch of religious and secular, it both lends credibility from religious to secular and vice versa. If, for example, our law says do not kill, and a god says do not kill, then our laws are "right with that god." A person at odds with secular laws cannot justify breaking them by referring instead to religious law and vice versa. This is not limited to the extremes of murder and the like, but also in how we treat each other. Ideally, this fusion of religious belief and secular law will mean that the laws and the beliefs make sense to the people holding them. The inevitable result of holding beliefs that make no sense is cognitive dissonance, and that comes with all its associated problems.

Psychological Benefits of Belief

Having covered the genetic and social benefits of religious belief we find ourselves discussing the most intuitive of reasons for belief—the psychological ones. Even the social benefits were truly based in psychology, more about making individuals feel safe and whole than making society safe and whole. The problem here is that the majority of individuals need to be in good condition for society to function well, so making the distinction between which benefits are social and which ones are mental is a bit of a game. Ideally, the social benefits also benefit the psyche of the individual, and when they don't, the society usually changes.

Again I'm going to limit the discussion here to the psychological *benefits* of belief. The theory here is that religious belief exists as a psychological entity because it has some psychological benefit. As with the social benefits, psychological benefits are not solely the domain of religious belief, can be accomplished by means other than religious belief and certainly are not provided by all forms of religious belief. To discuss this rationally, we first have to ask what the goals of psychology are. Since we assume the purpose of psychology is to have a healthy mind, then anything that is beneficial to achieving a healthy mind serves the same purpose as psychology. It has a psychological benefit, to use our previously discussed terminology.

As with all such statements, we have to define "psychologically healthy." Is it, as some would suggest, merely the state of being without significant psychological illness? Certainly there are people throughout the world that you and I would consider devoid of significant mental illness but not necessarily healthy! Likewise, we can't base psychological health on happiness, because I can assure you some of the worst psychological cases we can study involve people who are completely happy with their situations. The school of psychology by which the mind is being studied defines psychological wellness. To the neuroscientist, it is the operation of the brain within ideal working parameters, to the cognitive scholar, it is thought that works within ideal parameters, and to the behaviorist, it is behavior. As simple as that seems, psychology has few people who do not work across such boundaries. Psychological well-being, then, can be defined as the brain, thoughts and behaviors all working within ideal parameters.

What those parameters are can be judged on three basic levels. The first is sheer functionality. The child who is abused and develops a negative coping mechanism to stop the abuse or psychologically deal with it is working within the parameters of functionality. This is the most basic psychological state of function—the ability to think, feel and do at the minimum level needed to avoid dying or losing contact with reality. When this child grows up, he or she may not be able to hold a job, have a decent relationship or make responsible decisions, but the child grew up and has some basic knowledge about reality.

The second parameter is independence, which most of us achieve. This is essentially the ability to hold a job, have decent relationships and make responsible decisions. Note the use of the word "ability." This does not imply that the independence parameter of psychological well-being indicates that we will make the best decisions, but does imply that we have that capacity. Compared with the sheer functionality parameter, the difference is thinking through the result of our actions. The just-functioning individual is essentially working from a state of fear, moving from one fearful situation to another, with the essential goal of avoiding fear and pain. The independence parameter, on the other hand, allows fear and pain if they are seen as a means to an end.

This leaves us with a third parameter, beyond independence and into leadership — not merely leadership of armies or governments, but leadership of families, employees and friends. The ability to lead people is hardly something we need to survive, and certainly persons stuck in the independence or sheer functionality stages can lead if it means achieving their goals, however minimal those goals are. This parameter, in the triarchic view of the world I hold, is the "above average" parameter. The triarchic view sees most of existence as having three levels, which I term Not Functioning, Functioning and Functioning While Innovating, or "superfunctioning." A superfunctioning individual is not merely getting by, and not merely living well, but is making achievements that can be viewed as extraordinary in their efficacy.

Ideally, superfunctioning is the goal of all psychological assistance that is not based on repairing damaged mechanisms of thought or behavior. Put another way, superfunctioning is the goal of psychology once the baseline of average functioning has been achieved. I am hesitant to discuss this in terms of humanistic psychology, because I know from my personal experience of the study of psychology that the invocation of the names Maslow or Rogers instantly results in a core group of people blanking out all you have to say. I began my college studies in social work, and came around to biology by way of psychology, so I can speak with some authority on the different worlds represented by humanism on one side and physiology on the other.

That being acknowledged, a good holistic student recognizes the good in all fields that apply to a given situation, so I will use Maslow's Hierarchy of Needs to describe the path towards superfunctioning, although Dale Carnegie's *How to Win Friends and Influence People* or even Plato's *Republic* would probably do as well. Maslow's hierarchy is generally portrayed as a pyramid. At the bottom is what we need the most, and in the greatest quantity: survival. Without the base of survival, the next step up the pyramid becomes moot. As you climb the pyramid, equal height (but not equal width) is given to security, social acceptance, self-esteem and, at the top, self-actualization. Maslow's self-actualized individuals, like Plato's philosophers and Carnegie's influential elite, are superfunctioners.

Using Maslow's hierarchy, with the eventual goal of self-actualization, we can see where religion would fall in the psychological well-being department. It is not a quantity, like air or food, which we need for the baseline of survival. However, religious belief can be described in each of the next ascending steps, again, not as the sole provider of that step's goal, but as a tool toward that end, and it grows in its usefulness the higher you go. For example, religious belief can help establish a goal of security by teaching the individual that all things happen in a cycle or a pattern, and that all things happen for a reason. While not the true security of a steady home or caring parents, the belief that the world is not going to come abruptly to an end, or, that if it does, you'll be magically whisked away to safety, is a step towards thinking securely about yourself.

Of course, there is a physiological component of the need for security. A highly non-secure life inevitably leads to all the stress conditions we are familiar with: heart disease, hypertension, migraines and the like. Without the ability to know where you will spend the night or know where your food is coming from, you have less hope... and when you have no hope, things like suicide or toxic drug use seem like reasonable ideas. Therefore, unlike the things we need for survival, things we need for security allow us to continue to live. A wise person once said that you cannot think on the tragedy of your life and whether or not you should try to continue it when you are under the ocean gasping for air. Your body will do what it thinks will help you survive. Your mood, attitudes and religious beliefs will have little or no effect on what the body is going to do.

The next step up, social acceptance, covers part of the reasons for belief we discussed in the previous section of this topic. Mankind is a social animal, a political (literally "of the polis") animal, prone to make and live in society. Interestingly enough, this social acceptance at the smallest level — the level of the family — can be enough for some people. Other people need a broad social acceptance to feel right with the world. Religious belief, when shared, can create an instant community. Perhaps most interestingly, religious belief can create an illusion of community where there is not one. A lone Christian Roman, in the early days of the faith, could believe that he alone in his remote community was going to find the kingdom of god, simply because he was part of a far-flung community of Christians as a whole. An interesting aspect of that faith in particular was that any persecution, real or imagined, was seen as reinforcing membership in the community of Christians as a whole. We see this today occasionally in Wicca, where young, new members see real or imagined persecution as a flaw with the non-Wiccan community and as proof that they are somehow genuinely Wiccan. As a member of the gay community utterly accepted by my family for what I am, I can assure you that this "You're a real member of the minority community once you've been persecuted" phenomena is something intrinsic to human nature, not religion specifically.

The next level on Maslow's pyramid, and perhaps the focus of too much activity by psychologists, is self-esteem. As indicated previously, religion can give you an idea of self-esteem, both by teaching you to take what would normally be esteem-breaking situations — having your beliefs criticized — and turning them into esteem-building situations — like thinking that everyone who is criticizing you is wrong and going to hell. Religious belief, like other beliefs about our direction and ourselves, can be either esteem-building or esteem-shattering, depending on what the beliefs teach about the individual. Some religions teach that mankind is a dirty, rotten, horrible creature wriggling on the earth like a worm. Such a view of one's self is hardly beneficial to self-esteem, but if you can believe that everyone else is like that worm and you, by grace, by saying the right prayer, or whatever are not like that worm, it can be beneficial to your self-esteem. In my experience, religion has done as much harm as good to self-esteem, so I am uncomfortable labeling it a benefit to self-esteem. Certainly it *can* be a benefit, and that is a reason for us to hold beliefs, but it is certainly often enough a detriment.

The last level on Maslow's pyramid, the level of superfunctioning, is self-actualization. An individual whose needs are met on the parts of the pyramid below self-actualization is capable of this level — a level at which Maslow hypothesizes a person is utterly accepting of himself. While aware of his faults, the person is detached and autonomous, has strong relationships and liberal social values and is essentially an all-around good guy. The problem with this is that the more you read Maslow's idea of a self-actualized person the more it sounds like a list of traits that are not only not held by any one person but are often in stark contrast to each other. A perfectionist who feels his flaws deeply and painfully is not self-actualized when you focus on self-acceptance as a fundamental quality of self-actualization, but is self-actualized if you see awareness of imperfection as a fundamental quality of it. Ideally, we are told, a person in this self-actualized state of being is a balance of these contradictions, but the problem with Maslow's theory is that it was reverse-engineered from case studies of people who were successful and happy. As a result, he came up with a group of people with certain qualities, but not really a group of qualities manifest in each one of them.

As one of my friends put it, the only way to be seen as a self-actualized person is to be dead and unable to defend the interpretation of your thoughts as thoughts of the self-actualized. While I do not take that strong an edge, I am uncomfortable speaking of the attainment of the individual qualities of self-actualized people as attainment of a singular thing. People who are superfunctioners function as such in multiple ways, which often cannot be understood as a singular quality. To make it clearer, I've used the parable of the water main break in the past. In this parable a group of people are standing at the top of a hill when a water main break causes water to begin rushing down the hill. A few of the people, the "non-functioners" respond to the water rushing down the hill towards their homes in ways that do no one any good. They run around in circles, screaming "Water! Water!" They stay still and hope the water won't hurt their homes or get them wet. They run blindly in whatever direction they were facing. They chant at the water, or tell it to go away, all to no avail.

The next group of individuals, the functioners, each respond in ways that make more sense. One calls the water company, another tells his wife to get the sump pump going in the basement. A few run away, but they run toward higher ground. Several of them try to stop the water with tried and true methods-sand bags, closing all the windows, clearing off sewer grates. The third group, the superfunctioners, may try the same methods as the functioners, but seeing them not having enough of an effect, they begin to try different things. One fells a nearby tree to redirect the water into the street, another gets the functioners to form a bucket brigade and work together and a third starts digging a ditch. Some of the superfunctioners' ideas work, and some of them do not, but their quality lies in innovation.

Rather than call these superfunctioners self-actualized, I think of them as situationally innovative. The ones with the highest level of superfunctioning can apply that ability to anything they encounter — social problems, burnt dinners, bad news, emotional stress... it doesn't matter what the situation is, it is their ability to function above the norm in that situation that is important. People can look like non-functioners or superfunctioners because of knowledge. A civil engineer might not be a superfunctioner if he knows that if he digs a ditch the water will take his lower ground over the raised street. A child who has never seen rushing water may not be a non-functioner because she thinks it will respond to her telling it to go away. It is the way they think, not the knowledge they have that makes the difference. If that little girl drowns because she stands at the foot of her porch telling the water to go away while it rises slowly above her ankles while she could be climbing away from it we do have to wonder how functional she is. If the engineer drowns in the ditch because he simply cannot grasp the fact that he can't dig fast enough to have an effect, we must have similar questions about his functionality.

Whether you call people who work well on a psychological level functioners, self-actualized individuals, Buddhas or mages, it does not matter what the mechanism is that is making them so psychologically well off. We know that there are certain aspects of thought that help these people be so well off psychologically. These people are self-motivated, sure of themselves, not afraid to innovate and willing to take reasonable chances among other qualities. We know that religious belief can be a factor of many of those aspects of thought; beliefs *can* help a person achieve those states. Therefore, we know religious belief is a positive factor in some individual psychology. We can see religious belief as a tool toward some of the individual qualities that Maslow lumped into the state of self-actualization.

With this in mind, religious belief becomes one method by which a person can achieve superfunctioning. If it is positive, growth-inspiring and assists the person toward better knowledge of the self, the divine and the universe, religious belief has an inherent psychological benefit, leaving religious individuals in psychological states early psychology taught could only be reached with psychoanalysis. Religious beliefs, whether those of a fringe religion or of a mainstream one, can often do the same things as secular beliefs, and that simple fact is the result of contentions between religion and psychology going back decades. There is no bigger fear for some faiths than the fear that their adherents could find out that the benefits of their religion could be matched by therapy, and no bigger fear for many therapies than the fear that their adherents could find the same benefits in religion.

That being said, when we qualify religious belief as having a psychological reason to exist by virtue of its psychological benefit, we leave unanswered the question of whether or not it should exist. For example, Post-Traumatic

Stress Disorder (PTSD) exists, but very rarely benefits the individual's psyche. Many disorders have the benefit of allowing those afflicted by them to cope with unspeakable trauma but have the side effect of making it difficult to deal with normal life. Even if we leave disorders like clinical depression or schizophrenia out of the equation by virtue of their organic nature, we find ourselves faced with the fact that the human mind often develops things that are not beneficial to it. If religious beliefs can have psychological benefits, can they also have psychological detriments?

Healthy and Unhealthy Religious Beliefs

The inevitable result of discussion of the benefits of religious belief on people and society is a discussion of the problems beliefs can involve. These problematic belief systems have been called everything from toxic spirituality to cults and range from the physiologically destructive to the socially destructive. Certainly the socially destructive forms of religion needn't be discussed in our current world. The struggle of Abrahamic Religion against Abrahamic Religion (even perceived Abrahamic Religion, as in those attacks on the United States that assume we are all Christian) covers more than half of our evening news.

Few people would agree that sects of religions that encourage killing yourself and others, whether by suicide bombings, machine guns, hand grenades, poisoned food or drink or setting yourself on fire, are physiologically healthy. The other physiologically destructive beliefs are less coherent, and are perhaps told best in a parable a Christian doctor once emailed me:

A man, distraught over the death of his son is walking along the road when the tears in his eyes blind him to the drunk driver who swerves and kills him. He gets up to heaven whereupon he finds that his sorrow and anger are not only not gone, but also made stronger. Here he is, face to face with a god who just killed him and his family, and instead of feeling blissful, he feels miserable.

God reaches down and touches the man, and asks him how it is that he could be angry when he wanted to die and was dead and wanted his son to die and he was dead.

The man looks at God in shock, and assumes (correctly) that the question is some kind of test.

"How can you say that I wanted my son to die?," he says.

"Your actions tell me so," God says, "Three times I tried to help and three times you spurned me."

"How can you say that," the man says, "I never spurned you! I would never spurn you, let alone three times!"

God chuckles, and says, "I've heard that before." Then he shows the man the moment his son climbed out on the branch of the tree he would soon fall from. He shows the man the rope that lay at his feet as the man prayed his son would safely get down. "I gave man the ability to use tools, and here you spurn it for prayer. Prayer is a tool, but a rope is a better one in that case. I gave you a rope. What more could you wish?"

Next God shows the man his son's fall, a fall that could've been prevented had the man tossed the child the rope. God shows the man the stick jutting from the boy's leg and simultaneously, for he is God and can do that, shows the man the safety films he'd seen a dozen times in high school on how to deal with such an injury. "I gave mankind the ability to know how to heal himself and others, and the ability to teach others, the ability to create technology to share this knowledge, and what do you do?"

God shows the man touching the stick and praying that it be removed from the boy and that the wound be healed. He shows the man the fact that he called the films to man's memory. "I showed you how, and why, and you did not look! You prayed and I answered! What more could I do? I am not one to force you to action!"

Next God shows the man the one who answered the 911 call he had made. God congratulates the man, but sternly says, "See, here you did not expect that I should call you the ambulance, did you? Why is it alright to do for yourself only sometimes?"

The ambulance arrives, and the paramedics remove the stick, but the boy has lost a lot of blood, and the man refuses a blood transfusion on religious grounds. Here, God shows the man his fury, "I created man so that the blood of one, freely given, can save another! I gave man the cells, the knowledge to find them and type them! The knowledge to save each other! Here you throw that knowledge upon the ground, dare to trample it in my name because of a verse in my book a mere mortal claims to know the knowledge of. I have millions of people, and less than half of one percent believe that interpretation of the verse. Was that not clue enough? I gave you the knowledge that it is my will that you be fruitful and multiply, and have spared sons in the past, did that not impart some knowledge of my self to you? Eve gave you knowledge, as her descendent, of the difference between good and evil! Do not claim to not have known you were wrong!"

God shows the man his son die once again, and looks at the man in anger. "Only my son had my permission to die by his father's hand. You are not I, and your righteousness is the sin of Pride. Repent or face all of paradise with my scorn upon you, the true meaning of Hell."

...And with that, the man finds himself before the tree, the rope at his feet, and immediately throws the rope to the boy, who fashions a knot and climbs down to safety. His son looks at him, tears in his eyes and says "Thank God for that rope! And thank God you were there! I could've died."

The man held his son and wept, knowing
there are far worse things than death.

If the parable above makes your skin crawl, it should. It
has all of the subtlety of a Chick Tract, without the hatred
and stupid logical flaws that make them kitsch. Even
though it is inherently, desperately and unrepentantly
Christian (save where it reeks of Frank Capra), it shows the
basic theological differences between religious beliefs that
expect a god to interact with man in his most mundane
moments and those that teach the divine gave us these
brains for a reason. Religious beliefs that spurn, for example, medicine that saves lives, are not healthy from a
physiological standpoint when they cause people to die.
The concept of physiological health is pretty easy for us to
understand because sickness, death and pain are pretty
easy to perceive.

That's not to say prayer is a bad thing, it's just not a
substitution for action. It can give us an illusion of action
where we have no ability to act. If you are, oh, watching a
plane crash into a building, praying is just about the only
thing you can do. When our car went into a 65mph skid on
a sudden patch of icy road on US 15 one Christmas day,
Phoenix steered and prayed, I watched in terror and prayed
and my son screamed at the top of his lungs. We went 360
degrees, across four lanes and ended up facing the correct
direction in a lane parallel to the one we'd been in and two
lanes away from any traffic. Once we could breathe, we
thanked Phoenix, the gods and the car for all doing their
part to save us, but the fact remains that she didn't take her
hand off the wheel and hope everything went well; the road
had too many obstacles, and she steered away from them.
We missed a huge sign that would've totaled the car, several feet of concrete divider and going off into a ditch. Once
stopped, we could see we'd come within inches of about
seven things that would've resulted in severe injury.

At no time during that incident did we stop what we
were doing and decide to pray instead. On a personal note,
I think I stand as a testimony to the power of prayer. I walk
on a knee totaled on three different occasions with nothing
but pain, have a physical condition that requires occasional

hospitalization that has never struck when I could not afford to be hospitalized (despite that being the situation most of the time) and have numerous incidents in my life that fall well within the number of random events expected in my short time on earth and always happen at the moment I am best equipped to deal with them. I even met Phoenix, before she became my wife of 10 years, days after discovering I needed a roommate to get by and less than a month after she'd decided to move out of her apartment.

The difference between healthy and unhealthy beliefs above is that in a life full of prayer, I never once used *only* prayer, and that's probably the gist of the majority of toxic beliefs, the belief that you don't have to do things for yourself because your god will provide. It is great to think that your god will provide. I certainly subscribe to the belief that the divine doesn't "close a door without opening a window," but I think we can all think of persons who'd stand at the open window thinking how nice it would be for the door to open so they could leave or get fresh air.

In general, I define as toxic any belief that results in your acting one whit below your ability. If your belief that we are all dirty rotten sinners makes you avoid becoming as great a person as you can, I define that as a toxic belief for you. If your beliefs make you think that women are lesser than men and should have fewer rights, or that gay marriages aren't as valid as straight ones, those beliefs, the moment they affect the way you treat your fellow human beings, are also toxic.

Note the distinction made here between action and thought. Many people in this world think that all mankind are horrible rotten worms in the eyes of their god but nonetheless try to be the best worm they can be. Many people think that America is the enemy and never make a move against her, or that Israel is corrupt and never strap a bomb to their bodies. There are people who think that the reason their boss was so mean to them yesterday was because Mercury is retrograde but still try to reconcile with the boss immediately, regardless of the astrological implications of the day. All of these people have negative beliefs that are perfectly healthy because they are not allowing them to interfere with otherwise healthy relationships to reality.

Put most simply, a belief is unhealthy when it contributes to actions that are destructive to the mind, body, society or other people. A belief can be negative, even wrong, but it is not unhealthy unless and until it is a strong factor in creating an unhealthy life. If you are using your beliefs to violate or oppress people, including yourself, that is not quite the same as thinking that people should be violated or oppressed. We can live in a world where we hope people don't have negative beliefs, even if they aren't toxic, but as a proponent of free thought I believe that we should allow folk to think however they wish until those thoughts begin to affect their behavior.

An exercise I am fond of doing, both by myself and with my students, is to look at the negative things you are doing in life, smoking, for example, and trying to find the beliefs that allow you to do those things. Those beliefs may or may not be toxic, but they at least warrant trying to understand. As a personal example, I am a fairly hypercritical person. The reason I am is because I believe that people should always try their best, try to speak fairly, try to win people over to their side when they are right and give everyone the same amount of baseline respect. For example, if I met you on the street, I would treat you the same as the next guy over unless and until you did something to distinguish yourself from the masses.

For me, my hypercritical nature is turned toward no one with the level of ferocity it is turned toward myself. In the past, this has resulted in my not finishing things I've started because I can't get them right enough, dropping out of classes, fiddling with things that were finished enough already and much more. It has also resulted in a number of physiological conditions associated with intense and long-term stress. It was essential for me to examine my beliefs to keep this from becoming a set of completely toxic beliefs and change the direction my life was going. I had to change from a desire for perfection to a desire for the best me I can be in order for my life to be healthy. I will probably always have that struggle.

What I don't have now, even though I used to, are unhealthy beliefs about what the world expects of me. The beliefs are often negative, at the least some sort of borderline narcissism that dictates that while good enough is alright for the rest of humanity, I have to be better than that or else something terrible will happen. I may have fairly negative beliefs about what I'm doing, but as those negative beliefs are not affecting my functionality, they aren't unhealthy.

That may be, perhaps, the best lesson I can give you from this topic, and I'll end with it in classical fashion by restating it:

Any belief of yours which makes you miserable, which hurts people, damages society or damages your body should be examined in excruciating detail, and if necessary, changed. You are not required to believe that you are horrible, nor that life is miserable, nor must you involve yourself with those that believe as such. Put simply, you have the right to beliefs that make life worthwhile, whole, good and fun and the right to challenge any belief that does not affirm life and living in such a manner.

Recommended Reading for Topic Nine:

The Biological Basis for Morality, Edward O. Wilson
http://www.theatlantic.com/issues/98apr/biomoral.htm

The Neurobiology of Morals, Charles Jennings
http://www.nature.com/nsu/991021/991021-6.html

Collected works of Abraham Maslow
http://www.maslow.com/

Discussion Questions for Topic Nine:

9.1. What is a belief?

9.2. What is meant by "instinct is based on the belief that the instinctual action is preferable to inaction?"

9.3. Why is it "unfortunate" that there "is no Phineas Gage of Atheism?"

9.4. What are some socially beneficial aspects of belief?

9.5. What is meant by socially beneficial? Psychologically beneficial?

9.6. Must something be "good" to be beneficial? Give examples.

9.7. Is Maslow's theory a good definition of psychological health?

9.8. What is the difference between a healthy belief and an unhealthy one?

9.9. The author states that beliefs which cause a certain group of people to be violated or oppressed are only toxic when they result in the violation or oppression of those people. Do you agree? Are there limits to who should be given equal treatment or chances?

9.10 What unhealthy beliefs do you struggle with? How do you cope?

Wicca in Practice III: Mental Experiments and Validity Testing

In our modern world it is often convenient to relegate the running of simulations or validity testing to computers, but the idea goes back hundreds of years before the computer was invented. It is the core of the scientific method, the idea of creating a hypothesis and testing it. With some types of data, the experimentation is intuitive. If you wish to see if chemicals X and Y mix, then you mix them, right?

A student of macroscale chemistry knows this is untrue. The first step of such an experiment is conducted in the library and in the brain. Even if chemicals X and Y have never been mixed, chemicals similar to X and Y certainly may have been mixed. If these chemicals are so rare that they've never encountered each other, their cost—let alone the risk of explosion or another dangerous reaction—is enough to warrant an experiment in the mind before an experiment in the lab.

Mind experiments are exactly what they appear to be, running a simulation of the possible real experiment in your head or on paper. If chemical X acts like octane in all known situations, and chemical Y acts like water in all known simulations, you'd presuppose that they'd act like octane and water in your experiment, and you'd then run an experiment to see if that was how they acted. If they acted in a way other than expected, you'd need to run it a few times to see why it acted the way it did, maybe even developing a whole new branch of organic chemistry along the way, who knows?

The mind experiment in this problem serves as a specific type of logical testing—a validity test. A validity test answers the question of whether or not your expectations of a thing are valid. In the above example, the validity of presupposing chemical X will act like octane and chemical Y will act like water is questioned and backed up with research. The assumption may be wrong in the end, but you didn't make the assumption for no reason whatsoever.

Since this is a book on religion, I'll leave chemicals X and Y on the lab table where they lay in one vial with two layers. They seem happy that way, and did what I expected them to do (and—being a mad scientist—I *do* have an imp-like assistant to clean up such things).

A common belief of those who study religion, magic, metaphysics and the like is that things like science, history and study are detrimental to their studies. The fact that this ignorant hypothesis was foisted upon the world will never cease to amaze me, for it is absolutely untrue. If you wish to be taken seriously in your quest for knowledge, or to make real discoveries, you need to use as many resources as possible. No one source of knowledge will blind you to other sources, although it may make you reconsider some of your questions.

For example, let's look at a phenomena used in one movie that has tragically brought many youngsters into Wicca with grandiose ideas about the faith—the ability to change eye color with a simple spell. The producers of this movie had Wiccans and other magical practitioners on staff but still paid a huge chunk of change to have this done digitally. That, in and of itself, should clue you in to the validity of that spell. Nonetheless, let's imagine you wish to do this magically.

The first stop in your research should be your library. Get every book you can find on Witchcraft, magic and sorcery, and see if any of them tell you how. No? Perhaps a visit to the fashion section reveals the fact that most people have multi-chromatic eyes and by dressing in certain ways can change the way they look. For example, the pumpkin orange shirt I'm wearing right now makes my brown eyes look very green. My son's eyes, nearly the same color as mine, look black when he wears dark green or blue—but since you are looking for magic, not color theory, you put those down, as well as the history of contact lenses and a text on how the eye works. By now, you should begin to question the validity of the idea that a spell will change your eye color, but a few mind experiments may be in order.

In your mental notebook, or a real one, you write the following hypothesis:

A spell can change eye color without contact lenses or another physical device.

Now that you have a hypothesis, you can test the validity of the question. Let's look at the bigger picture: changing your eye color falls under the category of altering the body. People in the Western world are obsessed with this, especially when it comes to losing weight. There is nothing that hasn't been tried to get people to lose weight, and diets, hypnosis, drugs, even surgery are all over the place. Magic, however, is not. In fact, some of the best authors on Ceremonial Magic of the past fifty years or so have been, well, pleasantly plump, and this in a community that will often outright admit to abusing drugs known to make you scrawny.

If weight-loss magic isn't available, even at a premium, you have to ask yourself why. This is the first validity test of a new hypothesis that is relevant to the first one: *If magic is capable of altering the body, why isn't it being used for weight loss in a culture obsessed with weight loss?* Can you say with a high degree of validity that the culture is obsessed with weight loss? I certainly can. Can you say with a high degree of validity that magic isn't being used? Maybe, maybe not... So you refine your hypothesis further, knowing that a finding that magic is being used to lose weight has a lot of relevance to whether or not it can be used to alter the body in another way.

I'm not going to follow this mind experiment to the end, because it's a long process, but it is the foundation of logical discourse. For example, if a Christian tells you to turn him into a frog to prove your religion is real (something that happened to me) you have every right to ask by what means he's arrived at this conclusion. (In my case, I simply said "You first.") Nonetheless, I think that you can see the external use of mind experimentation if you put your brain to work. Rather than developing a hypothesis to see if what you are thinking makes sense, you turn it toward him: "Why would turning you into a frog prove a religion? Why must a religion be proven? What do you mean by religion?"

I find myself in the delicate position of trying to explain something that is simultaneously simple and complex. A mind experiment consists of coming up with a set of data and a set of situations... and then imagining that data being put in those situations. This mind experiment can be as simple as imagining an experiment that you can do in the real world or you can try imagining an experiment it is impossible to run. It consists of creating a set of hypotheses based on known phenomena and imagining the results. It is, essentially, running a computer simulation with a computer with faster processing speed than any we've made and the ability to deal with completely illogical events: the brain.

You do this already to some degree whenever you make a decision about anything. Engaging in mind experiments is nothing more than taking what your brain already does and extending it into realms of thought that you've been told you aren't capable of having. This is the core of this mental discipline, which anyone, regardless of IQ or background, can try.

Mind Experiments and Validity Testing in 5 Easy Steps:

1. Identify the question.
    i. Is it a valid question or is it based on a flawed understanding of the facts?
    ii. Is it part of a bigger question? If so, can you investigate an easier to study part of the bigger question?
    iii. Can it be made easier to study by narrowing its focus instead?
2. If necessary, revise the question, and go back to Step 1.
3. Imagine the answers to the question, or situations in which answers to the question would be found. If possible, do this in a format of "What would happen to data X if exposed to situation Y?"
4. Research, if possible, to back up your claims.
5. Experiment, if possible, to back up your claims.

One method that helps people is to imagine the whole thing as a game. The practice experiment is set up in such a manner. As another form of practice, you can try to reverse engineer what the hypothesis of that experiment was. How was the question narrowed or expanded to be more coherent, if at all?

Practice:

I used a version of this mind experiment in an evolutionary biology paper. The reason why I could not run an experiment should be obvious.

There are two sets of data, the level of altruism in a species and the type of food they are allowed. In all other ways, the herds are the same and they get the same amount of food. Like all herds, the individuals in each herd range from strong to weak, slow to fast, etc. There are no penalties for overeating and no benefit to overeating, although starving will result in death. In all animals, the altruistic or selfish qualities can be passed on to any young that are born, as well as strength, weakness, etc.

Types of Animals:

A: Completely Altruistic. They work as a herd and everyone gets the same amount of food.

B: Completely Selfish. They work as individuals; the strongest get the most food.

C: 50% Altruistic/50% Selfish. The herd is an even mixture.

D: 90% Altruistic/10% Selfish.

E: 90% Selfish/10% Altruistic.

These animals are placed on "playing fields," where the goal of the game is surviving to breed. Offspring has the same tendencies as parents. These are the playing fields, with the amount of food per season on each:

1. Infinite amount of non-hoardable food.

2. The exact amount of non-hoardable food required for all individuals to live.

3. Infinite amount of hoardable food.

4. The exact amount of hoardable food required for all individuals to live.

5. Less non-hoardable food than required for all individuals to live.

6. Less hoardable food than required for all to live.

Non-hoardable foot is essentially grasses. It cannot be stored, and an individual can spend a maximum of 20 hours a day eating it but only needs 8 or 9 hours at an average pace of eating. Hoardable food is essentially food pellets, which the animals can collect 3 times faster than they can eat. To make things easy, we'll assume a hoard is easy to defend, that it is in some mechanism like a hamster's cheek pouches, only infinite in capacity.

The primary goal of the game is to live to the end of the season and the second goal is to breed a new herd. Imagine that each herd is placed on field #1. Remember, they don't interact in any manner; each herd is the sole herd on the field each season. Which members of the herd live to the end of the season? Which herd has the most members go on to breed? Which *new* herd will have the average strength of their herd go up or down. (I arbitrarily chose 1 season as their life span in my paper)

On field #1, everyone should come out equal. This is the control field. Now try imagining it on the next fields. Take notes if you need to. Who wins the survival game? Pay special attention to group C. How rapidly does it cease to be 50/50 in successive herds?

Further Practice:

Conduct the following mental tests:

1. A man dies. His religious beliefs say his afterlife will be one way. Imagine that man in multiple different afterlives.

2. Take three deities you are familiar with and imagine them as one. In what way must they change, or in what way are their followers' beliefs wrong, if at all, to fit into the idea of all gods being one?

Mentally test the validity of these hypotheses:

1. Christianity is not a valid religion because Jesus hasn't shown up yet.

2. Magic can be used to lose weight.

Note: As this book was being edited, another thought experiment was proposed: "Why is this section in this book?" the resulting conversation was interesting enough that I suggest it highly for anyone studying this book with a group.

Topic Ten: Wicca and Science

As should be obvious by now, I'm of the opinion Wiccans need science. Why? What is science, anyway? What are some basic scientific concepts commonly misunderstood by Wiccans, at least from a reading of their books and webpages? Are religion and science enemies? Opposites?

Why Wiccans Need Science

Wiccan religion embraces the Hermetic axiom "As above, so below; as below, so above." It may surprise people to discover that the majority of Hermetic philosophers (whether Early Freemasons, Ceremonial Mages or others) are and have been involved in the scientific and technical professions. To the members of the lodge of lodges, the idea of an able bodied person sitting around earning a welfare check or sponging off mom and dad were anathema. Early Hermetic metaphysics in the United States was not merely a metaphysical system, but a social one, with rules for order and behavior. In the past, to be a mage required knowledge of both the workings of the spiritual world and the physical one — a knowledge earned by practice.

A good friend and Hermetic Mage expresses his disgust at lazy metaphysicists in no uncertain terms. He calls them black holes, and believes that their nature is to suck the marrow out of everything they encounter, and not in a positive, Dead Poet's Society kind of way, but by absorbing and degrading everything they touch. People who hang around them, he says, have their natural vibratory energies sucked away, just as a black hole sucks in light. They vibrate, he claims, at such a base level that they innately disrupt everything around them from magical practice to television signals.

While I am not sure I believe that, I do know that it is only in recent years that magic and non-Abrahamic religion have begun to be seen as in opposition to science and only quite recently has the idea of studying magic to the exclusion of science instead of as part of it developed. Crowley, for example, proposed magic as an unstudied field of science. Early Modern Wiccans were so enamored of science they based entire mythologies upon the flawed science of their time. In our short history as Wiccans, and in the longer history of alternative religions, science has been friend, not foe, and to those of us who are comfortable with both, the expectation that we'd reject science for Wicca is like the expectation that we'd reject our friends or family... it's not going to happen.

As always, we can understand the problem by looking closely at the terms we are using. A good definition of science might be "the body of evidence, conjecture and theory involved with the interpretation of the world in the most logical way, and the study of that material." That's a bit unwieldy, but it does the job well because it involves the three ways we interpret reality: experiencing, guessing and assuming. As we might expect, experiencing, guessing and assuming are not very effective ways of moving through life when you have very little information, but as you get more and more information they become more effective, and they each lead to more information.

Experiencing, guessing and assuming are also how we find our religious beliefs. Religious beliefs consist of experiences—we then guess the cause of them and make assumptions based on the data. Religion, therefore, has the same basis as science: the search for knowledge. Like a scientific theory, which can never be proven, only proven false, religious theory cannot be proven—with the technology we have, that is—only proven false. Therefore, just as scientific theories are best when they say much, have many chances to be challenged and still remain, a religion is best when it says much about life, is often challenged and never fails.

To set religion in opposition to science is to make it a theory which says little—only that it is right no matter what—and that ignores challenges to its claims. Far better are religions that make broad but simple claims—for example, that what you do comes back to you. Such religions withstand the tests of new experiences and have a much longer shelf life. As an example of a theory that didn't work well, early Christianity taught that the sun revolved around the earth, which was the center of the physical world just as god is the center of the spiritual one. In making this claim that was shown to be false, early Christianity set itself in opposition to science. It was a dangerous wager, because in showing one claim of Christianity to be false, an element of falseness, or at least of uncertainty, was added to the other claims of the religion.

Had early Christianity claimed, instead, that all things had a center around which they revolved, just as god is the center of the world, the theory not only would've been much broader but also would've added a level of truth to the religion with each discovery that worked in that manner, from gravity to the spin of electrons. By being too narrow and too literal, the religion missed an opportunity. Of course, there was no way for the developers of early Christianity to know this, but it makes a good example.

Wicca, therefore, in trying to be a religion that is inherently true, makes claims that are both broad and nonspecific– as above, so below, for example, and tries to make those claims within the bounds of science. So when Wicca says that an apple grows from a fertilized seed just as we grow from a fertilized egg, it is adding a level of truth to the religion that might not be otherwise apparent, while going with the scientific knowledge of the day. Note the claim is not that it takes two parents to make all things on earth. What Wicca often does teach is that life is often the result of two parents, but not always, therefore it is likely that in the divine, the world above, life is often the result of two parents, but not always.

Wiccans are in the active process of rendering their religion coherent to the masses. Therefore, an understanding of science is needed both in order to explain the religion to the outsider and to keep the religion relevant to today's world. As much as we like to claim Wicca is a religion that we can take and leave as we please, all Wiccans *do* have some investment in the continuance of the religion into the future. While we know we can leave it at any time, the thought of it not being there to come back to is a bummer. Just as certain millennial cults died out as their beliefs became less relevant, a Wicca that is irrelevant to the future will die out and its practitioners could find themselves wondering what they spent their years following.

An example of Wicca which is irrelevant to the future is the bastard stepchild of Wicca and ex-Christianity, a critter I like to refer to as the "I'm Wiccan because everyone else is Christian" beastie. If current sociological trends continue, Christians will continue to become less of a majority in the future. Therefore, any religion that bases itself on opposition to a Christian majority will find itself growing less and less relevant. This is paralleled by a specific type of Christianity that bases its beliefs on the fact that it is a bastion of goodness in an ever more multicultural, secular and therefore "evil" world. As the level of multiculturalism and secularism go up, that form of Christianity gets more relevant and the inverse form of Wicca gets less so. It is fair to no one for one religion to base its relevance on the irrelevance of another, and the cycle of relevance/irrelevance this leads to makes both religions unstable.

Unlike relevance to other religions, however, relevance to science is relevance to growth. The amount of scientific knowledge, the "body of evidence, conjecture and theory" is in a constant state of growth. As an example, a good friend of mine received the same degree I have, in the same field, and was required to know about half of what I was because he studied it 10 years before me. My sister, 15 years younger than me, has an interest in a similar field, and may find herself needing to know twice what I did. This is felt hardest in biology, but occurs in nearly every field of study. If religion is relevant to science, the religion grows as science does. If religion is not relevant to science, it declines as science grows.

Therefore, a basic understanding of science, when used as a framework for defining religious belief, or at least explaining or interpreting religious belief, is not only making the religion more coherent but making it more stable. Note that the religion is not changing much by being held to the scientific framework — only that the metaphors used to describe the religion are changing. To refer to an earlier example, few will claim that god is not the center of the Christian reality simply because the early discussions of Christianity got the position of the sun in the heavens wrong. This scientific flub, however, added an element of wrongness to the faith's claims that had no business being there. It is for that reason that Wiccans, each one an ambassador to the non-Wiccan majority, should try to speak from a position of knowledge rather than of ignorance. Like Christianity, Wicca will not be proven wrong by flubs of knowledge, but it will certainly distract from educated discussions of our beliefs.

Thus the need for science is three-fold. We need it to understand our world in a religion that says understanding the divine comes from understanding the mundane. We also need it to maintain relevance and growth in our religion, allowing our religion to speak to the reality of the world around us instead of to an imagined version that may grow further from truth over time. Lastly, we need to understand science as ambassadors of our faith, using metaphors that match reality rather than adding an element of wrongness to our claims by using metaphors that do not match reality. If we are to speak, as one book of shadows says, we must speak coherently. If we cannot be coherent, we must not speak at all.

Bad Science: The Truth about Genetics

Perhaps the place where most Wiccans slip up most in their discussions of reality is in the use of genetics to prove a point. Whether the claim is that Karma is passed in the genes or the claim is that Wicca is, strange and unusual claims about the reality of genetics are commonplace in the wide web of misinformation humans spew, and Wiccans seem to be no exception when it comes to spewing contentedly.

The first issue in genetics I'd like to cover is the idea that all traits and characteristics are passed down genetically, except for those that are learned. While amounts of neurotransmitters, brain structure and the like may have a heritable component, genetics doesn't work like that. You can't chop off a leg of a chromosome and slap on another and get a bull with a man's head, nor clip some code here and there and replicate a dead person's artistic ability. You can't clip a fragment of DNA, add it to some guy's sperm and make his offspring solve a complicated math problem the same way the person who was the fragment's originator does. Genes code for proteins, and while it is possible to add and subtract proteins, it's not possible — not yet at least — to make a gene that puts whole parts where they aren't. We can tell it to make extra limbs, limbs that wouldn't be there, even limbs like those of another animal, but not to grow another animal's limb. We can't have a cow that is beef on the left side and pork on the other, nor grow broccoli instead of fingernails. This is because what we do to make genetic changes is alter is the beginning stage of a chaos-based replication, which has no similarity to grafting, which is how they make trees that have apples on one side and plums on the other and similar things.

Let me explain chaos-based replication this way. When I was a child, I had one of the early spin art kits. These work by whirling a piece of paper around by means of a rubber-band driven "engine" and squeezing out drops of paint on the whirling paper. You get patterns that are never exactly the same, even if you very carefully do everything exactly the same way. If I wound the rubber band three times, re-leased it, dropped one drop of red paint after one second and one drop of yellow paint after one second, then re-peated this procedure on later papers, I'd get different amounts of color, different swirls.

If you imagine it at a molecular level, you can see that the centripetal force is moving the paint in a certain di-rection, but the make-up of the paint will give it choices on *how* to move in that general direction. If, for example, it tends to move at right angles every three millimeters, every three millimeters it has a choice of up or down. If you draw a line on your paper using a similar pattern, you can see how quickly the line changes and how after only a few dozen turns, the probability of replicating that line goes down. If you want to think of it in terms of math, when you make the first turn, you have a 50% chance of making the same turn as the line you want to replicate, when you make the second turn, you have a 50% chance of making the same second turn in addition to the 50% chance of making the first, and on and on. Even after four turns, the chance of replication is pretty low. It'd be like flipping a coin four times and getting heads, tails, heads, tails and then flipping it again and getting the same pattern. If it helps, think of the pattern as something easy to grasp. You have as much chance of replicating any pattern. Heads, tails, heads, tails is equally as likely as four heads.

We know that the body uses this technique to do a lot of things. It is making patterns, fractals, based on the size and shape of the molecules it is using to create things. While this can yield things that are terribly similar, there are extreme differences at the molecular level. It is generally thought that the arrangement of the neurons in the brain is one such fractal. Certainly the arrangement of dendrites is, but as that occurs later, and has a lot more factors than genes, we'll just discuss the arrangement of cells. As evidence of how this use of fractal patterns works, the patterns in the brains of identical twins, as well as their fingerprints and retinal capillaries are not identical. Two clones, for that's what identical twins are, will have differing (but quite similar) capacities for different things. They may be good at math, or art, but if you take scans of their brains while doing the same task (or even ask them to describe steps to doing the task) you'll usually see slightly different readings.

This is a little obscure and complicated; so let's imagine an impossible situation where it might be easy to understand. Let's imagine a quality we'll call "ability to paint like Monet" and that the ability to paint like Monet is found in a patch of brain that is exactly one layer of cells thick and takes up a square inch. If you possess this inch, and the cells make the exact same pattern, you and Monet, painting the same scene with the same materials, would turn out identical paintings. (This is impossible for a number of reasons, but imagine it nonetheless.)

If you had a pattern *similar* to the Monet inch, you'd paint similarly but not exactly, and as the pattern gets further and further from the Monet inch, your styles differ more and more. If we were trying to replicate this genetically, we'd find a gene that coded for that inch of brain (again, not possible, but imagine). That gene would code for cells to be put there, and would probably code for a general pattern of those cells, but would use randomness to assort them (like fingerprints). Thus your clone would share the cells, and the general pattern, but not the exact molecular pattern, just as twins often have whorls of the same character in their fingerprints while the actual arrangement of lines differs.

If you believe that the brain is the source for personality you can see, then, how two brains created from the same stuff could still differ. It's a bit like having two people building a brick wall from the same plan. The two walls may look alike in the grand scheme of things—after all, they are the same design—and they may have similarities based on the things the brick layers know, like how much mortar to use. However, if you were to examine their construction microscopically, you'd see huge differences: a slight angle here, a pattern in the mortar there, differences in the order the bricks were laid and which packs of bricks were opened first, etc. If there were a sudden way to reveal hidden differences, say a bunch of the bricks turned blue in the rain and were all enclosed on the right side of the third layer of each odd-number pack of 100 bricks, the difference would be striking, and little things like what order the bricklayer took the bricks from the pack would change the ways the walls looked. They'd still just be blue and regular brick color, of course, because that's the extent of the material available to make the wall.

The idea then, that you could inherit the ability to write the same limerick as a parent is flawed because it is based on a level of exact replication that the body does not use. What we inherit are bricks and plans for walls, not pre-made walls. We can inherit the ability to hear and recognize music, but we don't inherit the liking of a specific band or a specific song. We can learn those things, but we don't inherit them. Again, bricks and plans, not pre-made walls.

This goes for religion as well as songs. Over 80% of 1st generation Wiccans come from Christian families, so clearly religion is not heritable. (The next section discusses that 80% number.) The tendency toward certain thought patterns may be heritable, but an actual belief structure is not inherited. In order to demonstrate that it was, we'd need pretty impressive studies and possibly a new definition of heritability.

It is for this reason that there are no true "hereditary witches." There may be a genetic tendency for a type of beliefs and types of abilities, but there is no proof that beliefs and ways to use them are inherited. People who claim to be such (as opposed to meaning that, as hereditary witches, they have been taught by family members directly) have a lot to prove if their claims are to be believed.

While we are on the subject of genetics, a few Wiccans claim that things like genetically modified produce are not merely wrong but anti-Wiccan. Our beliefs actually say nothing about genetically modifying organisms, and rightfully so, because if they did we'd have to completely reject nature, which does it all the time. Such people rarely complain about the existence of wheat, which was genetically modified by virtue of breeding, or sweet corn, modified in the same way, but are quick to condemn the cheaper, faster and more reversible routes of doing the same thing. Rather than weigh in and say one side is right or wrong, I prefer to say that it is a very big picture indeed, and that a high level of knowledge is needed for anyone to decide what they think, and further that what they think may be quite situational. They may think it wrong to genetically modify olive trees to get bigger and better crops but right to genetically modify a rare flower to keep it from extinction. These issues, and many others, all require a coherence of thought that comes with knowing what you are talking about, and that's really the important part of the relationship between science and Wicca.

Since Wicca teaches that what is ethical must be decided based on the sum total of the data about a given situation, the ability to interpret that data is vital for an ethical existence. We are not a religion of books declaring a thing is bad or a thing is good, but a religion of individuals making decisions based on data and experience. Therefore, we must know a thing before we can make decisions about it. Knowledge is thwarted whenever we pass bad information to other people, and at least a tangential knowledge of the science behind the issues of the day is required to form coherent opinions.

Worse Science: The Truth about Statistics

Less common but still prevalent on the web and in a few Pagan books is a poor understanding of statistics. Statistics is the language of randomness, the way we look over a huge sea of data and pick out trends, finding meaning in the numbers, like the divine in our early creation story: by picking it out, isolating it and giving it a name.

The problem with statistics is that if you are untrained in understanding them, it is easy for people to use them to lie to you. The numbers themselves don't lie; it is the selective use of them that leads you astray. For example, think of a beach, pristine, with one piece of trash covering four square inches of it. If I wished to talk about how clean the beach was, I could say that of the one-hundred million square inches of beach, only four were polluted, or that the beach was completely clean except for a single piece of trash. I could even say that the beach was statistically pristine, because those 4 inches are way less than .05%, the level required for significance in most applications.

However, if I wanted you up in arms I could use the same exact data. I could say I went to the beach the other guy claimed was clean and found trash within minutes of arriving or that the section of beach I studied was 50% polluted. The fact that I only studied the eight square inches around and including the trash, of course, would be something I neglected to discuss. Those eight inches are called the threshold, or the scope, of my study, and it's the first thing you need to understand statistics.

Four out of five dentists might recommend a toothbrush, for example, but which five dentists? Is it five dentists who work for that company? If so, isn't it pretty relevant that a guy who works for the company wouldn't recommend the toothbrush? Can you imagine the statistics there? "The Scuzzbot toothbrush is so bad that 20% of the dentists employed by the company won't even recommend it." Both are the truth, mind you, but they are both saying dramatically different things.

The scope of the research is what is being questioned here, and a good study presents you with the scope of research right up front. To keep it simple, we'll discuss the

Scuzzbot toothbrush a little more. In their commercials, they claim four out of five dentists would recommend their product. Since we know that four out of five means nothing, we might get a listing of all the dentists in a state, say Delaware (it's nice and small and has a good cross section of rural, urban and suburban areas) and study them in Delaware. (Since a nationwide mailing would be very expensive!)

We poll all the Delaware dentists, one year apart, by mail. On the first one, we ask them what brand(s) of toothbrushes they would recommend. On the following mailing, we list a group of toothbrushes and ask which of the above they'd recommend. The first is a cold question, a little hard to manipulate, but there are some factors that immediately affect the responses. First, you're going to get a large group of people who discard the study altogether. Then you're going to get the people who are in the employ of the companies who are making the toothbrushes. Thankfully, DuPont is not a big maker of toothbrushes, and no major toothbrush companies are in the state, so that should be minimized. Lastly, you're going to feel the effects of advertising. Say the biggest toothbrush company in the world, for giggles we'll call it Hamilton, advertises a lot in Dover, Milton and Rehoboth Beach. Since you're not going to ask these people why they chose which toothbrush, it is likely those with no real preference are going to choose the one advertised on billboards on Route 1, billboards they see every commute.

Since we want to give Scuzzbot the benefit of the doubt, we'll put three lines for the answer. While the questions say which brand(s), in the past, we've noticed that the number of lines and their size affects the answers. If we made one small line, we'd only get one answer, but three larger lines means we're likely to get at least 3 answers. It is likely, we know, that if we had one line, Hamilton Toothbrushes, a well-established and well advertised company, would be the answer most people gave. Since we're being honest here, we realize this question is not a perfect representation of the dentists' recommendation, but in fact is testing for which toothbrush names spring to the mind of the dentists without a negative reaction when they receive the mailing.

Let's say on our test that 90% of the dentists write Hamilton, 72% write Scuzzbot, and 10% write "no preference." A bunch of others write other things, but one thing is true of our research: Hamilton appears on every list where the dentist expresses a preference, and Scuzzbot appears on four fifths of those lists as well. In statistical lingo, "among dentists with a preference, Scuzzbot toothbrushes are recommended by four out of five dentists." Note this doesn't say that every dentist with a preference chose Hamilton, because that factoid isn't helpful to the Scuzzbot people.

A year later, we list a bunch of brands, and Hamilton is still amongst them as well as a rare German wunderbrush, the VNQ, which is expensive but will do nearly anything you can imagine and is only discussed in dental journals. As always, people given a short list tend to check only one or two, and on this survey, the Scuzzbot does worse, as does the Hamilton. The VNQ, which none of these dentists has actually seen, does very well. These were the same people, mind you, who had the earlier statistics, and it demonstrates either a lack of conviction behind their preferences, or a huge change in the way they viewed toothbrushes in twelve months. Since we are working for Scuzzbot, we pay no attention to this second survey and chug right along with our commercials, saying four out of five dentists recommend it.

We're not lying, and if we say four out of five of the dentists we surveyed in Delaware who expressed a preference mentioned the Scuzzbot we're already being considerably more honest than most of the commercials out there, much more so if our study and its methodology are published somewhere where anyone can see it. As bad as we like to claim statistics are, that study is pretty honest, and does give us some knowledge about toothbrushes, even if it's not terribly relevant to anything.

Another thing often used to trick you is the average, also called a mean. As an example, imagine you have ten people. Nine of these people scrape by on $10,000 a year and the tenth makes $10,010,000 a year. The average income of this group is $1,010,000 a year—tell that to the nine people living well under the poverty level! We interpret means by a thing called the standard deviation. The standard deviation is the average of the amount away from the average of all members of a list, and here is probably something around three million dollars. A standard deviation of three million when the average is one million is saying that the numbers are nonsense, and is similar to surveys that say that a candidate is running twenty percentage points above his opponent, plus or minus one hundred percentage points.

The standard deviation is one of a whole bunch of tools we use to interpret data, but sometimes what it takes is simple mental stretching. A friend did a study of Wiccans she knew in the US, and estimated that 80.4% of first generation Wiccans began as Christians. This would seem at first to be really telling about the make up of Wicca, and make never-been-Christians like me seem to be very rare creatures. The problem here is that in studies of the American populace, between 83% and 89% of people describe themselves as Christian. Since her study sample was small, the difference between her results and the others may be nothing more than a factor of her sample. If 80% of first generation Wiccans in the United States were Christian and 80% of people in the United States identify as Christian, all that means is that Wicca draws a percentage of people from Christianity that is comparable to the percentage of people that are Christian in general.

Her study was interesting, however, in that former atheists (like myself) and former Jews were very well represented, contrary to their percentages in the American public. This would seem to indicate that members of some minority religions are more likely to cross over to Wicca than members of other minority religions. Since her sample was low, the relevance of her study is questionable, but it still provides a good example

Understanding statistics is especially important for members of minority religions because we are often the people who fall through the cracks of studies. If you see a poll that says 80% of the country is Christian, 5% is Buddhist, 10% is Muslim and 5% are Jews (a poll that would be very wrong!) it's easy to feel like you simply don't exist. Knowing how to dissect those statistics is a vital and important skill for our self-esteem and understanding the world. So next time you feel the need to say what an average person is, or what most Wiccans believe, or that 99% of all Wiccans are ex-Christians, refrain or explain.

Horrible Science: Equal and Opposite Reactions mean all the Good I do Generates Evil

Perhaps the worst example of misunderstood science I've experienced from the mouths of young Wiccans and others was the idea that since, as Newton tells us, every action has an equal and opposite reaction, every good act done in the world generates an evil one and the world works out neutrally because of it. I cannot begin to describe my reaction to this belief. Shock? Shame? Bewilderment? I'm not sure there is a word that describes the complex mixture of emotions this statement generated in me. It made my wife — the daughter of a physics professor and generally somewhat restrained — guffaw, but she wasn't standing in front of the person who said it, either.

If I hadn't encountered the same statement from another person a few years later on Beliefnet, I probably would've forgotten the entire episode. I'm generally of the opinion that if you hear a thing once it is a fluke, and if you hear it twice it's either a fluke or a trend. In this case I pray it's a fluke but I'm going to pretend it's a trend for the sake of discussion. It's not as if I've met tens of thousands of Wiccans, but if the people I've met have been a representative sample, this view is held by a few dozen folk who vacillate between confusion and anger about it. The first one even dismissed Wicca as a valid faith because that was part of our beliefs.

First I'll explain the problem with the physics of this idea. It hinges on the word opposite. Opposite has two related but distinct meanings in the English language. The first is the one we heard on Sesame Street and in our nursery rhymes, and is actually better described by the word antonym, with "opposite" pairs such as good and evil, light and darkness, mean and nice, etc. The second is the more technical use of the term and means the reverse or alternate, like the opposite side of a coin or piece of paper or the opposite direction. The complete extent of this problem is caused by seeing the phrase "equal and opposite" and using the first meaning, not the second. Rather than simply leave it at that, I'll explain.

If you had a spring, and that spring had a weird scale exactly in the middle, and you pushed that spring/scale against a wall, it would say that you and the wall were pushing with the same amount of force, you toward the wall and the wall away from the wall. Actually, there would be two sets of forces, you and the wall and the spring's compression, not to mention gravity, magnetism, wind and all those other forces we were always told to ignore in the first months of learning physics.

Metaphor works well in this situation, so imagine you are in a frictionless skating rink. Forgetting for a moment that you'd fall down because of the way our bodies are shaped, imagine the hand of the deity of your choice pushes you toward the north wall of this skating rink with just enough force to get you moving. When you hit the wall, even though the hand of your god pushed you north, you begin to go south with the same amount of speed that you were previously going north (the magic walls of the frictionless skating rink absorb none of the momentum.) You are now going *equally* and *opposite* of the force and direction you were going before.

The metaphysical version of this is that when you put energy, in the form of will, into the universe you get an equal and opposite reaction: the universe pushes back. Chaos, life, karma—whatever factors that you wish to consider—alter this equal and opposite energy just as friction, wind, gravity and magnetism alter the force you place on the wall. The important distinction here is that the Wiccan view of good and evil points out that energy has no good or evil. The electricity that powers the machine that keeps a great man alive is the same electricity that runs through an electric chair. It's not good or evil. It's just energy.

Related to this is a silly new trend in Wicca: to draw out energy, in the form of a spell or just a prayer and to say, as you focus it out into existence, "So long as this harms none," with the belief that those words will somehow stop something harmful from happening as a result of your actions. There is nothing wrong with hoping that your actions will have no negative effects. However, this type of disclaimer offends those of us who see magic as real. You see, to us, it is energy, just like electricity, or a bullet being propelled from a gun. I do not think anyone who says this "So long as it harms none" thing would be willing to point a gun at themselves, say "So long as this harms none" and pull the trigger. To those who see magic as energy, there is no difference.

Even though the problem at the core of this argument came from a misunderstanding of English, not of energy, the idea that magic is energy shows the need for a basic understanding of another of the sciences—physics. As with biology and statistics, you don't have to know or understand these things at a college level, you just need to have a basic understanding of the facts and language. Such an understanding can be grasped by watching a kid's science show on television, or reading a good how-to website. More importantly, those who teach need to be prepared and willing to fill in where their students lack knowledge, if they cannot answer a question, they need to learn to turn the students on to someone or something that can.

Science is not Wicca, and Wicca is not Science Once More

This brief discussion of science has left us once again in needing to have a disclaimer amongst the information. Wicca is not science, and science is not Wiccan. Knowledge of one may assist you in gaining knowledge of the other, but it does not assure knowledge of the other. Wiccan belief, however, consists of understanding that the divine created the world (or the world created itself) with the idea that as it is above, so it is below. We see the nature of atoms mirrored, if imperfectly, in the heavens. We see the creation of man mirrored, if imperfectly, in the evolution of animals around us. For those who believe the gods took an active hand in our creation, we see that hand mirrored in the farm animals humans have raised. For those who believe the gods have been hands off, we are mirrored in the animals never tamed by mankind's hands.

Science is a language, a language we use to communicate discoveries about the nature of the universe. Without that language, you cannot share the wonderful fruits of your introspection, prayers and knowledge. Without that language, you may struggle along for years feeling as if a simple problem that eludes you has made the universe impossible to understand, but with it you may see how others learned and hear how they have coped with the very same problem you have.

Science is about being open to new things, but not gullible. It's about learning how things are, while imagining how they could be. Nothing is more important or critical to an understanding of the universe than science. It will not restrict you, it will not judge you, and it makes no demands on you, which is more than can be said of any human being. To those who have not been taught to fear it—by teachers saying it was hard or by friends saying it was stupid or by any other means—it is inherently spiritual. It is even called the language of the gods.

Even when you know the reason for the perfect spiral of a snail's shell or for the patterns in clouds or fingerprints, you are not closed off to the voice of the gods that lies within them. Indeed, I would say you are tuned in to their voice. You can know how they did it, and that in all your life you'd never achieve that level of molecular perfection in your own art, and wonder why they did it and what the message could be for you.

Rather than take a position that religion is against it, Wicca turns the words of seeking—when, where, who, why, how, what—into sacred words. We wonder about why we are here and about all the other questions that easily spring to mind… and we recognize that even if life never results in an answer, the quest is enough. To those raised to see religion as anti-science, the transition into Wicca can be difficult, for it is a faith that not only is pro-science but teaches that science is part of a quest for knowledge we all need to make. This change is more than a paradigm shift or a change in attitude; it is a whole new world of thought.

This isn't to say we're all intellectuals sitting in ivory towers or monks living in caves near the tops of mountains. We teach ourselves to recognize that the knowledge held by gazing into a flower is as important as the knowledge learned from a book or class. The important part here is that we scorn those who would see one as more vital than the other. The voice of the divine must not be blocked out in any of the ways it chooses to talk to us—whether in dreams, in the matrix of DNA or in the dance of the stars in the heavens.

What we must not do, however, is assign our own hopes and motivations to those things. I can look at the action potential in the neuron and see the very spark of Zeus' lightning that Prometheus gave to his creation, without once thinking that those who don't see it are lesser beings or those with less faith. I can see the moon, and know all the myth and imagery surrounding her without thinking she will not rise again the next cycle, nor return to her previous shape at the appointed time. Rather than sift through the bulk of knowledge—Diana, made of green cheese, "one small step for man," 29.4 days—I can ask myself what all that knowledge means, or better yet just gawk at her beauty.

A wise friend once said that the glory of Wicca is that we can know so much about something that the knowledge becomes a mirror of that thing within us. I can know the moon, maybe better than I know myself, but in doing so I know one part of myself with certainty. It is, perhaps, not the most explicable phenomenon, but for those whose judgment of a religion as true or false relies on the tangibility of its phenomena, it is proof of the absolute reality of Wicca.

Recommended Reading for Topic Ten:
Science and Religion:
http://www.srforum.org/
Genetics:
http://www.dnafiles.org/home.html
And I strongly suggest *A Cartoon Guide to Genetics* by Larry
Gonick and Mark Wheelis. (Harper Perennial Library, 1991)
Statistics:
http://www.robertniles.com/stats/
http://m2.aol.com/johng101/lying.htm
http://hoa.aavso.org/mathtalk.htm
Physics:
http://www.insolitology.com/rationally/reason.htm

Discussion Questions for Topic Ten:

10.1. What are some of the reasons Wicca needs science?

10.2. What is meant by it being a "gamble" for Early Christians to teach the sun revolved around the earth?

10.3. Why would an acceptance of science in a religion lead to an increase in relevance over time?

10.4. What is the difference between grafting and altering something genetically?

10.5. How can the mean be misleading?

10.6. What is an equal and opposite reaction? How might that apply to energy directed toward the universe?

Topic Eleven: Proselytizing

What is proselytizing? What do Wiccans (and others) have against it? Do Wiccans do it, should Wiccans do it and how can I deal with it in my life?

What is Proselytizing and Why is it Wrong?

Proselytizing is the act of attempting to convert a person from their faith to your own by whatever means are allowed you within the legal system of the country you are doing it in. Rather than conversion by example, proselytizing uses words and often threats and lies to coerce you into changing faiths. Wiccans may be familiar with proselytizing as a result of a former faith. As you may know, members of these faiths are often prodded into proselytization with threats or rewards. Save a certain number of souls on a certain day and get a toaster oven, don't save enough and you go to hell.

What you must understand first about proselytizers is that they are caught in a web of lies before they even start. If, for example, you state that you feel proselytization is wrong because it involves attempting to correct an error in another person that you cannot even prove the existence of, you will hear such responses as "Proselytization is about honoring the dignity of another person because letting them be wrong is cruel," and "Your objection to my attempting to convert you to my faith is because you think there is no such thing as truth." A good rhetorician, or even a person with a sharp eye, can recognize these responses as non sequitur. Put simply, they have nothing to do with the objection raised whatsoever.

Rather than go into the reason why proselytizing is wrong, and the fact that it is wrong should be obvious enough, I'm going to discuss the doublespeak that is used to justify it by its proponents. First, however, I want to make a strong distinction. If I tried to persuade you that Darwin's theory of natural selection was much more correct than Lamarck's theory of acquired characteristics, I wouldn't be proselytizing, I'd be debating, or making a persuasive speech. The difference is that I know Lamarck's theory, what proof he had for it and why it doesn't work. I also know Darwin's theory, and why it is better, and I can offer proof to that effect.

If you can take the emotional nonsense out of a discussion of proselytizing you can see the difference. To make it clearer, I'll take another example of something that can only be proselytized about–the taste of food. I think that there is little in the world more wonderful tasting than cheesecake. A good, rich cheesecake with lemon curd is just about the most wonderful thing I can have to eat, and one with fresh raspberries and white chocolate is nearly as good. On the other hand, I can take or leave chocolate. With the exception of a certain combination of flavors — chocolate with mint, peanut butter, toffee or cheesecake — I don't really eat chocolate that often and when I do, I can't even stomach the cheap stuff. My wife is, put mildly, a chocoholic. She loves chocolate, even bad chocolate, and last Winter Solstice got about 8 pounds of it from family and friends who knew it would be eaten swiftly. She is pretty ambivalent about cheesecake, however.

My wife and I, like other people with different tastes, don't argue about which is better. She doesn't try to convince me that chocolate is the number one food in the world and I don't try to make her love cheesecake. To those not understanding the problem, it might seem that we don't argue about it because it is trivial, or because we love each other, but if that were so we'd see discussions about it all over the place. Part of the fun of being in a relationship is discussing the trivial, and if we avoid it because we love each other, why is it that I don't go into my local donut shop and go "how can you even think of getting donuts with that white cream in them when there is good custard right along side it" or try to explain to my neighbor that no, really, I think liver is disgusting and feeding it to her children is just mean.

The real reason we don't argue is because we assume that someone is eating something because they have preferences based on actual phenomena. We assume that the reason they don't like the flavor of things the same way we do is that they have actual different perceptions, just as people can see different things in art or nature. This speaks drasti-

cally to the first of the claims of your average proselyte—
that they proselytize because it is natural to do so.

In fact, it is quite unnatural to argue without cause. We
do not see it in the natural world, mirrored in animals, and
we certainly do not see it in normal society. Only the proselyte is concerned that your sensory phenomena of the divine must match his, and if it does not you must change.
Those that claim it is natural often cannot account for the
simple fact that the religions that promote it are the minority. It is a claim often made but never proven, and often
proven false.

Likewise, the proselyte who claims he does it because it
is natural is quite often of those religions that shun other
things that occur in the natural world, things like homo-
sexuality. It behooves the person discussing this with the
proselyte to bring up this small hypocrisy, of course. That it
is natural, alone, is not justification to these people, don't let
it be their justification to you. They may claim, as well, that
it is in their sacred book, a fact that often relies on misleading translations. You will note that few of those persons
obey all the laws of their holy book, and why they have
chosen this one, which, even translated horribly, is little
more than a suggestion, is yet another valid question.

It is difficult to condemn proselytization without con-
demning those sects of Christianity that use it, because it's
really not done that often outside of those sects, a fact which
should convince you, if nothing else can, of proselytizing's
non-biblical nature. The flaw lies not in Christianity but in
the justification of proselytization. Even in those few Christian sects that claim to proselytize only by means that do
not use manipulation and coercion, manipulation and coercion exist in their techniques because without them the
techniques always fail. The fact that they are claiming that
their religion is better than that of people they are proselytizing to is, in and of itself, a manipulation of reality. They
have no proof of this; it's just a claim.

In addition to those who defend proselytization by virtue of its being natural are those who defend it by virtue of
its fringe benefits. These include teaching that it fosters
communication, teaching that it increases the efficacy of the

church and even teaching that it assures you the good graces of the divine. The flaw in this so-called defense is that once again it comes from the arrogant assumption that the proselyte knows better than the one he is preaching at. As a mother who has spent long periods at home writing and raising children I can assure you that if and when I wish interreligious discourse I am quite capable of rustling it up myself. The proselyte's inappropriate decision to begin it when and where it is convenient to him flies in the face of human decency.

The last common defense of proselytizing is that somehow, by claiming to know better than that person their relationship with divine, claiming they have it wrong and you have it right and by all around considering their decisions on religious matters unimportant, you are affirming their dignity. No level of venomous vitriol, nor snide sarcasm, can accurately describe the depths of disgust such opinions bring out in me. Indeed, they apparently drive me to alliteration, a statesman's last recourse of ethical attention getting.

The theory behind this excuse of proselytizing is that you and I, the intended victims, have never heard the "good news" that we are not, as our faith teaches, all equals in the game of life loved as children by the divine. Instead, we are seen as worms in the eyes of an angry god. They feel they are morally obligated to tell us this, and that showing us we are wrong and not actually loved by the divine is something we should laud as being shown the error of our ways. There is something spiritually bankrupt and morally delinquent in teaching people that the next guy over is ignorant and must be corrected. It is an act that shows a lack of caring for the dignity of the people to whom it is being done. Put simply, to proselytize a person you must place their life experiences, choices, even their very worth, on a level far beneath your own.

Does proselytizing work?

The problem with taking a stand against proselytization, no matter how you feel it degrades the proselyte, nor how you feel it expresses disrespect for the victim, is that it's hard to get worked up over something that doesn't work. Proselytization is notoriously ineffective on adults and on people who hold minority religions, but these are the people who are most often targeted. Jews are perhaps the group gone after the hardest, but I lived in a Catholic neighborhood full of older Italian immigrants, and the proselytes swarmed around them like flies on a carcass, knocking on their doors, crashing their festivals and making a general nuisance of themselves.

In general, proselytizing doesn't work. More specifically, proselytizing adults who are of sound mind, secure in their faith or relationships, or otherwise not good targets is ineffective. It is for this reason that proselytes target the elderly, children and people in poor neighborhoods. They come during the middle of the weekday, or Saturday morning, when you are most likely to be doing housework or otherwise indisposed and when you are most likely to be dressed at your "worst." They, of course, are in their Sunday best and expect that when you open the door, hair mussed, maybe with paint on your face or a baby in your hand, this will somehow intimidate you.

As horrible as this sounds, it's fair, unlike the practice of proselytizing children. Few people in minority religions haven't heard the horror stories about children, again, mostly Jewish and Catholic, who have been selected for systematic proselytization. This action can range in technique from something not unlike the technique of kidnappers — come into our church for free candy and ice cream — to actual threats: join our church or you will suffer in a miserable lake of fire and pain. One friend in college told the story of going to what he was told was a sleepover birthday party as a child, and being told by the parents there that only saved people could stay the night. They'd told him that accepting Jesus as his personal savior was just something they did as a family, and there was no harm in it, and he could go back to being Jewish when he left.

He was about 12 at the time, and not an idiot, so he promptly left, taking his friends and younger brother with him. The scorn heaped on the son of those treacherous parents by those in the know was probably undeserved, but according to my friend, it would follow him right through high school—"Do I have to be saved to be your lab partner?"

I wish I could say my friend's experience was a truly rare thing, but he encountered a phenomenon that is growing more and more common (and will no doubt continue to grow if *Good News Club v. Milford Central School* is not promptly reconsidered). This phenomenon is the attempt by Christian bigots to assassinate the other faiths around them by going for the children, whose ideas of their parents' faiths may be oversimplified, and who may even have been raised to think that all faiths are equal and that their job is not to take a religious stand but to be children.

We must now, as members of minority religions, shield our children from proselytes with the same tools we use against pedophiles. The comparison is harsh but deserved, as both get their kicks by shattering innocence. I am not generally given to paranoia or excess, but my own child was home-schooled for several years. A strong factor in the decision to do so was that being made aware of proselytes and seeing them in action had led my son to begin to genuinely hate and mistrust Christians. Despite knowing many of the good kind, he began to feel they were after him, and he was mostly right.

A thing that is only effective on the un- and under-informed, the naïve, the inexperienced and the very young is hardly a thing of honor or of dignity. That it works on these folk not only does not justify the use of it but also seems to indicate that perhaps it would be best not done at all. Here, of course, I speak only of the quasi-acceptable proselytizing of so-called "legitimate" religions. Perhaps surprisingly even those groups that have the most heinous techniques do not approve of it when the proselytes are groups like the Branch Davidians or People's Temple. That they are impossible to distinguish from such groups from the point of view of their victims means nothing to them.

Proselytization and Secular Governments

Proselytization is a unique critter. Put simply, it is completely and utterly immoral and completely and utterly legal. As much as it pains me to say it, it *should* be legal. There should be some clause of some sort protecting those who are incapable of protecting themselves from it, or at least some overarching sense that it is repulsive enough that we'd all protect the weaker people from it, but it should not be outlawed.

That's not to say I don't think proselytization from door to door should not be banned as a nuisance. I feel this more or less about everyone who disturbs the sanctity of the home. As a pretty hard-core misanthrope I'm of the opinion that no one should come to the door ever, and if that is not possible, no one should come without calling and asking permission first. That's my particular kink, however. I am no fan of forced discussion, conducting most business by email or post, where I can choose to ignore a person's request for discourse by leaving it in my inbox. My phone has caller ID and often goes unanswered, and I'm a big fan of spying on who is at the door and not answering that, too. I am introspective, prefer to be left alone to my family and will go seek out unplanned socialization at a pub, restaurant or bookstore when I wish it. For some, that seems like an unhappy existence but it makes me exceedingly happy and is a core factor (or, if you prefer, quirk) of my personality.

My quirks aside, every church has the right to do what is needed for it to survive, provided the thing is legal. For some churches, these things are moral, like asking for donations or setting up an information booth. For other churches this is immoral, like proselytizing or trying to influence the law into giving it special privileges. In a just government, such influences fail, so the church isn't really immoral in doing it, just ineffective.

The core value in this "it's wrong but not illegal" position is the idea that government should not legislate morality. Unless a thing can be shown to have a clear danger to the society, that thing should be legal and all peoples who've done nothing to relinquish their rights should be given the same, equal rights. For example, secular governments that have some form of recognition for couples in contractual relationships should recognize all couples legally capable of entering into a contractual relationship. Secular governments that outlaw the manufacture of one drug on the basis that the sole purpose of the drug is to cause an addiction yielding to more sales should outlaw all drugs with that purpose. Such rational government may be beyond the capacity of a majority rule, but as majority rule is the best form of government we currently have offered to us, we'll have to make do.

What to do When they do it

Perhaps the only real thing that can be taught about proselytes is what works when trying to stop them. I can state that it's illogical and arrogant and demonstrate how. I can state that it's immoral, which is something you can only decide for yourself no matter what *I* say. I can say who they target and why, and the fact that they have the right to do it, even if it is the wrong thing to do, but I can't teach you anything more about them without it being nothing more than opinion. I've said nothing that cannot be verified, but also nothing particularly productive.

What I do know, from experience, practice and be-friending ex-proselytes is what does and does not work when it comes to getting them to leave you alone. These are most effective with the door-to-door types but can usually be altered to work with street preachers and their ilk. What does not work, I can assure you, is telling them you are busy or not interested. Both things will usually not get your house checked off on their map of the unsaved and they will simply be back next week.

In general, there are four types of things that work on proselytes: signs, shock, strong opinion, and knowledge. The first, signs, refers to actual signage, such as signs that state, "Proselytes are not welcome," and also to signs that you may follow a different religion, such as a small pentacle on the door or, in the case of Witnesses, Halloween or birthday decorations. Signage is only effective when they respect it, however, and not all groups do. A small plaque indicating that the people inside are happy in their faith and do not wish to change it will do quite nicely for the av-erage proselyte and, when ignored, changes the power dy-namic of the entire conversation. No longer are you the average Joe answering the door to the well-dressed well-intentioned young people, you are now the justifiably irate individual whose polite request has been ignored.

Shock works on an individual basis, and is good when the proselyte is a family member or neighbor you wish to get rid of. The type and level of shock you use should be carefully measured. If you tell the guy at the door you're too busy sacrificing cats to talk to him, you may find the ASPCA knocking at your door. If you tell the local gossip you are a lesbian, you'd best be prepared to have everyone know. One of my favorite shock tactics stems from the fact that as a never-been-Christian of European ancestry, knowledge of the Bible demonstrates that I am, in fact, without sin. In general, there are three definitions of sin used in the bible: violating a personal covenant with god (as in baptism), violating a biblical covenant (as in the "I am your only god because I saved you from slavery" of Exodus) and being descended from Adam and Eve (original sin), which is simply not true of non-Semitic peoples, as the Bibles verify in their constant revelation of peoples other than the Jews that the Jews encounter.

I find calmly explaining that I am without sin and am appalled that they would claim otherwise often works. When it does not, I find lifting a large stone and telling them that "As a being without sin, I believe your god entitles me to special privileges" usually does. Both things have been done in my life but not often, and are generally the result of answering the door after the doorbell has been rung repeatedly, a sign ignored and my marital privileges interrupted. In fact, the explanation of why I am without sin actually falls under the most important tactic of them all: knowledge (with a little bit of strong opinion thrown in to the mix).

Strong opinion, while no replacement for knowledge, does have its benefits. The proselytes have already expressed an opinion about your religion by coming to the door, and you have the right to object to it. Don't hold back; tell them what you really think. For example, one friend simply answers the door and tells them that she believes proselytes and missionaries, in having the pride to assume they know better than their god who is and is not saved, go promptly to hell upon death. She insists that if they prayed and thought about their actions they would see this as truth, and that they must leave at once because she will not be a party to their sin nor bear responsibility should they put their soul in mortal danger on her behalf. In thirty-five years of saying this, she says that twice she has had missionaries drop letters in her door saying that she was right and thanking her for showing them the truth of their actions.

The most effective technique, both for adults and children is knowledge—knowledge about your own faith and why you do things, as well as knowledge about the faiths of those you encounter. Studies have shown that child victims of Christian proselytization from Judaism are often from families in which the faith is tangential to family life. The missionaries are betting on the fact that these children don't know, for example, that you cannot be a Jew and follow Jesus, or that the children are unaware or under-aware of Jewish history and culture. This works equally well with children who are humanists or are raised in Eastern or Anabaptist-like religions. One friend remembers being told that even though her parents were Hindu, they wouldn't mind if she committed to Jesus as her personal savior. Being a smart cookie, of course, she asked her dad—whose opinion of American Christianity was quite low and was no doubt reduced further by the event.

Knowledge about their faith and the world in general helps as well. I once had a member of a doomsday cult sect of Christianity tell me that a copy of the book of Revelation was found at an archeological dig at Alexandria and carbon dated to 13 AD. When I said that Alexandria was under water, he claimed that the book was written on plates of pure copper. I then ordered him off of my porch as being a dirty liar and told him I hoped his god wasn't the one that had issues with bearing false witness, for certainly he was lying for god. As he left, I told him he was welcome to come back as soon as he could show me a single news story about the find or explain how plates of pure copper could be carbon dated. He never came back.

While these four techniques work well, a fifth, changing the power dynamic, is also effective. Tell them you are busy right now and that you'd like to arrange a meeting between them and your priest/ess (or coven, or friend), and try to set a date. Tell them you are not dressed appropriately right now or that you don't let people in without an appointment. Do whatever it takes to make it clear that you do not have an interest in playing their game and most of the time they will simply go away. Those that don't may become friends or even give up their proselytizing altogether. The amount of time and energy you put into it may vary and is, of course, up to you.

When Wiccans Proselytize

As has been said before, being a Wiccan is not a guarantee of being particularly moral. There are good Wiccans and bad ones… people who grasp and uphold the tenets of the faith and those that do not. Few Wiccans, however, have not been informed of our positions regarding proselytization, so while it may surprise you to find out some Wiccans proselytize, it may not surprise you to find out that those that do proselytize do so in unconventional ways.

The goal of proselytization is to get a person to change from their religion or point of view with the idea that yours is better for them than their current one, with no evidence that either is better than the other save personal opinion. We are most familiar with this in the form of street preachers or door-to-door proselytes, but subtler and more subversive forms of it exist, from demanding textbooks be changed to benefit your faith to demanding that people give up their holidays in favor of your own holidays.

If you subscribe to clipping services or mailing lists where you receive international news regarding Wiccans you are familiar with the stories of people doing anything to get their version of Wicca (or other forms of Paganism) out there regardless of their motives. I'm not speaking of things like Pagan Pride day, nor of students at secular schools suspended for wearing pentacles when the school's policy allows other religious jewelry, but campaigns to get special privileges (like wearing jewelry where it is *not* allowed of anyone, regardless of religion) and attention.

An example I recently encountered (not too far from my house, unfortunately) was when a woman and her children decided to make a few extra bucks by working a Halloween festival as mythical witches and conducting an ugliest witch contest. A fringe group of locals decided that this was highly objectionable to them, and contacted the media with their objections. A few things should be apparent to you right off the bat: this was a Halloween festival, not a celebration of the religious holiday of Samhain or November Eve, and these were mythical witches, not the real thing. Sadly, the idea for this protest was no doubt gleaned from some similar protests of things that really *were* objectionable.

For example, in the 1990s there was a rash of ill-thought-out Halloween "witch-burnings" in which groups dragged an effigy through the streets and set it ablaze. Wiccan groups, women's groups and many Christian groups objected to these because they were reenacting, for fun, the slaughter of hundreds of people for being different, old, or just having property someone else wanted. The Halloween festival in question was using an archetype, the mythical witch, which we should all recognize from the Wizard of Oz (and note the lack of protest whenever Oz is aired!), and which has nothing at all to do with Modern Witches or Wiccans — and very little to do with those persons killed for allegedly practicing Satan worship and heresy during the Witchcrazes. (The tangential relationship that *is* present is only there because the uninformed populace during the Witchcrazes didn't know that the witch-hunters made a distinction between fairy-tale witches and what they were seeking.) This Witch-contest and those Witch-burnings were not similar, but were treated as the same by protesters, for reasons I will not try to explain here.

The mythical witch costumes of the Witch contest were not about Modern Witches or Wiccans. The actresses said as much in the media, and an offer was made to give the "real" Witches an information booth, which quieted some of them, but others still complained until the contest was changed. Now while there is strong opinion that this media blitz was mostly the result of a shop owner wanting to get people into her shop, people wouldn't have gone for it unless they really felt that somehow they had the right to have the contest changed. This perception of a right to be involved whenever anyone uses the word Witch is no different than a perception that any religion should be yours.

That may seem difficult to grasp, but try to see it from a purely rational viewpoint: on the one hand there is this word "witch," a word with a few dozen perfectly valid definitions. On the other hand you have this group that falls under one of these definitions. Does this one group *really* have the right to dictate the use of the word, or is it overstepping its bounds to expect such a right? A student gave the best example of a similar possibility: a person from Hamburg objecting to certain fast-food sandwiches. I'm sure you can think of other possibilities in a similar vein... a person from Frankfurt objecting to hot dogs? ... an Irish town objecting to a humorous, five-line poem? Nowhere else in the English language does one perfectly valid definition trump another. We are quite confident in our ability to figure out the word from context, which is why Merriam-Webster online lists 42 definitions of "American" and 40 of "English" but only one definition of "American English."

With this knowledge, the reason for the complaints seems less than clear. Was it really, as some said, an individual's attempt to get her shop noticed? Was it just ignorance of the reality of other definitions of the word "witch," or was it the sinister beastie of proselytizing, the belief that as long as a belief exists contrary to yours you have to change that belief, no matter how or why it is held?

Perhaps this is not as clear an example to others as it is to me, so I'll refer instead to an example in which I was personally involved. When a church preached against the presence of Wiccans in their city, we leafleted the church with documents that said, essentially, that Wiccans were human and were open to dialogue with Christians. It answered specific allegations of their pastor, but wasn't designed to teach these people how to be Wiccan nor to belittle Christianity. The actual flyers were designed by committee and put up to a vote. Another flyer that fared well—until heartfelt speeches were made against it—was essentially a refutation of Christianity and a promotion of Wicca as the logical choice between the two.

I remember being pretty offended that this one was even on the table, and the astonishment that I felt when it genuinely seemed that the reaction to Wiccans being slandered was going to be attempting to convert the slanderers to Wicca. I understand wanting to correct allegations that are false. I do not understand seeing those false allegations as a reason to preach the need for others to convert to your faith, either directly or by attempting to demonstrate that their faith is illogical and yours is not.

Identifying your goals in anything is a good way to know proselytizing from regular discussion. Is your desire to inform the ignorant? Fine… but why? Is it because they have demonstrated a lack of knowledge or is it because you assume they lack knowledge? Is it to gain new members or show people that their faith is wrong? That second quality is often important to Wiccans who are ex-Christians, and there is a real psychological reason for it. Just as you wish to tell your friends about the boyfriend or girlfriend they haven't met, you often want to tell your former co-religionists all about your new religion. This is admirable, but there is a right and wrong way to do it.

Recommended Reading for Topic Eleven:

http://www.hvk.org/articles/1100/30.html (This is really an excellent piece!)

http://www.religioustolerance.org/chi_decl.htm

http://www.progressivehumanism.com/stopproselytizing.html

http://www.atheists.org/flash.line/colo7.htm

http://www.jhuger.com/kisshank.mv (This satire perhaps expresses best of all what proselytizing sounds like to people who don't believe what you are teaching.)

http://paganwiccan.about.com/library/weekly/aa100802proselytize.htm

Discussion questions for Topic Eleven:

11.1. What are some of the definitions of proselytizing given in this topic?

11.2. What are some of the justifications for it?

11.3. How valid is the author's refutation of those justifications?

11.4. What are some of the historical rules/ordains of Wicca that forbid proselytizing?

11.5. What is meant up proselytizing being immoral but legal? Why the distinction?

11.6. What are the drawbacks and benefits of the techniques for fending off proselytes?

11.7. Some examples are given of subtle proselytization. What is the main way to avoid this?

Topic Twelve: Wicca 666: Facts about Satanism for the non-Satanist

What is Satanism? I know Wicca isn't satanic, but what is? What's this LHP, RHP stuff? What do you mean by good needing evil being "silly"? Are there different types of Satanists? How do they feel about Wiccans?

Wicca is not Satanism. What is?

Scarcely a single newcomer to Wicca refrains, in his/her first few minutes of web-crafting, from telling you that Wicca is not satanic. Wiccans who have been in the religion for more than a few minutes know, of course, that Wicca is not satanic, despite the claims of liars and fools to the contrary, so this claim is simply not meant for us, but for the dozens of people who wish to claim otherwise. I use the quantifier dozens on purpose. There is a very miniscule contingent of Christians, specifically, whose goal is to prove that Wicca is satanic. In the past, these people have claimed to be former High Priests (but could not offer a single name of a covener or teacher), but the tendency of Wiccan organizations to sue those who claim to be former members who are not has brought that to a halt.

Similarly, these people used to claim that they'd sacrificed scores of infants and children, but as the common practice upon hearing these things is now to call the police, this too has dwindled to a halt. Let me make this clear: if a woman comes into your church or home and confesses that she has killed people as a result of her former religion the only ethical thing to do is call the cops. Murderers are not allowed to go unpunished just because they claim they used to follow Satanism. If you go on Jerry Springer and say you killed people, be prepared to recant that statement or be prosecuted for murder. I, at least, will make the call, and I'd hope anyone else with a shred of decency would.

That tangent over with—and let me refrain even from naming the names of Christian speakers who claim to have killed or been witness to a killing and have not spent a second in jail for murder or conspiracy—we can get back to the real discussion. Wicca is not Satanism. Duh. Every Wiccan knows that! The issue here is the simple fact that few Wiccans know what Satanism is, beyond the fact that it is not what they follow. I created this topic with the idea that you cannot merely claim you are not something, you must understand that something to speak about it with any authority.

First, we have to look at what Abrahamicists, Christians specifically, mean when they say "Satanic," because the fact remains that the word has multiple definitions, and some of them are so broad that Wiccans (as well as Catholics, Mormons, Protestants and others) fall under those definitions. Such definitions are nonsense, and asking a person what they mean when they say "Satanic" is really the only way to even begin such a discussion:

Common Definitions of "Satanic" Used By Abrahamicists:
1.   Not of the same religion as the one using the term. (For example, some Christians refer to Jews as "Satanic.")
2.   Not of the same denomination as the one using the term. (For example, some Protestants refer to Catholics as Satanic, and vice versa.)
3.   Secular. (As in non-religious education, capitalism or laws not based in the Bible.)
4.   Magical or Metaphysical in nature or appearance. (Ranging from misunderstood science to astrology.)
5.   The actual worship (or following) of Satan or use of the term Satanic to describe yourself.

Of these five definitions, I only count the last as a genuine definition of Satanism. In the Bible, whenever Satan appears, people know who he is. Jesus and other characters in the Bible do not refer to Satan as the gods of other people. As you can see, Wicca, as well as every other religion in existence, falls into the first two definitions and everything else falls into the third. Definitions that are *that* broad are clearly nonsense, especially since so many better words to use exist.

The fourth definition, satanic as magical or metaphysical, is based on the idea that magic of any kind is explicitly forbidden in the Bibles. The problem with this is that while specific magical acts are prohibited in the Bibles, everything metaphysical certainly isn't, or else every prophet, messiah and being in the Bibles is satanic. There exist metaphysical traditions in every Abrahamic religion, even if they are obscure. Even then, most of what is considered "satanic" in Wicca based on this definition falls under Christian practice as well—things like praying.

The last definition, the worship of Satan or self-proclamation of Satanism sounds forthright and upfront, but in actuality, the idea is highly controversial and convoluted. The reasons why a group or person takes the label "Satanism" are many and varied, and I hope to make them at least somewhat clear. To be clear however, know this one thing: You cannot be a Satanist and be unaware of it.

Those that choose the term Satanism do so for many and varied reasons. They may do it to shock, to protest or simply because what they believe matches what another person has called Satanism. I feel a Wiccan like me, whose very religion used the term Witchcraft for decades for the exact same reasons, has no business lecturing people on what they call themselves. It may be telling, however, that unlike many modern Witches I've encountered, I have never heard a Satanist cry foul when someone used the term in a way they didn't like, only when they dictated things about individual Satanists that simply were not true.

How Modern Satanists define Satanism

My definition is much broader than that of many Modern Satanists. LaVeyan Satanists, for example, have historically considered all the other Satanists to be *poseurs* and would object (and have objected in the past) to their religion being called anything but Satanism with no names and modifiers added. As with limiting the term Pagan to only those you agree with, I'm uncomfortable labeling even the furthest fringe that uses the term Satanist as anything but what they call themselves. That fringe is, however, a crappy example of Satanism, the equivalent of our Wiccan wannabes or Christian yes men. That being said, I do believe the definitions of Satanism used by Satanists to be valid and worthy of study. If nothing else, the fact that the people most likely to be shown as examples of Satanism by the press are often the ones furthest in practice from Modern

Satanists is instructive, and that difference is worth our time.

In my experience in dealing with general peace-making between minority religions, I've found a few Satanists whose definitions reflected an exceptional coherence of thought. Chief amongst those Satanists is Jashan A'al (Valeska Scholl), who has often provided excellent and challenging commentary on interfaith lists and bulletin boards. She stands, in my estimation, in a very small group of excellent web and independent authors — a list that also includes Drew Campbell and John J. Coughlin, mentioned in the first half of this book. A'al identifies two main types of Satanism: Traditional Satanists, who fall into the "actual worship (or following)" half of my definition; and Modern Satanists, who fit the other half.

Traditional Satanists believe that Satan is a genuine being. The exact nature of that being varies from group to group, but only a minority limits their perception to that of the Abrahamic anti-deity. A'al notes, and I concur, that the majority of these Abrahamic Satanists fit what she calls the "Manson-worshipping, gothic, high school dropout" stereotype[69]. Their philosophy is often rooted in Christian beliefs of what a Satanist is, which is highly contrary to the philosophy of most Satanists, Traditional or Modern, who have no desire to allow their religion to be dictated by them by practitioners of another religion.

One Traditional Satanist and dear friend who I'll call Peter (who describes himself as a literal Satanist) expressed his relationship with Satan as that of a child to a distant grandfather. The Abrahamic god he'd followed in the first half of his life was wrong, he'd discovered, on so very many points that any being the Abrahamic god condemned or disliked was probably the better deity. Peter said the difference was similar to his experience as the child of an immigrant. His father wanted to be everything American, even refusing to speak his native tongue or teach it to his children. When his grandfather immigrated, Peter discovered a

[69] Satanic Denominations- Traditional http://www.lightbringer.net

whole culture that had been denied him by his father's obsession on being an American, a culture he felt was better in very many ways and a culture he would grow to be a part of (except in his religious affiliation) in the future. "Satan," he told me with a chuckle, "is exactly like my grandfather, who probably spins in his grave whenever I say it. He is the reality I missed because the culture around me insisted I deny it."

To him, Satan represents everything the Abrahamic god does not. He is a god without jealousy, who doesn't want people converted to his cause, let alone killed for not following him. Peter will gladly point to images of September 11th, 2001 or bombings in Israel and say *That* is the adversary." Even his beliefs on the stories of the Bibles are both amusing and thought provoking. Every time he sees something on the rapture, he says, he gets hopeful. "A day when all the annoying people of God go away? *If only...*"

Peter describes himself as a literal Satanist and a Pagan Satanist, and believes that Satan is embodied in deities like Bacchus. He describes principles of Bacchus that mirror the tenets of most Satanic philosophies—that man is the center of his universe, that those who lose themselves in drugs or alcohol (as opposed to sensible use) deserve to get hangovers, crash their cars and rip their kids to shreds (as in *The Bacchae.*) He also believes, as most Satanists do, that you get what you earn, and as a successful professional he earns a great deal. As a sort of quasi-Hellenist, he is a triachist, believing that man exists in an in-between state, a state between god and animal. This seems at first contrary to most Satanists who, like A'al, believe that man is an animal like any other[70], but is really reflective of the differences in the deity concept. Many Literal or Traditional Satanists believe that mankind alone is capable of communicating with the divine and we are therefore superior to animals. To use Peter's own words "We are naked apes with the voices and tools of gods."

---

[70] Defining Satanism http://www.lightbringer.net

Unlike Peter, most Satanists are Modern Satanists, which he calls "metaphoric Satanists." Modern Satanists do not see Satan as an actual entity but instead as a representation of parts of their belief. A'al divides Modern Satanic thought into three varieties, which she insists are just her personal labels, not any sort of classification. As with the earlier discussion of types of polytheism, these labels are not mutually exclusive and Modern Satanists may fall in more than one category, or even between categories.

The first of A'al's "flavors" is that of the Naturalist, people who see Satan, she says, "as the natural force of the universe, the 'underlying current' of nature." Like the magic ether of some Ceremonial Mages, this current, called Satan, is not good, evil, intelligent or sentient, it just **is**, and may be tapped into with the right training. It is no surprise then that the practice of tapping this current may be called Satanic Magic. Perhaps a valid criticism of it is that it is simply slapping a new name on an old practice. I'm hesitant to say that, though, because I sense a difference in the textural nature between the two that I can't use worldview alone to account for.

The second variety, which A'al terms "Psychologic," is similar to the Shadow-Self school of (Jungian) Witchcraft, and is based on the idea that the very id or inner animal that most of society seeks to hide and tamp down deep within the unconscious — The Satanic Self — must be recognized and dealt with. This is reflected, in part, by the Church of Satan's philosophy of living life to the fullest, or the Ceremonial Mage's quest for true will (both of which provide admonitions against involving the unwilling in your fulfillment, I might add). It even bears a resemblance, though it makes me uncomfortable to admit it, the Apollonian commandment to "Know thyself."

Once again, it is the contextual usage of the terms that matters. The Apollonian, Jungian, Satanist and Ceremonial Mage can all recognize inherent similarity in the ideas, but vast differences in the context. I liken it to the cheeseburger I once had at a Chinese restaurant (a long story, perhaps for a later work). It met all the criteria for being a cheeseburger — a formed patty of beef and melted cheese served on a toasted bun with some toppings and sauces. It looked like something I would get at any fast-food place, save for the bean sprouts sticking out of it, but it tasted completely different. If you asked me to describe a cheeseburger to you, this would be the last cheeseburger I would use in my description. To the chef, however, it was the perfect cheeseburger. These similarities may be a full frontal assault on the schema we place our data in, but recognition of the differences in the creation of the schemas is part of the key to understanding the reasons people are so often dissimilar.

The last of A'al's flavors of Satanism is that of the symbolist. She says the symbolists "view Satan as a mental/mythical archetype, as the 'Adversary' or the 'Lightbringer.'" To them, Satan is fictional but powerful nonetheless, embodying concepts they find powerful or important, qualities like free will or independence. Peter refers to such people as "nothing more than atheists with attitude," and A'al, in her work, acknowledges that this and similar views of Modern Satanism are common amongst traditionalists.

Whether they see Satan as real or a metaphor, as the id or a symbol, most Satanists agree on a few core beliefs. A'al covers these beliefs in the "Defining Satanism" section of her webpage. What may shock you, even more than any of the words, are the innate similarities between Satanism and parts of Rational Wicca. Once again, the difference is more contextual than literal. At the risk of sounding like a new age bunny, I will say that, having considered Satanism as a possibility when I first left Atheism, the two have vastly different vibes. Both can get the job done but, just as choosing between two proficient lovers, sometimes the ability is simply not enough and you have to go with the one with the right vibes. That analogy, of course, raises the specter of following both, but as my open relationship has been monogamous for longer than I can remember, I have (conveniently) no business even commenting upon that.

The first core belief that A'al discusses was the one I mentioned earlier, the belief of man as animal. Traditional Satanists share this belief, but at least in Peter's case, this is to a lesser degree. He, unlike A'al, distinguishes between the needs of the animal (which he terms the "meat") and the needs of the mind. He insists that the mind is the difference between man and the rest of the animals and that it does, indeed, make us the better animal. To A'al, this is no doubt an example of what she calls "species-centric thought processes" on her website. Both beliefs, however, are rooted in the refusal to deny that man is an animal, complete with instincts and needs. Denying these needs becomes, to the Satanist, a personal choice, something that, if done, is done because the Satanist desires to do so, not because society says so. A'al's website, as well as my conversations with Satanists, drove one highly admirable quality of their religion home, and hard. Satanists, like Rational Wiccans, don't put much stock in what society tells them to do. The reasons why we don't flow with the whims of society are somewhat different, but the result is similar.

Likewise, Satanists generally believe in self-responsibility, autonomy, Magic (whether as a metaphysical, mental or physical entity) and a focus on *this* life and *this* world, things that are highly familiar to the Rational or Post-Modern Wiccan and need no explanation. As uncomfortable as we are to admit it, Satanists believe a lot of the same things we do with a highly different context. Fortunately for us, it is usually their context that our mutual enemies define them by, so it is unlikely that the informed amongst them are likely to get confused between the two.

You will note that throughout this section, I did not refer to children being kidnapped and raped, dogs and cats being sacrificed, selling your soul or any of the things that generally follow "I am not a Satanist, Satanists do things like…." on the average neophyte Wiccan's website. Massive child or animal sacrifice and similar things would be easily documented in police reports and none of the Satanists I know do such things so to discuss them beyond the realm of their extreme rarity would be an insult to your intelligence.

Diabolic Imagery in Wicca: Good needs Evil

Wiccans often cry foul when they are accused of having diabolical world views, but very often the reasons for such claims come from the very words those Wiccans use to describe their beliefs. An example of this diabolical double talk is the near constant claim by a group of Wiccans that light needs darkness, good needs evil and men must know hate in order to know love.

I have never seen anything else cause the waves of confusion that penetrate many Wiccan faces the first time the response to this statement is "Why?" The claim that good *needs* evil is, in fact, unsubstantiated dogma, nothing more or less than something we tend to accept as true because other people say it is. This dogma, nonetheless, explains the weird combination of condemnation with acceptance for fictional or fringe forms of Traditional Satanism that many people in Wicca express.

The theory that good cannot exist without evil is based on one of those basic truths of philosophy, that good and evil, like hot and cold, will exist somewhere no matter how different those places are. To give you an example, there are fish in hot springs in North America that can die of cold at temperatures some of us would find uncomfortably warm in our bath water. To these fish, a day we would consider oppressively hot, even deadly, is nothing more than balmy. If we imagine that their ideal temperature is between 95F and 105F then 90 is cold and 110 is hot. To your average human these temperatures are just plain hot. In general, anything near or above the body's normal 96.8 degrees is miserable for us.

To make it explicitly clear, I'll relate my own experiences living in Southeastern Pennsylvania. When I was there, the temperature would regularly be in the low 30s during the winter. The entire time it was in the low 30s, people would glare at me, often in nothing more than pants, boots, a sweatshirt, hat and gloves, and affirm that I must be *freezing*. To me, it was nippy, but not cold enough to warrant more than the layers I had on. Especially if I was shoveling, where moving around in bulky clothes is half of the work

I am quite possibly the only person in reality who can honestly say I walked through two miles of snow and ice to get to school. When I was growing up the rule was that if you lived two miles from school, bussing was free. I lived 1.98 miles from school, and since I didn't live one block over, bussing came to a buck a day, which I could not afford. As a result I walked four miles, five days a week, for three months at a time, in Syracuse, NY's winter. I own parkas, hats, gloves, scarves, mittens and more, and always have. On the few days in Pennsylvania where the wind-chill began with a minus sign I wore them all. For me, cold is single-digit. Cold is what it is right now as I eye the neighbor's thermometer in Buffalo, NY: 8 degrees, with two feet of snow on the ground and a few inches more blowing around. I like this cold. It interferes with my arthritis, so I like it best from a window, but I like this a lot more than the oppressive summers of Pennsylvania.

For me, it begins to get oppressive around 82 degrees. Like those fish, I seem to have a 10 degree comfort range, between about 70 and 80. When it's 85 degrees, I turn the air conditioner down to 72, draw the curtains and drink lemonade. From about March until October, I was physically miserable in Pennsylvania. Cold isn't like hot, because you can only shed so many layers of clothes. To me, anything over 80 was too much, and while it regularly got over 80 back home, it didn't stay that way all summer, nor refrain from dropping below 80 during the night. A typical Syracuse August can have a 20 degree drop between the day and the night, and I can remember a few days where I wore a swimsuit one day and a jacket the next, but long protracted heat is something I remember only very rarely.

You cannot tell me it was not hot at 85 degrees in Pennsylvania. My body pretty much considers everything that high and above the same. Nonetheless, weather reporters regularly said that the 85 degree weather was a break from the heat, and that 95 wasn't as bad as 98. Obviously, to them, there was a difference, and they mentioned it regularly.

Good and evil work the same way. We live in a culture where things are generally good. If you told a person living in Afghanistan in 2003 that they were going to have 10% of the people who wanted jobs unable to find work, 40% making less than $5.00 per hour and fifteen murders a month in the cities, that person would be hard pressed to complain when comparing that with his current status. When we see numbers like that in this country, we scream and complain and cry havoc. The theory here is that even in those places where "evil" is not apparent to us it is still in existence. It's seen here like the hot and cold in my example above.

To use another metaphor, if only one car accident happened in a given year, and that accident was the fault of the weather and resulted in the death of a small girl, we'd probably see that as a triumph over the evils of traffic accidents. If, however, this one accident happened in a place where there had never been an accident before, the death of that girl would be the lead news story for day after day. Her death would be seen as a sign of horrible things. To put it in perspective, if that girl was killed in our world of daily traffic deaths, the loss would be just as profound to her parents, but the culture wouldn't care.

So that's the theory that is misused, that the knowledge of good and evil exists regardless of the proportion of good and evil in existence. In a perfect world, the perfect people would still find something to label as evil, even if it was considered a utopia to our eyes. Compare this, if you can, to the belief that in order to *understand* the nature of love, or goodness, or light, you need to *first* understand hate, or evil, or darkness, ignoring, of course, that by this law of opposites, you'd also need to first understand love to understand hate.

The difference between the idea of good and evil being seen by all peoples and the idea of good needing evil might, at first, seem vague. Both account for the idea that poles exist. One says that the poles exist regardless of the space between them and the other says that having or understanding one pole is needed to have or understand the other. We've discussed mind experiments, so can we try to use them here. Can a thing exist without its polar opposite or is it, as I believe, merely that we can claim to better understand a thing by declaring an understanding (or the existence) of a polar opposite?

It's important to understand that these definitions and explanations only work where we accept the opposites as valid opposites. For example, darkness is often assumed to be the absence of light, but hate is called the opposite of love when the absence of love would be apathy. These definitions seem to vary, but in general I've picked ones where if you went up to someone and asked for the opposite of a given quantity they'd give you the same opposite I've used.

Imagine, now, that you are in a room and you can see everything in it. If you had suddenly awoken in that room, with no memory of the past where you had been able to see or not see, would you not understand that there was a difference between seeing and not seeing? I don't even mean the difference between closing your eyes and opening them. In that brief instance between looking at an object to your right and looking at an object to your left you have expressed knowledge of the quantity of not seeing, even though your memory only has memory of seeing. If you could not understand that difference, you never would've turned your head to see another object because you would assume that what you were seeing was the end all and be all of sight.

That's a bit obscure, so imagine instead the pure joy of an infant for its mother. A child who has never known abandonment or true pain or true hunger is quite capable of knowing that he is absolutely ecstatic to be held by his mother. In fact, in reducing true love to a thing that can only be understood by experiencing hate, and saying that a being must have experienced hate to know love we are condoning abuse, in a round about way. That is not to say that those who teach that you must know hate to know love and vice versa are suggesting we go out and abuse children, merely that they are reducing the horror of child abuse to something that is quasi-acceptable. At least the abused child, in this point of view, can know love better for having been abused.

The main problem with this worldview is that it doesn't quite work. If, indeed, knowing the opposite of a thing made you better appreciate it we'd all appreciate good television, good food and good writing, having endured their opposites. In fact, if this were true it would be our greatest persons who had suffered the most, and very often we applaud the persons with disabilities or tragic histories for just surviving (and rightfully so). If we actually believed that knowing hardship made you appreciate the good things in life better, our culture would expect that every abused or disabled individual would be an expert on love, ability and the rest. In fact, as any psychologist will tell you, it is often the people abused the most that have the hardest time understanding love and non-abusive relationships.

It's important to understand that in this worldview, where the only way to appreciate a thing is to know its opposite, Wicca requires Satanism, even a false idea of it, as a foil. It is something that Wiccans with this worldview can point to, claim to not be and therefore feel that they have accurately described themselves. The fact that this sort of literary device isn't needed in the real world is unimportant. If there is a Wicca, there must be an anti-Wicca, and we often do the injustice of claiming that anti-Wicca is Satanism. If Satanism could be said to be anti-anything it would be said to be anti-Christian, and even that is stretching the definition of Satanism.

The Left Hand Path, the Right Hand Path and the Center

Another example of diabolic imagery used in Wicca comes from Ceremonial Magic. It is the idea of the three "paths" of magic, the Left Hand Path, the Right Hand Path and the center. A poor understanding of this idea is very prevalent and that poor understanding describes the paths as evil, good and neutral. I will resist the obvious slam that people who see things in this way have likely involved themselves in too many role playing games, because the division of magic into black, white and gray happened long before any role playing games were invented.

The problem here is that the concept of the three paths was created to discuss concepts that are, by their nature, difficult to discuss. From the point of view of Ceremonial Magic, the Left Hand Path and Right Hand Path don't really refer to good and evil but to the two basic methods by which any act can take place—benefiting only one's self to the exclusion of others, and benefiting others to the exclusion of one's self. The center path is seen as ideal in any case, but the idea is that the extremes of any situation can be broken down into these two decisions—the decision to act purely in one's own self interest and the ability to act purely against one's own interests.

I often describe myself as a Right Hand Pather, because I am constantly finding myself in situations where I am not acting in my own best interests. Some of these situations are noble and altruistic, but just as often they are selfish in an obscure kind of way. Wanting my son to excel, I removed him from middle school where he was foundering, in part because of a fear of proselytes and in part because of a strong disparity between the level of his reading and his math. The decision was to home school him until High School, but I was required to remove myself from a graduate program in the process. It seems high-minded and altruistic to the outsider, but it was nothing more or less than my animal nature wanting to make my progeny survive to successfully pass on his genes and have an effective adulthood. (Also, perhaps, the knowledge that I could maintain his reading level while improving his math level if I altered the ratio of time spent on math and reading. A child who, for example, reads the first four Harry Potter books at nine years old, does *not* need to be spending two hours a day reading chapter books. Instead, he spends 30 minutes a day reading a chapter of a level-appropriate novel and answering a few questions. Thirty minutes on math, however, is not acceptable, and in one month of home schooling with a heavy math curriculum he went from level testing at 3rd grade to level testing at 6th, a full year above his age group.)

The Right and Left Hand Paths don't truly describe people but choices. While originally they may have been emotionally linked to Jesus' dividing mankind into sheep and goats — a goat here, thanks... an ornery, capering, independent goat — they have usually been associated with the decisions that lay before us, the original "on the one hand and on the other" situations. By his nature, the Wiccan tries to go forward on the Center path, but often falls on the Right. The ideal Wiccan can balance his completely selfless acts with those that keep his personal needs met. These paths, again, are not about good or evil, but about those things that help the self to the exclusion of others and vice versa. They are just filters we use to interpret data, not worldviews on good and evil.

Wicca does not fall under any real definitions of Satanism!

Wicca, as has been said, is not satanic. It does not fall under biblical definitions of Satan worship (and neither do any religions that are actually discussed in the Bibles) and it is nothing that Modern Satanists, traditional or otherwise, recognize. I have reached the highest levels of my faith and can tell you, with absolute honesty, that you never reach a level where you find out our gods are "really" Satan because not only does no such level exist but also the fact remains that our gods are not Satan, have not been Satan, will not be Satan and those who claim they are Satan are either deluded or lying—most likely lying.

This is why those who have authored books on the imagined truth of Wicca as Satanism cannot demonstrate to what Wiccan groups they belonged in the past, nor give a single reference for their alleged former practices. The second they claim to have been taught that Wicca is really Satanism by a Wiccan, they will be hit so hard by the hammer of truth, and its accompanying lawyers, that the world will be reeling. I do not care if they are a nondenominational minister or the Pope, we have the numbers and money to defend ourselves from attack with weapons those early Wiccans who claimed kinship with those hung for Witchcraft could not have imagined: Truth, Lawyers and Sheer Numbers.

They know this, and as a result they focus instead on innuendo and vague testimony from shadowy figures that are apparently above the law as well as the truth. Outright slander is met with force and unity, so they rely on the shadow realm of untruth that can be proven neither true nor false. You will note, however, that in doing so they have already lost the battle. The public is too well educated to be lied to for an extensive amount of time, even subtly, and these fringe groups of anti-Wiccans run the risk of being seen as the real "satanic underground."

The unity that allows us to fight defamation of our religion (and occasionally tempts us to yell "defamation!" when something isn't) was not possible twenty or thirty years ago, and is perhaps the single best accomplishment of Wicca in the past few decades. This is highlighted by our willingness to communicate and our presence on the Internet and in the media. While we've yet to have a millionaire athlete make our religion acceptable to the public, nor have we had a brilliant cross-genre musical star floor the world with her announcement that she was Wiccan, we're making strides toward acceptance every day, strides that are most effective when we work together and don't try to make the outsider, whether Christian or merely cowan, uncomfortable. This is not to say that we need to pander to them, as I'm sure you understand. Those that would be uncomfortable that we exist deserve their discomfort.

Recommended Reading for Topic Twelve:

Former Satanists and Wiccans who never were:
http://users.cybercity.dk/~ccc44406/smwane/English.ht
m
http://www.masonicinfo.com/schnoebelen.htm
Modern Satanism:
http://www.lightbringer.net

Discussions Questions for Topic Twelve:

12.1. What is the justification for putting a section on Satanism in this book?

12.2. What definitions of Satanism does Wicca fall under?
What does labeling these definitions nonsense mean?

12.3. What is the difference between the author's accepted
definition and the ones used by Satanists?

12.4. My friend "Peter" describes his Satanism as purely reactionary but nonetheless rational. What do you think
he means and do you agree?

12.5. Peter describes his Satanism as Pagan, and sees Pan,
Hades and similar deities amongst those that have been
labeled Satan in the past. How do you feel about that?

12.6. A'al's portrayal of Satanism is what Peter called
"Atheism with attitude." How valid is that challenge?

12.7. Does good "need" evil?

12.8. What are the Right Hand and Left Hand paths?

Wicca in Practice IV: Forming an Ethical Code

Morality is, very simply, living our life ethically, within the structure of our religion and our philosophy. It is living our life with morals, ideals and archetypes that, by example, teach us the difference between right and wrong.

> — *All One Wicca,* Chapter Two.

As I described in *All One Wicca,* forming an ethical code can begin simply by identifying things that you find wrong in the universe and making a decision to not participate in those things. It is a deceptively simple idea, that what you want done for and to you, and what you don't want done for and to you, are powerful indicators of what is right and what is wrong. The reason it is deceptively simple is because it is really easy to look at what we can call the "small ethics," the ones based on your own feelings and thoughts, and assume that the really big ethics can come from the exact same thought processes.

For example, you probably want to continue living. Death is not something you're looking forward to, and an early death would be particularly annoying, so your "small ethic" of not killing anyone works. However, if you are anything like me, you're probably willing to die to help certain people in your life. If my son needed a heart transplant, and mine was the only match, you can be pretty sure that I'd take a bullet in the brain right there in the hospital. It's not about wanting to die or being altruistic, in fact, from an evolutionary point of view it is pretty selfish, wanting the genes to go on and picking the unit more likely to breed and sacrificing the one less likely to breed.

Being of a biological slant, I justify it like that, rather than use buzz words like "maternal instinct," but I think you get the idea. A small ethic can work great at the small level, but you need to look at a bigger level on a regular basis. It is this multi-leveled, multi-layered understanding of reality that is at the core of the majority of religious discussions of ethics. We ask ourselves what our gods would expect us to do in the situation and balance the many small ethics that apply to a situation — don't hurt anyone, don't kill anyone, don't make a mess on the hospital floor.

Creating a code of ethics can begin by finding a list of things to avoid doing, but in reality, such a code should primarily reflect the main foci of your life. For example, my family motto, translated, is "The Quality (or the Divine Attribute) of Love, The Quality of Beauty (the term I use for beauty is the one you'd use for a temple, not a person,) the Quality of Liberty and the Knowledge of Truth." The subtle differences between the idea of love as a quality or divinity and love as a verb are important, but I hardly need to give you a lecture on verbs and nouns. The point is to show the filter that all my personal ethics are drawn through. If it does not involve the furtherance of truth, love, perfection of form and liberty, it is hard for me to justify doing it. If, in addition to not furthering these things, it violates my personal list of don'ts, well then, I not only can't justify doing it but I can't justify doing it while maintaining my previous form of ethical code. Worse still, I then compare it to what I know of the Divine's plan for my life. If I have said not to do a thing, and it goes against the things I have as foci for my life, and I know my gods are against it not only am I being unethical and untrue to myself in doing such a thing, but I'm also rejecting my religion.

This is a bit deep and hard to understand. It consists of knowing one's self on three levels: the basest level of yes and no that we develop as children, the middle level of seeing each action we take as furthering an inner set of foci or life goals and the ultimate level of doing what we are shown is best for us by the divine. Each of these levels is achieved with another layer of work, introspection and prayer. It is not hard to develop a list of dos and don'ts; it is difficult but not impossible to identify the main foci of your life; and it is highly difficult to glean more than a mere fraction of the divine's plan for you. Work is the key factor in all of these. No one said Wicca was easy. There are religions where you will be told what is and isn't right at all times, religions that compartmentalize each section of life into little boxes. If, at any time, you find Wicca too hard, seek those faiths out, by all means.

Practice:

1. Make a list of things that you consider wrong. Try to categorize these into broad ideas. From this, make a list of things that you consider wrong to do ever, wrong to do sometimes and wrong to do in certain situations.

2. Try to identify a handful of ideals or beliefs that each make up a core focus of your life. Why did you choose each one? Is there an order to them; is one more important than the rest? In my list, for example, knowledge of truth trumps everything else. Why do you think you chose these things?

3. Using prayer, meditation, research into your primary deities and more, what do you think are the main goals your god(s) would have for you? Are they hands off, letting you do whatever you wish or are they focused on certain parts of your life? With what level of certainty do you feel these beliefs?

Appendix I: A Glossary of Terms

A much more extensive dictionary of Paganism is found in All One Wicca. *This glossary only uses words that were undefined in the text.*

Abrahamic: Of or pertaining to the religions founded from various mythos including Abraham, including Judaism, Islam, Christianity and modern versions of those faiths.

Ásatrú: It is very difficult to define the term without using a term-like Paganism, Heathenry or Reconstructionism-that some practitioners disagree with. My definition is simply Nordic Reconstructionism, although I liked the phrase "The reincarnation of Tacitus' Religio Germania" when a friend and Roman Reconstructionist used it.

Bible, Greek: The body of Abrahamic text written in Greek, including the New Testament and similar works.

Bible, Hebrew: The body of Abrahamic text written in Hebrew.

Coven: A group of Wiccans and/or Witches practicing ritual together.

Cult: In its original use, a small sect of religion dedicated to the worship of one god, often in a polytheistic culture. Cults had their own initiatory rites, standards of living and membership requirements.

Deity: A term for a god using the Latin root. Most words in English use the Greek root as in theology, theologian, and theocracy. Often misspelled "diety."

Dianicism: A collective term for a number of religious beliefs, most often a feminist spirituality similar to that outlined in *The Spiral Dance*.

Faith poem: Like some of the psalms, a poem dedicated to describing parts of religious belief. Often some liberty is taken with the beliefs or rites in their creation, so it is important to distinguish between faith poems and lists of rules like ordains or commandments.

Folkway: A tradition, custom, or typical mode of behavior and thought of a specific culture.

Imperialism (religious): The action of attempting to simultaneously spread one's religion and incorporate aspects of other religions into it in an attempt to make it larger and larger.

Mazeway: A collection of interpretations of experiences at the individual level that forms a basis for religious thought or the idea of self or even the concept of the position of one's self in relation to the universe.

More: (more-ay) A deeply held cultural belief, often involving appearance or behavior.

Outer/Inner Circle or Outer/Inner Court: In much of traditional Wicca, a division is made between new practitioners and old within a group. An inner court member may have access to anything from the hidden names of the Divine used in the circle to the addresses, phone numbers and genuine names of members. Usually some show of trust is expected before entry into the inner circle is allowed, such as signing an oath to not reveal confidential information.

Paradox: Statements or ideas seemingly at odds with reality or whose only solutions are illogical.

Solitary: Short for solitary practitioner. A person who practices Wicca and/or Witchcraft without another person's involvement.

Theology: The study of gods, masculine, feminine or other.

UberGod: Pejorative term for deities said to be the actual one deity in monotheistic versions of Pantheism.

Vedic Religions: Religions based on the Vedas or the culture of their creation.

Appendix II: An Abbreviated Bibliography

A'al, Jashan. *The Ascendancy Websites*, http://www.lightbringer.net

Alpha, et al. *The Ranting Witches*. http://rw.faithweb.net

Christ, Carol P. <u>Laughter of Aphrodite: Reflections on a Journey to The Goddess</u>. San Francisco: Harper and Row, 1987

Coughlin, John J. *The Evolution of Wiccan Ethics*. http://www.waningmoon.com/ethics/index.shtml

Geisler, Norman L. <u>Primitive Monotheism</u> *Christian Apologetics Journal, Volume 1, No.1*, Spring 1998. [Southern Evangelical Seminary]

Goldenberg, Naomi R <u>Changing of The Gods: Feminism and the End of Traditional Religion</u>. Boston: Beacon, 1979

Ronald Hutton's <u>Triumph of the Moon: A History of Modern Pagan Witchcraft</u>, Oxford, 2001

Stanley Milgram <u>Obedience to Authority: An Experimental View</u>. New York: Harper/Collins, 1983

Starhawk. <u>The Spiral Dance: A Rebirth of the Ancient Religion of The Great Goddess</u>. San Francisco: Harper and Row, 1979

Ontario Consultants For Religious Tolerance, http://www.religioustolerance.org

Appendix III: Self-Test

What this test is: This test is a collection of topics you should've covered in a year and a day of studying Wicca. If you read through these questions and find you know all of the answers, it may be that this book is above your level of study. If you find most of the questions beyond your ability, then it is likely this book will prove difficult to understand. If you are somewhere in the middle, you are in our target audience.

What this test is not: This test is *not* a reading comprehension test that can be answered by reading everything I have written. It is not a test of Witch-ness, nor a test of proficiency in Wicca. It is not a test of UEW or any other tradition. It is not comprehensive; the questions represent a random assortment of knowledge. While there are definitive answers to many questions, this test is not of whether or not you get the question right but of whether or not you are familiar with the question, that's why I do not provide answers. A question you understand, even if you don't know the answer, is indicative of the fact that you have covered that material. Questions are rated, quite subjectively, from 1-8 with 1 being really easy and 8 being really hard. Some are multiple choice, others are fill in the blank and still others are cold answers. They are sorted randomly.

1. It has been said that British Traditional Wicca is, by its nature, eclectic. What is the justification for this claim? (7)

2. What is a Priapic wand? What plant material is commonly carved on the more symbolic ones? (5)

3. What are some of the traditions associated with the Summer Solstice? (2)

4. What is the astronomical definition of a solstice? How is it characterized in Summer? In Winter? (3)

5. What is the difference between a solitary practitioner and a coven member?(1)

6. List two of the parallel stories to the kidnap of Persephone in mythology outside of Greece or Rome.(4)

7. What is the element and color commonly associated with the South? Why have they been historically linked with that direction (2)

8. Can a coven member practice alone? Is it encouraged?(2)

9. Wiccan is to Pagan Religion as Christian is to.....(1)
a. Heathen Religion   b. Irrational Religion   c. Judaism
        d. Abrahamic Religion

10.What was the gist of the "Old Law" that is generally considered an attempt by Gardner to replace Doreen Valiente with someone young and pretty? (3)

11. Define "Kathenotheism."(8)

12. What is the culture Yule is predominantly based in? What language does the word come from? (5)

13. What is portrayed in the Villa of the Mysteries? How is this relevant to Traditional Wicca?(8)

14. What is ancestor worship? Give examples.(3)

15. Who popularized the movement known by the Greek word Thelema? (2)

16. What is the direction a Wiccan circle commonly starts from? (1)

17. Which of the following is not commonly used in a Wiccan Ceremony?(1)
a. a knife   b. a lock of hair   c. wine or ale   d. bread

18. What did Gardner call the religion of the Wica?(4)

19. What is meant by the term pantheon? What is The Pantheon? (3)

20. Why is the temple to Athena on the Acropolis called the Parthenon? Who else could have temples called by that term? (7)

21. Which of the following (if any) are true:
All Wiccans are Witches
All Witches are Wiccans
All Pagans are Wiccans
All Wiccans are Pagan
Defend your answer. (2)

22. What is non-linear reincarnation? How can it account for the number of people who think they were famous in a past life? (6)

23. What is the Doctrine of Signatures? How was it fundamental to early herbalism? (5)

24. As of 2002, Wicca was: (2)
a. about 1000 years old. b. approaching 20,000 years old. c. around 50 years old   d.100 years old.

25. Environmentalism:(3)
a. is not a part of Wicca
b. was not historically part of Wicca but now commonly is
c. was in Wicca at the beginning.
d. is vital to Wiccan belief
e. b and d
f. b and c

26. What is wrong with the following statement? "Wiccans only do white magic."(2)

27. Who initiated putting a "k" on Magic to distinguish it from stage magic, and what else does it mean?(3)

28. Why is self-initiation technically not possible? What is the name commonly given that rite?(3)

29. What is the transmigration of souls theory of theosophy? How does it differ from Buddhism?(4)

30. Which would be against The Wiccan Rede?(1)
a. killing a person
b. punching a person
c. biting a person
d. all of the above.
e. all of the above but a Wiccan would do any of those things if it prevented greater harm.
f. none of the above are always against the Rede, the situation matters.

31. What is the next best line: Joe is a traditional Ceremonial Magician. He thinks his house is full of negative spirits. He does a ritual to drive them out. When his housemate comes home, he says:(5)
a. That smells like sage.
b. What smells like rotten eggs?
c. Why are there crucifixes all over the house?
d. Why is there salt around the perimeter of the house?
Defend your answer.

32. Who wrote Rede of the Wiccae? (2)

33. Are all gods one God, according to *Wicca*?(2)

34. What is a "cone of power" (1)

35. Is Wicca Celtic? (2)

36. Are angels or archangels traditionally used in Wicca? (2)

37. Name the two men who are credited with speaking to the Guardians of the Watchtowers. What did those Guardians have to say about Wicca?(4)

38. What is Theban Script? Is it a language, a runic alphabet, a pictographic alphabet or a substitution alphabet? (5)

39. Who was Gerald Gardner?(1)

40. What is a Book of Shadows? Why is it called that?(2)

41. What goddesses are usually associated with the Maiden, Mother and Crone? Were they thus associated by their original worshippers? (3)

42. What is meant by "a space of this world and not of it" in some Wiccan rituals?(1)

43. What is a handfasting? How long do they last? (2)

44. _____ is to Wicca as denomination is to Christianity.(1)

45. The Summerland and reincarnation are two semi-contrasting theories about the afterlife in Wicca. Explain two of the ways the existence of both has been rationalized. (5)

46. Why is it untrue to say that Wicca is matrifocal in its historic manifestations? (7)

47. Who coined the term "thealogy" and why does it apply to Dianicism but not Wicca? (6)

48. What is the difference between pantheism, panentheism and monotheism? (8)

49. How does the idea of Karma espoused by some Wiccans vary from the concept of Karma in Eastern Religions?(3)

50. What is meant by "three-fold" return? Is it espoused by all Wiccans?(2)

Appendix IV: Dramatis Personae

The following persons are mentioned, at least tangentially, in this book. A brief description of who each person is, as well as their year of birth (and death, if dead) is included herein .

Raymond Buckland (1934-) Author of The Complete Book of Witchcraft. Instrumental in bringing traditional Wicca to the United States even as new traditions were developing independently of Gardner and Sanders in the US.

Darwin, Charles (1809 -1882) Much maligned author whose theory of natural selection is, quite possibly the least understood statement of the obvious in over a thousand years.

Fortune, Dion (1890-1940) Occultist who was heavily influential on the founders of Early Modern Wicca but quite adamantly affirmed she was not a witch and whose spiritual descendants also claim as much.

Gage, Phineas (1823-1860) Railway construction foreman whose accident with a tamping rod allowed neuroscience to both claim that so-called "moral" behavior was in a part of the brain and to get past decades of prejudice that painted the science of localization of function as phrenology.

Gardner, Gerald (1884-1964) Author of the first commercially available books on Early Modern Wicca, Gardner is closer than anyone else to a "founder" of Early Modern Wicca.

Goldenberg, Naomi (1947-) Originator of the term "Thealogy" to speak of Goddess-based Theology.

Greyarrow, Gérard (1938-1990) One of the original six Silver Chalice Members, secondary founder of what would become UEW.

Maslow, Abraham (1908-1970) One of the primary voices of humanist psychology whose concepts of Self-Actualization and the Hierarchy of Needs would have a profound effect on Wicca.

Sanders, Alex (1916-1988) The so-called "King of the Witches" and founder of the Alexandrian tradition, it may be that Sanders' best contribution to early Modern Wicca was the idea of many traditions, even if it was not his intention that his "new old tradition" be seen that way.

Tomas, Jayne (1942-1994) One of the original six Silver Chalice Members, founder of what would become UEW.

Valiente, Doreen (1922-1999) Author of many books on Early Modern Wicca, Valiente gave us the common forms of the Charge of the Goddess and other liturgy. She, perhaps more than anyone on this list, can be said to be a "co-founder" of Modern Wicca.

Zimbardo, Phillip(1933-) Psychologist whose materials on cults, as well as his experiments on conformity, were highly influential in the development of the Modern Wiccan worldview that any organization is bad for religion. His prison study is the most mentioned, no holds barred, on websites that discuss Wicca from a Psychological viewpoint! Perhaps the most amusing thing about this influence is that it is the *psychologists and sociologists* within Post-Modern Wicca who are most loudly refuting this idea of *any* organization as bad. Perhaps this dichotomy between those who've read the professional articles on the experiments and those who've read the pop articles says something about the intellectual haves and have nots in our society, but I may be biased.

Appendix V: Websites

The following is a by no means comprehensive list of websites I use regularly and that students of Wicca will find highly useful:

Wicca in General:
http://www.witchvox.com [The Witches Voice]
http://www.waningmoon.com
http://www.allonewicca.com

Fair Criticism of Wicca/Satire:
http://www.fluffbunnytrad.com
http://www.cyberwitch.com/wychwood/Library/whenIs
ACeltNotACelt.htm
http://wicca.timerift.net

The CUEW Family:
http://www.cuew.org
[The webpage of The UEW tradition]
http://www.allonewicca.com
[Companion website for *All One Wicca*]
http://wwwcuew.org/cffn/
[Coven of the Far Flung Net]

Appendix VI: How to Seek Permissions.

In order to prepare this book, all persons whose work was used in more than a fair use manner were contacted and asked for permission for their work to be used and if the manner in which it was going to be used was acceptable. When I was highly familiar with the individual, as in Tamryn Wyrmstar, the email I used (because it is my preferred form of communication) said nothing more than "Can I quote your material on 'Rede of the Wiccae' in the next book?" If the material was fair use, the permissions I sought were more touch and go. In general, I sent emails to everyone, and if the email bounced or was not returned, I made sure that the material I used constituted fair use.

What actually *is* fair use is a complicated question. In general, while material from a book or book-sized website must be 250 words or less to constitute fair use, this is just a rubber rule for the individual. This material, no matter how short, must usually be used in a review or satire, or a critique of a person's point of view. No matter how "fair" your fair use is, an author has the right to complain, threaten to sue, claim to have banished you to the astral plane and the like. While I've never been at the receiving end of that type of abuse (at least, not for this purpose) it's common enough that the writers groups I belong to all talk about it — both using it and being the victim of it.

For that reason, I strongly suggest people who wish to seek permissions to quote the works of Wiccan and Pagan authors, whether on their webpages or in their materials, use a form letter similar to the one below for any materials longer than a simple sentence or a short list of terms. Please note that this is a letter for use with materials that would otherwise fall under fair use. Other materials not in the public domain require much more detailed requests and explicit permission:

> Dear Ms./Mr./Dr.[full name of author]
> My name is [your full name.] [If you have it, add some SHORT biographical material here.] I am working on a project

that could be assisted by the use of a quote from your material. The project is [full description of project.] The quote I am interested in is [full text of quote.] I feel that using this quote is the best possible direction my project could be taking at this point.

Although the use of your quote clearly constitutes fair use, I would rather not operate in a vacuum. Therefore, I am asking for your permission for the use of the material, which of course will be credited to you. While I would like a reply to this letter, one is not necessary. If I receive no reply, I will use the materials within the fair use statue of US copyright law. If, however, you object to my use of your materials, please contact me at once so I may remove them.

Keep up the wonderful work,
[Your full name]

If I am the person you wish to quote specifically, I'm generally open to it. For webpages, your material must, of course, not violate the webpage content rules of your service provider. Likewise, I don't approve of having my material, properly cited or otherwise, on any webpage that violates the copyright rights of anyone else. For more explicit directions, to seek permissions or even to ask about the right way to use someone else's files, you may contact me at kaatryn@macmorgan.org

About The Cover Image:

The picture on the cover is of fragments of a coated crystal smashed with a hammer and viewed at about 100X magnification. It was shot with a digital camera hooked up to a microscope. When the light source was properly arranged, in a dark field or light field setting, the image of the crystal was black and white. When the light source was skewed at an angle, however, colors emerged.

I chose this picture for several reasons. First, it comes from my final project in the very same awesome upper level class at Temple University I mention in the anecdote about the title of this book. Secondly, it represents a core fact I hope you learn from reading this book, if you don't know it already- you can stumble around without knowing what you are doing and get results, but there is a better way. In theory, I could have messed around with all the knobs on the microscope and got this image, but since I knew the colors in the crystal I could see with the naked eye were the result of light coming in at angles, I knew that skewing the light would probably have some effect on the image.

Just as the best abstract artists know how to do all the basics, knowledge of the core basics in Wicca are required to know how to do new things. "Whatever works" is not something you can live by just by mucking around. In order to find what works, you first need to know what "working" entails. Just as that means artists start by drawing bowls of fruit and photomicrographers start by looking at mouse guts, it means Wiccans start with the Rede and the basic circle.

K. MacMorgan-Douglas

About this Edition:

This edition was prepared with the help of students of the Coven of the Far Flung Net and the staff at Covenstead Press. There are several differences, which mainly include typographical revisions and clarifications. Essentially, this edition has been refined in preparation for its sequel: *Wicca 334*.

Collectively, Wicca 333 and 334 are known as *A Master Class in Wicca*. I am aware that not everyone is familiar with the term master class, but it refers to a seminar, usually quite small, in which a person thoroughly schooled in a topic teaches and works with a group of students who are also very schooled in a topic. In other words, it is a course with informed participants in which the participants study one or two aspects of what they know in depth, in this case aspects of belief. As many of my readers know, 333 and 334 are, in many ways, collaborative efforts. My students, friends and family had a large amount of input into what I discussed. There is not a single topic in either book that wasn't suggested by a student — the true participants in the master class.

In addition, with the assistance of Tamryn Wyrmstar, an appropriate conformation for the capitalization of god in the books was created. As many people know, most style guides are in conflict over when the word god is capitalized. Tamryn has established his own guideline, in which god is not capitalized unless it is being used by Abrahamic religionists or others to describe the name of their deity. Anywhere in which the proper name of god is not being used is not capitalized, contrary to a lot of Western tradition. Thus, a Christian may be quoted as saying "You will be punished by God," but that quote may be reported as "He believes his god will punish you."

This edition would not be possible without the gracious help of Llysse Smith Wylle, who was instrumental in many of the edits. Any terrific improvement between editions is her fault, anything that's gotten worse is mine.

CPSIA information can be obtained
at www.ICGtesting.com
Printed in the USA
LVHW091021130420
653235LV00001B/89

9 780615 175355